INTELLIGENT INFORMATION PROCESSING IV

IFIP – The International Federation for Information Processing

IFIP was founded in 1960 under the auspices of UNESCO, following the First World Computer Congress held in Paris the previous year. An umbrella organization for societies working in information processing, IFIP's aim is two-fold: to support information processing within its member countries and to encourage technology transfer to developing nations. As its mission statement clearly states,

> *IFIP's mission is to be the leading, truly international, apolitical organization which encourages and assists in the development, exploitation and application of information technology for the benefit of all people.*

IFIP is a non-profitmaking organization, run almost solely by 2500 volunteers. It operates through a number of technical committees, which organize events and publications. IFIP's events range from an international congress to local seminars, but the most important are:

- The IFIP World Computer Congress, held every second year;
- Open conferences;
- Working conferences.

The flagship event is the IFIP World Computer Congress, at which both invited and contributed papers are presented. Contributed papers are rigorously refereed and the rejection rate is high.

As with the Congress, participation in the open conferences is open to all and papers may be invited or submitted. Again, submitted papers are stringently refereed.

The working conferences are structured differently. They are usually run by a working group and attendance is small and by invitation only. Their purpose is to create an atmosphere conducive to innovation and development. Refereeing is less rigorous and papers are subjected to extensive group discussion.

Publications arising from IFIP events vary. The papers presented at the IFIP World Computer Congress and at open conferences are published as conference proceedings, while the results of the working conferences are often published as collections of selected and edited papers.

Any national society whose primary activity is in information may apply to become a full member of IFIP, although full membership is restricted to one society per country. Full members are entitled to vote at the annual General Assembly, National societies preferring a less committed involvement may apply for associate or corresponding membership. Associate members enjoy the same benefits as full members, but without voting rights. Corresponding members are not represented in IFIP bodies. Affiliated membership is open to non-national societies, and individual and honorary membership schemes are also offered.

INTELLIGENT INFORMATION PROCESSING IV

5th IFIP International Conference on Intelligent Information Processing, October 19-22, 2008, Beijing, China

Edited by

Zhongzhi Shi
Institute of Computing Technology
Chinese Academy of Sciences, China

E. Mercier-Laurent
MODEME, IAE Research Center
Lyon University, France

D. Leake
Indiana University
USA

Springer

Intelligent Information Processing IV

Edited by Zhongzhi Shi, E. Mercier-Laurent and D. Leake

p. cm. (IFIP International Federation for Information Processing, a Springer Series in Computer Science)

ISSN: 1571-5736 / 1861-2288 (Internet)

ISBN: 978-1-4419-4686-7 e-ISBN: 978-0-387-87685-6

Printed on acid-free paper

9 8 7 6 5 4 3 2 1

springer.com

General Chairs

Danielle Boulanger (France)
B. Wah(USA)
T. Nishida (Japan)

Program Chairs

Z. Shi (China)
E. Mercier-Laurent (France)
D. Leake (USA)

Program Committee

A. Aamodt (Norway)
S. A. AL-Dobai (Saudi Arabia)
J. Alvarez (France)
E. Auriol (France)
A. Bernardi (Germany)
B.Braunschweig (France)
JF.Cabestaing (France)
I. Cohen (USA)
R. Chbeir (France)
H. Dai (Australia)
S. Dustdar (Austria)
Y. Ding (Austria)
JL. Ermine (France)
P. Estraillier (France)
W. Fan (UK)
D. Feng (Australia/HK)
JG Ganascia (France)
Y. Gao (China)
Q. He (China)
O.Herzog (Germany)
T.Honkela (Finland)
Z. Huang (Netherlands)
T. Ishida (Japan)
G. Kayakutlu (Turkey)
N. Makoto (Japan)
P. Martinez (Italy)
R.Mizoguchi (Japan)

G. Osipov(Russia)
M. Owoc (Poland)
R. Pfeifer (Switzerland)
A. Rafea (Egypt)
F. Segond (France)
K. Shimohara (Japan)
M. Stumptner (Australia)
K. Su (China)
IJ. Timm (Germany)

Additional Reviewers

Dapeng Zhang, Institute of Computing Technology, CAS, China
Fen Lin, Institute of Computing Technology, CAS, China
Jiewen Luo, Institute of Computing Technology, CAS, China
Changlin Wan, Institute of Computing Technology, CAS, China
Zhiqing Li, Institute of Computing Technology, CAS, China
Jie Liu, Institute of Computing Technologies, CAS, China

Welcome Address

Dear Colleagues,

Welcome to the 5th IFIP International Conference on Intelligent Information Processing. We would like to extend to you our warmest welcome and sincere greetings. As the world proceeds quickly into the Information Age, it encounters both successes and challenges, and it is well recognized nowadays that Intelligent Information Processing provides the key to the Information Age and to mastering many of these challenges. Intelligent Information Processing supports the most advanced productive tools that are said to be able to change human life and the world itself. However, the path is never a straight one and every new technology brings with it a spate of new research problems to be tackled by researchers; as a result we are not running out of topics; rather the demand is ever increasing. This conference provides a forum for engineers and scientists in academia, university and industry to present their latest research findings in all aspects of Intelligent Information Processing.

This is the 5th IFIP International Conference on Intelligent Information Processing. We received over more than 50 papers, of which 22 papers are included in this program as regular papers and 5 as short papers. We are grateful for the dedicated work of both the authors and the referees, and we hope these proceedings will continue to bear fruit over the years to come. All papers submitted were reviewed by several referees.

A conference such as this cannot succeed without help from many individuals who contributed their valuable time and expertise. We want to express our sincere gratitude to the program committee members and referees, who invested many hours for reviews and deliberations. They provided detailed and constructive review reports that will significantly improve the papers included in the program.

We are very grateful to have the sponsorship of the following organizations: IFIP TC12, Chinese Association of Artificial Intelligence, Institute of Computing Technology, Chinese Academy of Sciences.

We hope all of you enjoy this diverse and interesting Program!

Zhongzhi Shi, China
Eunika Mercier-Laurent, France
David Leake, USA
IIP2008 Program Committee Chairs

Contents

Cognition-based Intelligent Information Processing

Image Processing

Virtual Organization and Applications

Risk Management and Computational Linguistics

Keynote Speaker: Phillip C-y Sheu

Title: Semantic Computing

Abstract: This talk highlights the past, present and future of semantic computing that brings together those disciplines concerned with connecting the (often vaguely-formulated) intentions of humans with computational content. This connection can go both ways: retrieving, using and manipulating existing content according to user's goals ("do what the user means"); and creating, rearranging, and managing content that matches the author's intentions ("do what the author means").

The content addressed in SC includes, but is not limited to, structured and semi-structured data, multimedia data, text, programs, services and, even, network behavior. This connection between content and the user is made via (1) Semantic Analysis, which analyzes content with the goal of converting it to meaning (semantics); (2)Semantic Integration, which integrates content and semantics from multiple sources; (3)Semantic Applications, which utilize content and semantics to solve problems; and (4)Semantic Interfaces, which attempt to interpret users' intentions expressed in natural language or other communicative forms.

The field Semantic Computing applies technologies in natural language processing, data and knowledge engineering, software engineering, computer systems and networks, signal processing and pattern recognition, and any combination of the above to extract, access, transform and synthesize the semantics as well as the contents of multimedia, texts, services and structured data.

Bio-Sketch: Dr. Phillip C-Y. Sheu is currently a professor of EECS and Biomedical Engineering at the University of California, Irvine. He also serves as the Founding Director of the Institute for Semantic Computing, an international research organization that connects industry, government and academia to promote semantic technologies. He received his Ph.D. and M.S. degrees from the University of California at Berkeley in Electrical Engineering and Computer Science in 1986 and 1982, respectively. From 1986 to 1988, he was an assistant professor at School of Electrical Engineering, Purdue University. From 1989 to 1993, he was an associate professor of Electrical and Computer Engineering at Rutgers University.

He has published two books: (1) Intelligent Robotic Planning Systems and (2) Software Engineering and Environment - An Object-Oriented Perspective, and more than 100 papers in object-relational data and knowledge engineering and their applications. His current research interests include semantic computing and complex biomedical systems. He is a Fellow of IEEE and the founding editor-in-Chief of the International Journal of Semantic Computing. He is also a co-editor of the forth-coming book "Semantic Computing" (Wiley/IEEE Press, Eds. Phillip Sheu, Heather Yu, C.V. Ramamoorthy, Aravind Joshi and L.A. Zadeh, 2008).

Keynote Speaker: Ning Zhong

Title: Towards Brain-inspired Web Intelligence

Abstract: Artificial Intelligence (AI) has been mainly studied within the realm of computer based technologies. Various computational models and knowledge based systems have been developed for automated reasoning, learning, and problem-solving. However, there still exist several grand challenges. The AI research has not produced major breakthrough recently due to a lack of understanding of human brains and natural intelligence. In addition, most of the AI models and systems will not work well when dealing with large-scale, dynamically changing, open and distributed information sources at a Web scale.

The next major advances in artificial intelligence and Web intelligence are most likely to be brought by an in-depth understanding of human intelligence and its application in the design and implementation of systems with human-level intelligence. To prepare us ready for the great opportunity, this talk outlines a unified framework for the study of brain inspired Web intelligence (WI) by exploring the latest results from brain informatics (BI). This leads to profound advances in the analysis and understanding of data, knowledge, intelligence and wisdom, as well as their inter-relationships, organization and creation process. The fast-evolving WI research and development initiatives are now moving towards understanding the multi-facet nature of intelligence in depth and incorporating it on a Web scale. The recently developed instrumentation (fMRI etc.) and advanced IT are causing an impending revolution in WI research and development, making it possible for us to pursue the new frontier of intelligence science and develop human-level Web intelligence.

Bio-Sketch: Ning Zhong received the Ph.D. degree in the Interdisciplinary Course on Advanced Science and Technology from the University of Tokyo. He is currently head of Knowledge Information Systems Laboratory, and a professor in Department of Life Science and Informatics at Maebashi Institute of Technology, Japan. He is also director and an adjunct professor in the International WIC Institute (WICI), Beijing University of Technology.

He has conducted research in the areas of knowledge discovery and data mining, rough sets and granular-soft computing, Web intelligence, intelligent agents, brain informatics, and knowledge information systems, with over 200 journal and conference publications and 20 books. He is the editor-in-chief of the Web Intelligence and Agent Systems journal (IOS Press), associate editor of IEEE Transactions on Knowledge and Data Engineering, and the Knowledge and Information Systems journal (Springer), a member of the editorial board of Transactions on Rough Sets (Springer), and the editorial board of Advanced Information and Knowledge Processing(AI&KP) book series

(Springer), Frontiers in AI and Applications book series (IOS Press), Chapman&Hall/CRC Data Mining and Knowledge Discovery book series, and editor (the area of intelligent systems) of the Encyclopedia of Computer Science and Engineering (Wiley).

He is the co-chair of Web Intelligence Consortium (WIC), chair of the IEEE Computer Society Technical Committee on Intelligent Informatics (TCII), member of the steering committee of IEEE International Conferences on Data Mining (ICDM), vice chair of IEEE Computational Intelligence Society Technical Committee on Granular Computing, the steering committee of International Rough Set Society.

He has served or is currently serving on the program committees of over 100 international conferences and workshops, including IEEE ICDM'02(conference chair), IEEE ICDM'06 (program chair), IEEE/WIC WI-IAT'03(conference chair), IEEE/WIC/ACM WI-IAT'04 (program chair), and IJCAI'03 (advisory committee member).

He was awarded the best paper awards of AMT'06, JSAI'03, IEEE TCCI/ICDM Outstanding Service Award in 2004, and Pacific-Asia Conference on Knowledge Discovery and Data Mining (PAKDD) Most Influential Paper Award (1999-2008).

Keynote Speaker: Zongben Xu

Title: Data Mining Technologies Inspired from Visual Principle

Abstract: In this talk we review the recent work done by our group on data mining (DM) technologies deduced from simulating visual principle. Through viewing a DM problem as a cognition problems and treading a data set as an image with each light point located at a datum position, we developed a series of high efficient algorithms for clustering, classification and regression via mimicking visual principles. In pattern recognition, human eyes seem to possess a singular aptitude to group objects and find important structure in an efficient way. Thus, a DM algorithm simulating visual system may solve some basic problems in DM research. From this point of view, we proposed a new approach for data clustering by modeling the blurring effect of lateral retinal interconnections based on scale space theory. In this approach, as the data image blurs, smaller light blobs merge into large ones until the whole image becomes one light blob at a low enough level of resolution. By identifying each blob with a cluster, the blurring process then generates a family of clustering along the hierarchy. The proposed approach provides unique solutions to many long standing problems, such as the cluster validity and the sensitivity to initialization problems, in clustering. We extended such an approach to classification and regression problems, through combatively employing the Weber's law in physiology and the cell response classification facts. The resultant classification and regression algorithms are proven to be very efficient and solve the problems of model selection and applicability to huge size of data set in DM technologies. We finally applied the similar idea to the difficult parameter setting problem in support vector machine (SVM). Viewing the parameter setting problem as a recognition problem of choosing a visual scale at which the global and local structures of a data set can be preserved, and the difference between the two structures be maximized in the feature space, we derived a direct parameter setting formula for the Gaussian SVM. The simulations and applications show that the suggested formula significantly outperforms the known model selection methods in terms of efficiency and precision.

The advantages of the proposed approaches are: 1) The derived algorithms are computational stable and insensitive to initialization and they are totally free from solving difficult global optimization problems. 2) They facilitate the construction of new checks on DM validity and provide the final DM result a significant degree of robustness to noise in data and change in scale. 3) They are free from model selection in application. 4) The DM results are highly consistent with those perceived by our human eyes. 5) They provide unified frameworks for scale-related DM algorithms recently derived from many other fields such as estimation theory, recurrent signal processing, information theory and statistical mechanics, and artificial neural networks.

Bio-Sketch: Zongben Xu received his MS degree in Mathematics in 1981 and PhD degree in applied Mathematics in 1987 from Xi'an Jiaotong University, China. In 1998, he was a post-doctoral researcher in the Department of Mathematics, The University of Strathclyde (UK), He worked as a research fellow in the Department of Computer Science and Engineering from 1992 to 1994, and 1996 to 1997, at The Chinese University of Hong Kong; a visiting professor in the University of Essex (UK) in 2001, and Napoli University (Italy) in 2002. He has been with the Faculty of Science and Institute for Information and System Sciences at Xi`an Jiaotong University since 1982, where he was promoted to associate professor in 1987 and full professor in 1991, and now serves as professor of Mathematics and computer science, director of the Institute for Information and System Sciences, and vice president of Xi'an Jiaotong University. In 2007, he was appointed as a Chief Scientist of National Basic Research Program of China (973 Project).

Professor Xu currently makes several important services for government and professional societies, including Consultant Expert for National (973) Program in Key Basic Science Research and Development (Information group), Ministry of Science and Technology of China; Evaluation Committee Member for Mathematics Degree, Academic Degree Commission of the Chinese Council; Committee Member in Scientific Committee of Education Ministry of China (Mathematics and Physics Group); Vice-Director of the Teaching Guidance Committee for Mathematics and Statistics Majors, the Education Ministry of China; Director of the Teaching Guidance Committee for Mathematics Education, the Education Ministry of China; Member in the Expert Evaluation Committee for Natural Science Foundation of China (Computer Science Group), The National Committee for Natural Science Foundation of China; Vice-president of Computational Intelligence Society of China; Editor-in-chief of the Textbooks on Information and Computational Sciences, Higher Education Press of China; Co-editor of nine national and international journals.

Professor Xu has published over 150 academic papers on non-linear functional analysis, optimization techniques, neural networks, evolutionary computation, and data mining algorithms, most of which are in international journals. His current research interests include non-linear analysis, machine learning and computational intelligence. Dr. Xu holds the title "Owner of Chinese PhD Degree Having Outstanding Achievements" awarded by the Chinese State Education Commission (CSEC) and the Academic Degree Commission of the Chinese Council in 1991. He is owner of the National Natural Science Award of China in 2007.

A Context Model for Service Composition Based on Dynamic Description Logic

Wenjia Niu[1,2], Zhongzhi Shi[1] and Liang Chang[1,2]

[1]Key Laboratory of Intelligent Information Processing, Institute of Computing Technology, Chinese Academy of Sciences,100080,Beijing,China

[2]Graduate School of the Chinese Academy of Sciences,100039,Beijing,China
{niuwenjia, shizz, changl}@ics.ict.ac.cn

Abstract: A service composition task for service broker is to discovery and compose provider's services to satisfy user's request. Many researchers model the context utilizing ontology-based or attribute-based method to assist service composition. We propose a new context model by combining the context logic with the dynamic description logic (DDL), where user' context, provider's context and broker's context are described by DDL separately and reasoned under the context logic. The reasoning results finally can be used to discovery and compose services intelligently. We evaluate this model on a simple, yet realistic example, and the results show that our context model provides a practical solution.

Key words: context model, context logic, semantic web service, DDL

1. Introduction

Since the term *context-aware computing* was first introduced in 1994 [15], a large number of definitions of the term *context* have been proposed in the area of computer science. Zimmermann [19] proposed an operational definition of context based on Dey's work [7], in which the context is

"*Context is any information that can be used to characterize the situation of an entity . Elements for the description of this context information fall into five categories: individuality, activity, location, time, and relations. The activity predominantly determines the relevancy of context elements in specific situations, and the location and time primarily drive the creation of relations between entities and enable the exchange of context information among entities*".

The context information in the semantic web services has been modeled to help discovery and compose services recently. However, this context information is rarely modeled as uniform context logic. For instance, the user preference context

---

Please use the following format when citing this chapter:

Niu, W., Shi, Z. and Chang, L., 2008, in IFIP International Federation for Information Processing, Volume 288; *Intelligent Information Processing IV*; Zhongzhi Shi, E. Mercier-Laurent, D. Leake; (Boston: Springer), pp. 7–16.

is modeled using description logic [3]. In general, the methods of modeling context fall into two categories: logic-based [2] [3] and non-logic-based [8] [9] [10] (e.g., attribute-based and ontology-based). The logic-based context model lacks operational definition of context and the non-logic-based model lacks logic representing and reasoning on context, so we try to integrate context logic and operational context in our context model.

The context logic [4, 12] is an extension of first order logic in which sentences are not simply true, but are true within a context. The key extension is a modality ***ist(context, formula)***, read "is true", which takes two arguments: a context and a formula. It asserts that the formula is true in the specified context. Contexts are logical individuals and, as such, can be quantified by logic languages. Description Logics (DLs) is a choice to describe contexts for its ability in representing and reasoning static knowledge. But in semantic web service, DLs cannot effectively represent and reason dynamic knowledge(e.g., service). A dynamic description logic (DDL) was proposed to represent and reason knowledge of static and dynamic [16], which can be taken as a proper logic base for semantic web services. So DDL is chosen to quantify the static and dynamic context information effectively. By combining the context logic and DDL, we proposed a DDL-based context model, in which web services are composed adapt to all contexts of user and provider and broker.

The remainder of this paper is organized as follows. Section 2 presents what's the context information of semantic web service composition. Section 3 presents the context modeling based on DDL and the context logic theory in semantic web services composition. In Section 4, we discuss the evaluation of our model through context reasoning in a realistic example. Section 5 overviews related work and conclusions.

2. Context in Semantic Web Services

According to the operational definition above, there are five main elements for description of an entity context[19]: *individuality*, *time*, *location*, *activity* and *relations*.

In the web service composition process, there exist three roles: the user, the service provider and the service broker. We generalize three contexts corresponding to the three roles separately, which are user context, provider context and broker context. The attributes of user context include user profile, user preference, time, location, and goal. The attributes of provider context include provider profile, time, location, and action. The attributes of broker context include broker profile, time, location, and resources. Fig.1 shows the description of context attributes of each context.

User Context

User profile: corresponds to the user's personal information.

User preference: corresponds to the user's preference on the service he wants to get.

Time, Location: inform use's time and location when sending a service request.

Goal: indicates what the users want to get from services.

Provider Context

Provider profile: corresponds to the provider information, such as provider name.

Time, Location: inform service provider's time and location when receiving a request.

Action: indicates the function description of service.

Broker Context

Broker profile: corresponds to the broker information, such as broker name.

Time, Location: indicates broker's time and location when receiving a request from user.

Resource: indicates service status and user status in composition process.

Fig. 1. Description of Context Attributes

Different from [13][14], the service's function description is defined as a context attribute in our model for two reasons. Firstly, according to the definition of context [19], the service's function is a kind of information that can be used to characterize the situation of the service. Secondly, the context information should be used for not only personalized application but also functionally composing web services.

3. DDL-based Context Model

In this section, we present our idea of extending the classical architecture of web services, which takes into account a context model of the service composition process. Then we introduce the context representation using the DDL language and the context reasoning in our context model.

3.1. Context model in Web Service Architecture

Traditionally, the architecture of WS (see Fig.2) is composed of three entities: the service provider builds the service and publishes its description to a service broker. The user needs are translated into requests that are carried on by the broker. Once the service is found, the user will obtain direct interaction with the service.

Our contribution aims to add to this architecture a context model, which is dedicated to context representation and reasoning. This model is centralized in the broker. In Fig.2, different steps are proposed to integrating the context model in the classical architecture of web services. The different steps are: 1) Provider describe their services using web service description language (WSDL). 2) The user launches his request to the broker (with format SOAP). 3) The context model (CM) captures the users' context. 4) The CM captures the providers' context. 5) The CM captures the broker's context. 6) The CM logically represents and reasoning the contexts, and the reasoning results are transformed into a service composition scheme and delivered to the user. 7) The communication between the user and the provider is done in a traditional way via SOAP.

Our context model consists of two function modules: representing module is responsible to give a logic formalization of context and reasoning module is responsible to reason on context. These two modules can be integrated into a uniform context logic system, meant as the triple $\Sigma=(L,\Lambda,\Delta)$, where L is a context logic language, Λ is a set of axioms and Δ is a set of reasoning rules. As mentioned in Sec.1, the key syntax of context logic is ***ist(context, formula)***, which ***context*** represents a logical individual and, as such, will be described by the DDL language. Context embodies an individual's subjective perspective which characterizes the individual's situation, so user's context, provider's context and broker's context are described separately by the DDL language, but logically connected by *bridge rules(BR)* in context logic system. A distributed reasoning algorithm is taken to reason about contexts of user's, provider's and broker's. As for the capture of context and the transformation between logic language and SOAP format, they are out of this paper's scope..

3.2. Context Representation

A DDL knowledge base consists of a TBox, an ABox and an ActionBox [5]. The Tbox contains assertions about concepts (e.g., *Person*) and roles (e.g., *hasAge*). The ABox contains assertions about individuals (e.g., *PETER*). The ActionBox contains assertions about actions (e.g., *BuyMovieTicket(JOHN, TICKET)*). π is a action. An atomic action is a pair *(P,E)*, where, *P* ,*E* are two finite set of formulas used to describe precondition and effect accordingly.

We depict a simple scenario to show how to describe contexts in web services composition and what's the difference of each context.

Example 1.(The movie scenario) PETER are going to see a movie when he is driving, so he would like to get the movie information and buy a ticket online. To achieve this, he will publish his request to a service broker through his smart phone. After receiving the request, the broker will try to find and compose proper services for PETER. There exist two services *BuyTicket* service and *GetMovieInfor* service provided by a provider, which can meet the PETER's request. According to the TBox, contexts are described by the DDL language as follows.

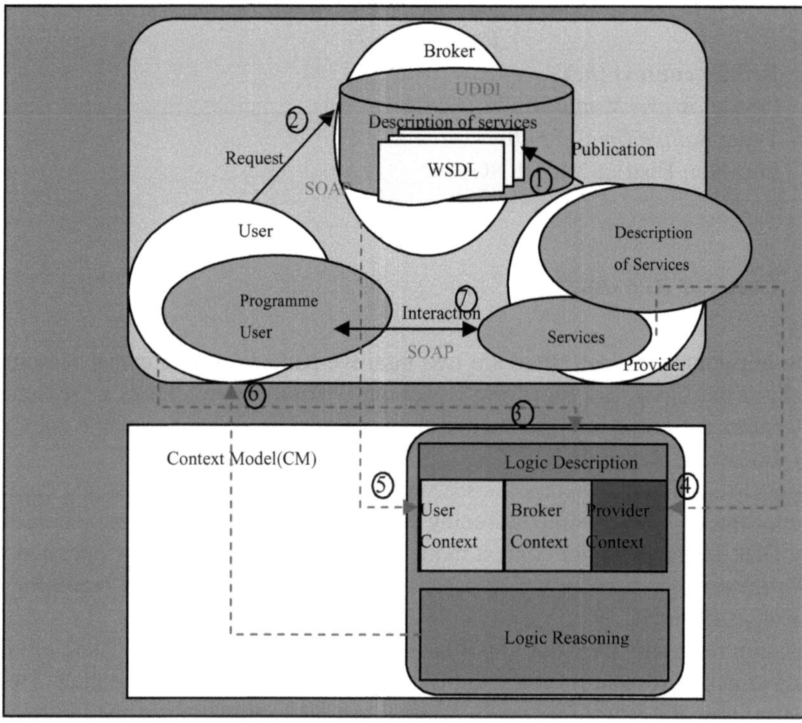

Fig. 2. Architecture of web service based on context

- **User context (*uc*)**

  Profile: $Person(PETER) \cap (InCar(PETER)) \cap Male(PETER) \cap (\exists hasAge.\{20\}(PETER)) \cap hasMoney(PETER,230)$

  Preference: $Movie(x) \cap \exists hasMovieGenre.\{Love\}(x)$

  Time: $BeijingTime(17{:}00)$

  Location: $District(HAIDIAN)$

  Goal: $Own(PETER,x) \cap Ticket(x) \cap hasInformation(PETER,y) \cap Information(y)$

- **Provider context (*pc*)**

  Profile: $ProviderName(PEOPLEMOVIE)$

  Time: $BeijingTime(17{:}00)$

  Location: $District(XUANWU)$

  Action: $BuyTicket(x,y) \equiv (\{Person(x), \neg Own(y), Ticket(y), hasMoney(x,z), Money(z)\}, \{Own(y)\})$

  $GetMovieInfor(x,z) \equiv (\{Person(x)\}, \{Movie(z), MovieGenre(y), (\exists hasMovieGenre.\{y\}(z)), BeginTime(t), (\exists hasBe-$

ginTime.{t}(z)),TicketPrice(p), (∃hasTicket-Price.{p}(z))})

- **Broker context (*bc*)**
  Profile: *BrokerName(SWSBROKER)*
  Time: *BeijingTime(17:00)*
  Location: District(XICHENG)

3.3. Context Reasoning

In our context model, there are two intuitive patterns of contextual reasoning: localized reasoning and transform reasoning. With these two kinds of reasoning, the context reasoning can operate in a single context as well span several contexts.

1)Localized Reasoning

Localized reasoning refers the reasoning process is always in a single context, which contains whatever the reasoning process needs. Since a context is described by a DDL language in our context model, localized reasoning can be operated in a DDL reasoning system in which basic reasoning in DL and action reasoning are typically supported.

Action reasoning plays an important role in localized reasoning. There are four kinds of action reasoning: realizability, executability, projection and plan. To understand how the reasoning works, we still use the example mentioned in Sec.3.2 and suppose that the $D_{S,}$ the set of formulas to describe the state, is: *{Person(PETER),(InCar(PETER)),Male(PETER), (∃hasAge.{20}(PETER)),hasMoney(PETER,230), Ticket(TITANIC-TICKET),¬own(TITANIC-TICKET), Movie(TITANIC), hasTicket(TITANIC,1);* The TBox D_T is showed in Fig.4 and The RBox D is supposed to be *null.*

Realizability: An action π is realizable *w.r.t.* the RBox D_R and TBox D_T iff there exists a model $M=(W,I)$ of both D_R and D_T such that there exists some states $w,w'\in W$ with $(w,w')\in\pi^I$. *Executability*: An action π is executable on states described by D_S iff for any model $M=(W,I)$ of both D_R and D_T, and for any state $w\in W$ with $(M,w)|=D_S$, there exists a model $M'=(W',I')$ of both D_R and D_T,such that $W\subseteq W',I'(Wi)=I(Wi)$, for each $(M',w)|=D_S$, and $(w,w')\in\pi^I$ for some state $w'\in W'$. In the example 1, the action "*BuyTicket(PETER,TITANIC-TICKET)*" is executable, but the complex action "*BuyTicket(PETER,TITANIC-TICKET), BuyTicket(PETER, TITANIC-TICKET)*" is not executable.

Projection: A formula ψ is a consequence of applying π on states described by D_S iff for any model $M=(W,I)$ of both D_R and D_T, and for any states $w,w'\in W$:if $(M,w)|=D_S$ and $(w,w')\in\pi^I$., then $(M,w')|=\psi'$.

Plan: Let ψ be a formula and Σ be a set of actions. Let $\pi_1,\ldots\pi_n$ be a sequence of actions with each action coming from Σ. Then, the sequence $\pi_1,\ldots\pi_n$ is a plan for ψ relative to D_S iff (i) the sequence-action $\pi_1,\ldots\pi_n$ is executable on states described by D_S and (ii) ψ is a consequence $\pi_1,\ldots\pi_n$ of applying on states described by D_S. For example, the action sequence "*BuyTicket(PETER, TITANIC-TICKET), GetMovieInfor(PETER, TITANIC-INFOR)*" is a plan for the goal *own(PETER,TITANIC-TICKET)*$\cap$*hasInformation(PETER, TITANIC-INFOR).*

2)Transform Reasoning

Context bridging allows us to state that a certain property holds between elements of two different contexts. In our model, the basic notion toward the definition of bridge rules are: a bridge rule from *i* to *j* is a statement of one of the six following forms, $i:C \xrightarrow{\subseteq} j:E, i:C \xrightarrow{\supseteq} j:E, i:C \xrightarrow{\equiv} j:E,$ $i:\alpha \xrightarrow{\subseteq} j:\beta, i:\alpha \xrightarrow{\supseteq} j:\beta, i:\alpha \xrightarrow{\equiv} j:\beta$, where *C* and *E* are either concepts or roles of the DDL languages DDL_i and DDL_j respectively, α and β are actions of DDL_i and DDL_j respectively.

The idea of transform reasoning is mapping a context logic into a global DDL_G, then utilizing the DDL_G's reasoning to realize the context reasoning, which is similar to the reasoning of distributed description logic[1]. Suppose the family of the dynamic description logic is $\{DDL_i\}(i\in I)$, the bridge rules are $BR_{i,j}(i,j\in I)$, the individuals are $IN_{i,j}(i,j\in I)$, we proposed a reasoning algorithm named transform reasoning(see Algorithm 1).

4. Case Study

We now put our context model on the simple scenario introduced in Example 1 to show how reasoning and service composition work.

Example 2.(The movie scenario revisited) The context logic contains three contexts: user context, provider context and broker context, which are described in DDL languages DDL_{uc}, DDL_{pc} and DDL_{bc} respectively. The bridge rules are :

$$uc:Information \xrightarrow{\supseteq} pc:\exists hasMovieGenre.MovieGenre$$

$$uc:Information \xrightarrow{\supseteq} pc:\exists hasBeginTime.BeginTime$$

$$uc:Information \xrightarrow{\supseteq} pc:\exists hasTicketPRice.TicketPRice$$

$$uc:Person \xrightarrow{\equiv} pc:Person, uc:Movie \xrightarrow{\equiv} pc:Movie$$

$$uc:MovieGenre \xrightarrow{\equiv} pc:MovieGenre, uc:BeijingTime \xrightarrow{\equiv} pc:BeijingTime$$

$$uc:District \xrightarrow{\equiv} pc:District, uc:Ticket \xrightarrow{\equiv} pc:Ticket$$

$$uc:Money \xrightarrow{\equiv} pc:Money, uc:Own \xrightarrow{\equiv} pc:Own$$

Algorithm 1. Transform Reasoning

//define an operator # from concepts/roles/actions of DDL_i to DDL_G
M are concepts/roles/actions in DDL_i
$\#(i:M)$ define $i:M$ as primitive concepts/roles/actions in DDL_G
If (ρ is a concept constructor taking k arguments in DDL_i)
Then $\#(\rho(M_1,\ldots,M_k)) = i:\rho(\#(i:M_1),\ldots,\#(i:M_k))$
//generate TBox in DDL_G
For axioms $C \sqsubseteq E$ in DDL_i
  add $\#(i:C) \sqsubseteq \#(i:E)$ into DDL_G
End For
For each bridge rules
IF($i:C \xrightarrow{\sqsubseteq} j:E$)**Then add** $\#(i:C) \sqsubseteq \#(j:E)$ into DDL_G
IF($i:C \xrightarrow{\sqsupseteq} j:E$)**Then add** $\#(i:C) \sqsupseteq \#(j:E)$ into DDL_G
IF($i:C \xrightarrow{\equiv} j:E$)**Then add** $\#(i:C) \equiv \#(j:E)$ into DDL_G
End For
add $\bot \sqsubseteq C$, $C \sqsubseteq_{\top} C$ into DDL_G ,C are concepts/roles/actions
//generate ABox in DDL_G
For $C(a) \in ABox_i$, where C are concepts/roles/actions in DDL_i
  add $\#(i:C(i:a))$ into DDL_G
End For
Action reasoning in DDL_G

According to the transform reasoning algorithm, the context logic can be mapped into a global logic DDL_G, in which the TBox is as follows:

uc:Information⊒pc.∃hasMovieGenre.MovieGenre
uc:Information⊒pc.∃hasBeginTime.BeginTime
uc:Information⊒pc.∃hasTicketPRice.TicketPRice,uc:Person≡pc:Perso
uc:Movie≡pc:Movie, uc:MovieGenre≡pc:MovieGenre,
uc:BeijingTime≡pc:BeijingTime
uc:District≡pc:District, uc:Ticket≡pc:Ticket, uc:Money≡pc:Money,
uc:Own≡pc:Own.

Suppose the state D_s in DDL_{pc} is:

{uc:Person(uc:PETER),uc:InCar(uc:PETER),uc:*Male(uc:PETER),*
uc:∃hasAge.{20}(uc:PETER),uc: *hasMoney(uc:PETER,uc:230),*
pc:Ticket(pc:TITANIC-TICKET),uc:¬own(uc:PETER,uc:TITANIC-TICKET),
pc: Movie(pc:TITANIC),pc: hasTicket(pc:TITANIC,pc:1)}

Finally, according to action reasoning in DDL_G, it is found that the action sequence "*pc:BuyTicket(pc:PETER,pc:TITANIC-TICKET),pc:GetMovieInfor(pc:PETER,pc:TITANIC-IFOR)*" is a plan for the user's goal of getting the information and buying an online ticket: *uc:own(uc:PETER,uc:TITANIC-TICKET)⊓uc:hasInformation(uc:PETER,uc:TITANIC-INFOR).*

The reasoning results show that the two services : *GetMovieInfor* and *BuyTicket* can be composed to meet the user's request.

5. Related Work and Conclusion

The context has been modeled as ontology-based model or list of attributes in context-aware computing and web services: S.K.Mostefaoui[15] proposed a framework by combination of context-aware computing and agent technology, in which contextual information is exploited for service discovery and composition; Z.Maamar[11] proposed an agent-based and context-oriented approach, in which agent is characterized by context information; Chen[6] describe a framework for an agent based pervasive computing environment, in which contexts are explicitly represented using ontology languages allowing independently developed agents to exploit common ontologies to share knowledge and interoperate; Qiu[14] proposed an ontology-based framework for the context-aware composition of web services, where the context model are structured based on the upper ontology OWL-S.

In semantic web area, the context logic theory is successfully introduced to model context for building a contextualized ontology[2] (C-OWL), whose contents are kept local, and mapped with the contents of other ontologies via context mappings. [17] integrated a context model in web services, in which comprehensive structured context profiles(CSCP) format is used to describe context information. 6.Conclusion

In this paper, we proposed a new context model in semantic web services composition. This context model aims to deliver a list of adapted web services according to user's and provider's and broker's context. By combining the context logic with DDL, our model can discovery and compose web services through logical reasoning. To our best knowledge, the combination of context logic and DDL to assist and achieve the service composition is a new try in web services area, and the case study evaluates our approach effective.

Acknowledgements

This work was partially supported by the National Basic Research Program of China (No. 2007CB311004), the National Natural Science Foundation of China (No. 90604017, 60775035) and the National High-Tech Research and Development Plan of China (No. 2007AA01Z132).

References

[1]A.Borgida, L.Serafini: Distributed description logics: assimilating information from peer sources. Journal of Data Semantics,1(1), 153-184(2003).

[2]P.Bouquet, F.Giunchiglia, Harmelen.: C-OWL: Contextualizing Ontologies. International Semantic Web Conference 2003, 164-179(2003).

[3]A.H. Bunningen, L. Feng, and P.M.G. Apers, Using Description Logics to Model Context Aware Query Preferences. *CTIT Technical Report TR-CTIT-06-17*(2006).

[4]S. Buvac, I. Mason: Propositional logic of context. Proceedings of the eleventh national conference on artificial intelligence(1993).

[5]L. Chang, F. Lin, Z.Shi: A Dynamic Description Logic for Representation and Reasoning About Actions. *KSEM 2007*, 115-127(2007)

[6]H.Chen, T.Finin, A. Joshi: An ontology for context-aware pervasive computing environments. *Special Issue on Ontologies for Distributed Systems. Knowledge Engineering Review*, 3(18), 197-207(2004).

[7]A.K.Dey: Understanding and Using Context. *Personal Ubiquitous Computing* 5(1), 4–7(2001).

[8]S.Iga, M. Shinnishi, M. Nakatomi.: Context Gallery: A Service-Oriented Framework to Facilitate Context Information Sharing. *APWeb 2006*, 1096-1106(2006).

[9]O.Khriyenko, V. Terziyan: Context Description Framework for the Semantic Web, *Context Representation and Reasoning Workshop at CONTEXT 2005.*

[10]C.Lee and S.Helal: Context Attributes: An Approach to Enable Context-awareness for Service Discovery. *SAINT 2003*, 22-30(2003).

[11]Z.Maamar, S.K.Mostefaoui, H.Yahyaoui: Toward an Agent-based and context-oriented approach for Web services composition. *IEEE Transaction on Knowledge and Data ngineering* ,17(5), 686-697(2005).

[12]J. McCarthy: Notes on formalizing context. Proceedings of the thirteenth international joint conference on artificial intelligence(1993).

[13] S.K.Mostefaoui, B.Hirsbrunner: Toward a Context-Based Service Composition Framework. Proceedings of the International Conference on Web Services(ICWS'03), 42-45(2003).

[14]L.Qiu, L. Chang, F. Lin, and Zhongzhi Shi: Context Optimization of AI planning for Semantic Web Services Composition. *Journal of Service-Oriented Computing and Applications,* 117-128(2007).

[15]B.N.Schilit, Adams, N.I., R.Want: Context-Aware Computing Applications. *Proceedings of the Workshop on Mobile Computing Systems and Applications*, 85–90 (1994).

[16]Z.Shi, M.Dong, Y.Jiang, H.Zhang: A Logic Foundation for the Semantic Web. *Science in China*, Series F, 48(2), 161-178(2005).

[17]B.Soukkarieh, F.Sedes: Integrating a Context Model in Web Services. *ICWS* ,1195-1196 (2007).

[18]T.Strang, C.Linnhoff–Popien: A Context Modeling Survey. *Workshop on Advanced Context Modelling, Reasoning and Management* (2004).

[19]A.Zimmermann, Andreas Lorenz, and Reinhard Oppermann:An Operational Definition of Context. CONTEXT 2007, 558-571(2007).

Evaluation of Ontologies and DL Reasoners

Muhammad Fahad, Muhammad Abdul Qadir and Syed Adnan Hussain Shah

Mohammad Ali Jinnah University, Islamabad, Pakistan.

mhd.fahad@gmail.com, {aqadir,adnan}@jinnah.edu.pk

Abstract: Ontology driven architecture has revolutionized the inference system by allowing interoperability and efficient reasoning between heterogeneous multi-vendors systems. Sound reasoning support is highly important for sound semantic web ontologies which can only be possible if state-of-the-art Description Logic Reasoners were capable enough to identify inconsistency and classify taxonomy in ontologies. We have discussed existing ontological errors and design anomalies, and provided a case study incorporating these errors. We have evaluated consistency, subsumption, and satisfiability of DL reasoners on the case study. Experiment with DL reasoners opens up number of issues that were not incorporated within their followed algorithms. Especially circulatory errors and various types of semantic inconsistency errors that may cause serious side effects need to be detected by DL reasoners for sound reasoning from ontologies. The evaluation of DL reasoners on Automobile ontology helps in updating the subsumption, satisfiability and consistency checking algorithms for OWL ontologies, especially the new constructs of OWL 1.1.

1 Introduction

Ontology has revolutionized the inference system by allowing interoperability between heterogeneous multi-vendors systems and semantic web applications [17]. Well formed ontologies can only furnish the semantics for emerging semantic web and provide reasoning capability that they require. Due to their expressive power and reasoning capabilities, they are being used in wide range of applications and knowledge based systems [1]. Like any other dependable component of a system, Ontology has to go through a repetitive process of refinement and evaluation during its development lifecycle so that they can serve their purposes and make their user safer in the application.

Several approaches for evaluation of taxonomic knowledge on ontologies are contributed in the research literature. Ontologies can be evaluated by considering design principles [6,7], maintenance issues [2] , use in an application [13] and predictions from their results, peer review [16] , comparison with a golden stan-

---

Please use the following format when citing this chapter:

Fahad, M., Qadir, M.A. and Shah, S.A.H., 2008, in IFIP International Federation for Information Processing, Volume 288; *Intelligent Information Processing IV*; Zhongzhi Shi, E. Mercier-Laurent, D. Leake; (Boston: Springer), pp. 17–27.

dard [10] or reference ontology library [13] or manipulation of data [3]. These approaches evaluate the ontologies from different frame of references that enable better reasoning support for fulfillment of sound semantic web vision.

Sound semantic web ontologies have to create balance between computational complexity needed for reasoning mechanisms and expressive power of the concepts defined [11]. Initial ontologies RDF and RDFS [1], provide very limited expressive power that is not very rich to represent semantics related with a domain. OWL and its newly formed specie OWL 1.1 provide much expressive power and sparked the inference engines by providing the suitable reasoning support. Though the DL reasoners were long before the existence of OWL ontologies, but new dialects of OWL ontologies need some more reasoning and inference services. These languages especially OWL 1.1 opens up new challenges [21] for DL reasoners to check subsumption, consistency and satisfiability from ontologies developed for sound semantic web environment.

One of the benchmark for DL reasoners is presented by Pan with realistic ontologies to check the time taken by these reasoners [20]. The experiment was dealt with 135 ontologies, and DL reasoners timeout and aborted operations were counted and reported. The experiment helped out in optimizing the algorithms followed by DL reasoners. The one conducted by us differs and is unique as it helps out identifying deficiencies and incompleteness in their algorithms.

This paper is based on our line of research [4,5,12,14,15] on evaluation of ontologies. In [17, 18], we presented the ontology evaluation framework for OWL ontologies and extended the ontology error taxonomy initially formed by Gomez. In this paper, we provide a case study on design anomalies and taxonomic errors. We have formed Automobile ontology and seeded all types of errors to promote learning and understandability of ontological errors. This ontology also acts as a test data for evaluation of Description Logic Reasoners, and helps in finding some of the deficiencies in the algorithms followed by them.

Rest of the paper is organized as follows: section 2 presents the types of ontological error and their classification. The same section builds the case study of Automobile ontology with these errors. Section 3 discusses the evaluation of state-of-the-art DL reasoners and our experiment details. Section 4 concludes the paper.

2 Taxonomic Errors and Design Anomalies

Gomez-Perez [6,7,8] identified three main classes of taxonomic errors that might occur when modelling the conceptualization into taxonomies. These classes of errors are Inconsistency, Incompleteness and Redundancy. We have extended these classes by incorporating more errors in each class by evaluation of online ontologies [17,18]. We seeded these errors in automobile ontology, as shown in Fig.1, which acts as benchmark for DL reasoners later on. Table 1 and 2 provide the important axioms for understanding the ontological errors. The top level description of errors in automobile ontology is provided by subsections.

Table 1. Important axioms of concepts in Automobile ontology.

Owner $\subseteq \exists$ drives MotorVehicle
Passenger $\subseteq \exists$ involves MotorVehicle $\sqcap \exists$ hasreserved MotorVehicle
VehicleOwner $\subseteq$ owns ≥ 1 MotorVehicle
NoOwner $\subseteq$ owns $= 0$ MotorVehicle
Owner2Vehicle $\subseteq$ owns $= 2$ PassengerVehicle
Owner4Vehicle $\subseteq$ owns $= 4$ PassengerVehicle
OwnerManyVehicle $\subseteq$ owns ≥ 3 PessangerVehicle $\sqcap$ owns ≤ 8 PassengerVehicle
Ownerlessthan3Vehicle $\subseteq$ owns ≤ 2 PassengerVehicle
OwnerSomeVehicle $\subseteq \exists$ owns PassengerVehicle
OnwerAllVehicle $\subseteq \forall$ owns PassengerVehicle
BikeOwner $\subseteq \exists$ hasBike Bike
Bike $\subseteq$ HondaMotorBike U YamahaMotorBike
Men $\subseteq$ Peson $\sqcap \forall$ hasGender Male
Women $\subseteq$ Peson $\sqcap \forall$ hasGender Female

Table 2. Disjointness and Property information in Automobile ontology.

Property(Domain, Range)	**Disjoint Axioms (Class1 ┤ Class2)**
owns(VehicleOwner, MotorVehicle)	Driver ┤ Passenger
owns(Owner, MotorVehcicle)	MotorVehicle ┤ Plane
drives(Driver, MotorVehicle)	PIA ┤ Truck
hasReserved(Driver, MotorVehicle)	Male ┤ Female
involves(Pessenger, MotorVehicle)	Coach ┤ Van
Functional hasBike(BikeOnwer, Bike)	Pejjero ┤ Jeep
hasRegisterationNo(MotorVehicle, RegisterationNo)	YamahaMotorBike ┤ HondaMotorBikc

2.1 Inconsistency Errors

There are mainly three types of errors that cause inconsistency and contradictions during the reasoning from the ontology. These are Circulatory errors, Partition errors and Semantic inconsistency errors.

Circulatory errors occur when a class is defined as a subclass or superclass of itself at any level of hierarchy in the ontology [7]. In automobile ontology, circulatory error on concept *Class_2* occurs as it is specified as subclass of *Class_5*. OWL ontologies provide constructs to form property hierarchies by specifying *MobilinkNo* as subproperty of *MobileNo* and *MobileNo* as subproperty of *ContactNo*. Circulatory error in property hierarchy [17] occurs by specifying *MobilinkNo* as subproperty of *ContactNo*.

Partition errors occur while decomposition of concept into many subconcept. A common class/property/instance in disjoint decomposition and partition error occurs when ontologists create the class/instance (or property) that belongs to various disjoint classes (or disjoint properties) [7]. In automobile ontology, *MiniVan* as subclass of two disjoint classes *Coach* and *Van* creates inconsistency of this type. Likewise common property in disjoint decomposition of properties creates inconsistency in property hierarchy [17]. We seeded instance *myMiniVan123* which serves as common instance between disjoint classes. Moreover when concepts are disjoint then they should not use the properties of their disjoint concepts. Concept *Passenger* ($\subseteq \exists$ *hasReserved MotorVehicle*) being disjoint with *Driver* constitutes this type of inconsistency by using property *hasReserved*.

External instance in exhaustive decomposition occurs when one or more instances of base class do not belong to any of the subclasses [7]. In automobile ontology, we seeded *SaudiAirWays* as instance of *Plane* that does not belong to *PIA* and *BritishAirWays* subclasses.

Semantic Inconsistency errors occur when ontologists make an incorrect class hierarchy by classifying a concept as a subclass of a concept to which it does not really belong [7]. For example the ontologist classifies the concept *Airbus* as a subclass of the concept *Train*. Or the same might have happened when classifying instances. We identify mainly three reasons due to which incorrect semantic classification originates [5] and categorized Semantic inconsistency errors into three subclasses.

Weaker domain specified by subclass error [5] occurs when classes that represent the larger domain are kept subclasses of concept that possess smaller domain. In automobile ontology, the semantic inconsistency of this type occurs as more generalized concept *OnwerSomeVehicle* $\subseteq \exists$ *owns PassengerVehicle* is created as a subclass of the concept *Onwer4vehicle* $\subseteq$ *owns* $= 4$ *PassengerVehicle.*

Domain breach specified by subclass error [5] occurs when a subclass adds more features but the additional features are violating the existing features of their superclasses. In automobile ontology, *OwnerManyVehicle* $\subseteq$ *owns* ≥ 3 *PessangerVehicle* $\sqcap \leq 8$ *PassengerVehicle* concept as a subclass of *Onwer4Vehicle* concept breaches the domain.

Disjoint domain specified by subclass error [5] occur when ontologists specify concept as subclass of a concept having disjoint domain. In automobile ontology, *NoOwner* concept as a subclass of *OnwerVehicle* concept, *Onwer2Vechicle* and *Onwerlessthan3Vehicle* as subclasses of *Onwer4Vehicle* shows the disjoint domain specified by subclass error. Moreover, *Women* $\subseteq$ *Person* $\sqcap$ $\forall$ *hasGender.Female* as a subclass of *Men* $\subseteq$ *Person* $\sqcap$ $\forall$ *hasGender.Male*, as *Male* is disjoint with *Female* constitutes the error of this category. Similarly, these semantic inconsistency errors can be applied same to the instances of superclasses and subclasses to check whether they have conformance with each other.

2.2 Incompleteness Errors

Sometimes ontologists classify concepts but overlook some of the important information about them. Such incompleteness often creates ambiguity and lacks reasoning mechanisms. The following subsections give the overview of incompleteness errors.

Incomplete Concept Classification error [7] occurs when ontologists overlook some of the concepts present in the domain while classification of particular concept. In automobile ontology, *Plane* concept is incompletely classified by ignoring *SaudiAirways*, *ShaheenExpress, etc,* types of planes.

Partition Errors occur when ontologist omits important axioms or information about the classification of concept. Disjoint Knowledge Omission error [7] occurs when ontologists classify the concept into many subclasses, but omits disjoint knowledge axiom between them. In automobile ontology, disjoint axiom between *PassengerVehicle* and *LoaderVehicle* is ignored. We experienced catastrophic results by disjoint knowledge omission between user and Administrator in *Access_Policy* ontology [14]. Similarly disjoint axiom between properties create incompleteness error in property partitioning [17].

Exhaustive knowledge Omission occurs when ontologists do not follow the completeness constraint while decomposition of concept into subclasses [7]. In automobile ontology, ontologist models the *Coach*, and *Van* classes as disjoint subclasses of *PassengerVehicle* concept, but does not specify that whether this classification forms an exhaustive decomposition.

For powerful reasoning and enhanced inference, OWL ontology provides some tags that can be associated with properties of classes [1]. OWL functional and inverse-functional tags associated with properties indicate how many times a domain concept can be associated with range concept via a property. Sometimes ontologists do not give significance to these property tags and do not declare datatype or object properties as functional or inverse-functional. As a result machine can not reason about a property effectively leading to serious complications [15]. In automobile ontology, *hasRegisterationNo* as an object property between *MotorVehicle* and *RegisterationNo* is an example of functional object property due to the fact that every subject *Vehicle* has only one registeration number. Ignoring Functional tag with *RegisterationNo* allows property to have more than one values leading to inconsistency. One of the main reason for such inconsistency is that ontologist has ignored that OWL ontology by default supports multi-values for datatype property and object property. In this example, *hasRegisterationNo* property also needs to be specified as inverse-functional property as it uniquely identifies the subject.

Sufficient knowledge Omission Error (SKO) [12] occurs when concept has only *Necessary description*, i.e., defined only by the basic criteria of subclass-of, and does not have *sufficient description* that elaborates the characteristics of concept and defines the context in terms of other concepts. In automobile ontology, *PIA* and *BritishAirWays* concepts need sufficient knowledge to interpret and distinguish them while reasoning.

2.3 Redundancy Errors

Redundancy occurs when particular information is inferred more than once from the relations, classes and instances found in ontology. The following are the types of redundancies that might be made when developing taxonomies.
Redundancies of *SubclassOf* error [7] occur when ontologists specify classes that have more than one *SubclassOf* relation directly or indirectly. In automobile ontology specifying *Jeep* as a subclass of *PassengerVehicle* and *MotorVehicle*, creates redundancy as *PassengerVehicle* is already a *subclassOf MotorVechicle*. Here indirect *SubclassOf* relation exists between *Jeep* and *MotorVehicle* creating redundancy of this type. Similarly, redundancy of *SubpropertyOf* can exist while building property hierarchies [17]. Redundancies of *InstanceOf* relation [7] occur when ontologists specify instance *myJeep* as an *InstanceOf MotorVehicle* and *PassengerVehicle* concepts.

Identical formal definition of classes, properties or instances may occur when ontologist defines different (or same) names of two classes, properties or instances respectively, but provides the same formal definition. In automobile ontology, *Driver* $\subseteq \exists$ *drives MotorVehicle* and *Owner* $\subseteq \exists$ *drives MotorVehicle* specifies identical formal definition of classes.

Redundancy of Disjoint Relation (RDR) [12] occurs when the concept is explicitly defined as disjoint with other concepts more than once. In automobile ontology, disjoint axiom between *PIA* and *Truck* creates RDR error as *MotorVehicle* and *Plane* concepts were already disjoint with each other. Fig. 1 shows the class hierarchy of Automobile ontology.

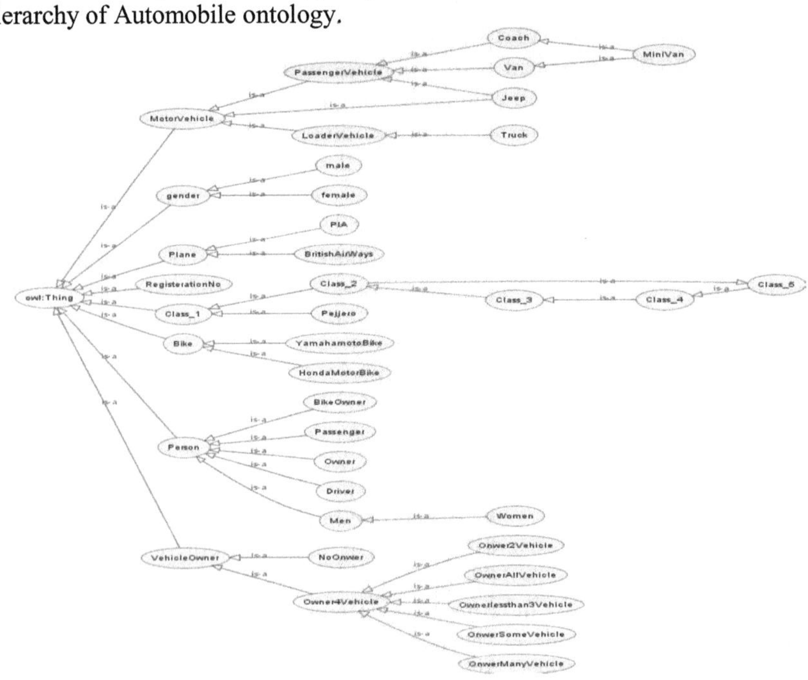

Fig. 1. Class hierarchy of Automobile ontology.

2.4 Design Anomalies in Ontologies

Besides taxonomic errors, Baumeister and Seipel [2] identified some design anomalies that prohibit simplicity and maintainability of taxonomic structures within ontology. These do not cause inaccurate reasoning about concepts, but point to problematic and badly designed areas in ontology. Identification and removal of these anomalies should be necessary for improving the usability, and providing better maintainability of ontology.

Property Clumps: The repeated group of datatype properties (name, model, color, price, etc.) in class *MotorVehicle* and *Bike* create property clump.

Chain of Inheritance: In automobile ontology, *Class_1* to *Class_5* creates chain of inheritance as these concepts have no appropriate descriptions in the ontology except inherited child.

Lazy Concepts: A leaf concept that is not instantiated and never used in the application is called the lazy concept. In automobile ontology we have created many lazy concepts, *Truck* concept is one of the example of this kind.

Lonely Disjoints: We moved the concept *Pejjero* from the *PassengerVehicle* hierarchy somewhere in the other hierarchy, creating lonely disjoint with *Jeep* concept.

3 Description Logic Reasoners and Ontology Errors

In this section, we are evaluating the state-of-the-art Description Logic (DL) reasoners by providing them the ontology seeded with the errors described in above section 2. The evaluation of DL reasoners helps us to build more powerful algorithms so that reasoning from ontologies can be enhanced to fulfill the goals of semantic web. The experiment was performed on three state-of-the-art DL reasoners Pellet, FaCT++, and Racer. The salient features of these reasoners and experiment details are explained below.

Racer: Racer was implemented in Lisp to demonstrate the tableaux calculus for SHIQ, and follows the multiple optimization strategies for better reasoning support including dependency-directed backtracking, transformation of axioms, model caching and merging, etc, [19].

Pellet: Pellet employs reasoning on SHIN (D) and SHON (D) and implemented in Java with the strategies of TBox partitioning, nominal support, absorption, semantic branching, lazy unfolding, dependency directed backjumping [21]. Datatype reasoning, individual reasoning, and optimization in Abox query answering makes it more attractive for sound semantic web applications.

FaCT++: FaCT++ [22] an improved version of FaCT [23] employs tableaux algorithms for SHOIQ description logic and implemented in C++ but has very limited user interface and services as compared to other reasoners. The strategies followed are absorption, model merging, told cycle elimination, synonym replacement, ordering heuristics and taxonomic classification.

Experiment Discussion: The automobile ontology that was seeded with various types of errors is taken as the test data. These errors and anomalies were seeded very intelligently so that performance of consistency, subsumption, satisfiability, and tableaux algorithm efficiency can be measured. Due to space limitations, the only necessary errors were discussed above and here also we discuss our high level findings from experiment. The experiment was conducted on FaCT++1.1.11 (uploaded date: March 28, 08), Pellet 1.5.1 (uploaded date: Oct 26, 07) and Racer 1.9.0 versions.

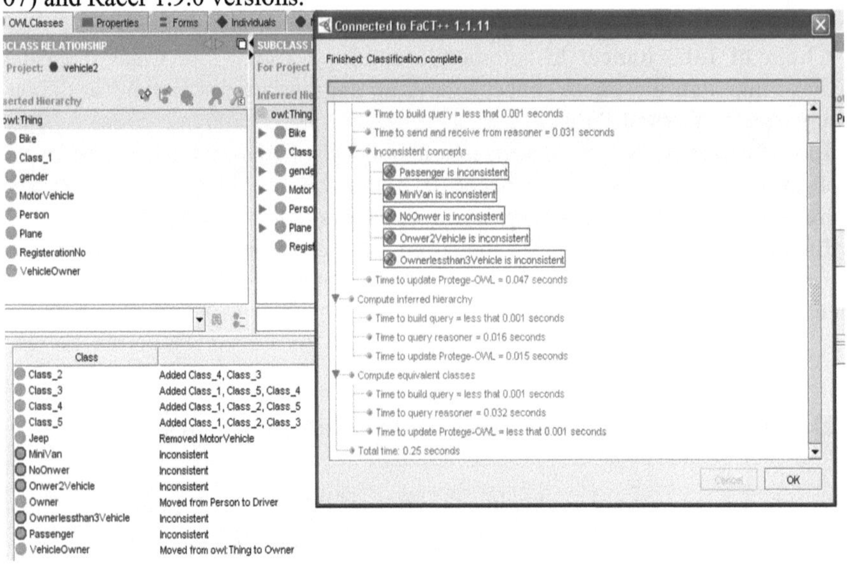

Fig. 2. Results produced by FaCT++ Reasoner

By consistency checking on automobile ontology, only some of the errors were detected. The inconsistent concepts (*Passenger, MiniVehicle, Owner2Vehicle, NoOwner, Onwerlessthan3Vehicle*) were detected by all the three DL reasoners. These inconsistent concepts are described along the errors above. Inconsistency of type common property in disjoint decomposition of properties is detected by only FaCT++. Redundancy of subclassOf error on concept *Jeep* was detected and in classified taxonomy superclass *MotorVehicle* was removed, as shown in classify taxonomy results *'Removed Motorvehicle'* in left down side of Figure 2. But some very important situations were not detected highlighting their deficiencies. One of the important aspects during reasoning from ontologies is that it should detect circles from taxonomies and get himself out from traversing circles again and again. According to Gomez [7], circle in hierarchy is error and should be detected and removed. This experiment highlights deficiency in their algorithms that they are not capable of handling circulatory errors in class hierarchies and property hierarchies. Circulatory error at *Class_2* was detected and all the subsumptions were reasoned as shown in the inferred class hierarchy by FaCT++ DL reasoners in

Figure 3, and added superclasses for all the classes in the circle as shown in Figure 2 (down left side). We again performed this experiment by making a circulatory error of distance 10. This time the inferred class hierarchy looks like a network of subsumption relations, making infeasible reasoning. Again performing the same experiment with a circulatory error with long chain of inheritance made the three DL reasoners crash. Imagine the consequences of circulatory error in ontology developed for critical application where strong reasoning with shorter answer time is required.

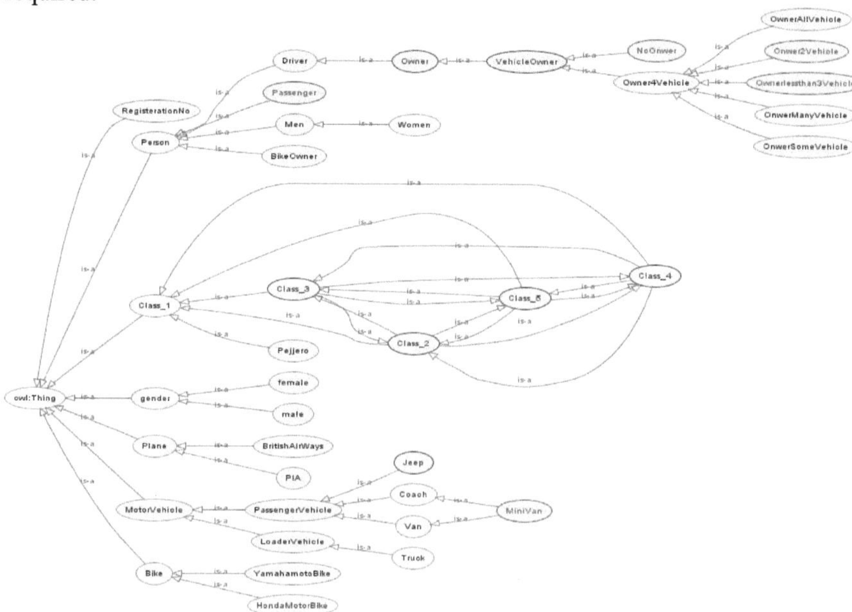

Fig. 3. Inferred class hierarchy

Besides circulatory, these reasoners have not identified various types of semantic inconsistency errors. Especially concept *Women* as a subclass of *Men*, with explicit description about disjointness between *Male* and *Female* can be detected as they also specify disjoint domains, but was not detected. Domain breach by specifying *OnwerManyVehicle* as subclass of *Onwer4Vehicle*, and *OnwerSomeVehicle* as weaker domain specified by subclass errors were also not detected.

Incompleteness as informal errors were not detected, as we know that incompleteness can only be manually detected by tester's domain knowledge and analysis of spot spots of ontologies by previous knowledge or populated data. Functional Property omission with *hasRegisterationNo* allowed creating several inconsistent registration numbers for a single vehicle. Disjoint knowledge omission, sufficient knowledge omission and exhaustive knowledge omission errors were also not detected.

Although the redundancy of subclass-of is detected and the arc from concept *Jeep* to concept *MotorVehicle* was deleted in the inferred hierarchy, but this was not always desirable. Sometimes that arc (between concept c and its ancestor) would be the actual one and the other arc (between concept c and its parent) would be the erroneous, but DL reasoners always does the same. Other types of redundancy like redundancy of disjoint relations, identical formal definitions were also not detected. On basis of common property *owns*, concept *VehicleOwner* is inferred as subclass of *Owner* concept and the hierarchy of *VehicleOwner* is moved to it. The overall experiment concludes that current state-of-the-art DL reasoners should be upgraded with respect of these errors and anomalies. Sound reasoning support is highly important for sound semantic web environment which can only be possible if these reasoners were capable enough identifying inconsistencies in ontologies.

5 Conclusion

Ontology driven architecture has revolutionized the inference system by allowing interoperability between heterogeneous multi-vendors systems. We have identified that accurate ontologies free from errors enable more intelligent interoperability, provide better reasoning mechanisms, improve the accuracy of ontology mapping and merging and combined use of them can be made possible. We have discussed existing ontological errors and design anomalies, and provided a case study that promotes understanding about these. Experiment with DL reasoners opens up number of issues that were not incorporated within their followed algorithms. Especially circulatory errors and various types of semantic inconsistency errors may cause serious side effects, and need to be detected by DL reasoners for sound reasoning from ontologies. The evaluation of DL reasoners on Automobile ontology helps in updating the subsumption, satisfiability and consistency checking algorithms for OWL ontologies, especially the new constructs of OWL 1.1.

References

1. G. Antoniou, and F.V. Harmelen, A Semantic Web Primer. MIT Press Cambridge, ISBN 0-262-01210-3, 2004.
2. J. Baumeister, and D.S. Seipel, Owls–Design Anomalies in Ontologies, 18th Intl. Floida Artificial Intelligence Research Society Conference (FLAIRS), pp 251-220, 2005.
3. C. Brewster et al, Data driven ontology evaluation. Proceedings of Intl. Conf. on Language Resources and Evaluation, Lisbon, 2004.
4. M. Fahad, M.A. Qadir, M.W. Noshairwan, N. Iftikhar,. DKP-OM: A Semantic Based Ontology Merger. In Proc. 3rd International conference on Semantic Technologies, I-Semantics 5-7 September 2007, Journal of Universal Computer Science (J.UCS). 2007a

5. M. Fahad, M.A. Qadir, W. Noshairwan, Semantic Inconsistency Errors in Ontologies. Proc. of GRC 07, Silicon Valley USA. IEEE CS. pp 283-286, 2007b.
6. A. Gomez-Perez, Some ideas and examples to evaluate ontologies. KSL, Stanford University., 1994.
7. A. Gomez-Perez, M.F. Lopez, and O.C. Garcia, Ontological Engineering: With Examples from the Areas of Knowledge Management, E-Commerce and the Semantic Web. Springer ISBN:1-85253-55j-3, 2001.
8. A. Gomez-Perez et al., Evaluation of Taxonomic Knowledge on Ontologies and Knowledge-Based Systems. Intl. Workshop on Knowledge Acquisition, Modeling and Management., 1999.
9. C. Jelmini, and S. M-Maillet, OWL-based reasoning with retractable inference", In RIAO Conference Proceedings 2004.
10. A. Maedche and S. Staab, Measuring similarity betwe- en ontologies. Proc. CIKM 2002. LNAI vol. 2473, 2002.
11. D. Nardi, et al. 2000. The Description Logic Handbook: Theory, Implementation, and Applications.
12. W. Noshairwan, M.A. Qadir, M.A., M. Fahad, Sufficient Knowledge Omission error and Redundant Disjoint Relation in Ontology. InProc. 5th Atlantic Web Intelligence Conference June 25-27, France, 2007a.
13. R. Porzel, R. Malaka, A task-based approach for ontology evaluation. ECAI Workshop Ont. Learning and Population, 2004.
14. M.A. Qadir, W. Noshairwan, Warnings for Disjoint Knowledge Omission in Ontologies. Second International Conference on internet and Web Applications and Services (ICIW07). IEEE, p. 45, 2007a.
15. M.A. Qadir, M. Fahad, S.A.H. Shah, Incompleteness Errors in Ontologies. Proc. of Intl GRC 07, USA. IEEE Computer Society. pp 279-282, 2007b.
16. K. Supekar, A peer-review approach for ontology evaluation. Proc. 8th Intl. Protégé Conference, Madrid, Spain, July 18–21, 2005.
17. M. Fahad, and M.A. Qadir, A Framework for ontology evaluation. 16th Intl. Proceeding of Conceptual Structures. July 2008, France. Vol-354, pages 149-158, 2008a.
18. M. Fahad, M.A. Qadir, M.W. Noshairwan, Ontological Errors: Inconsistency, Incompleteness and Redundancy. (to appear) In proc. 10th International Conference on Enterprise Information Systems (ICEIS'08). June 2008. Barcelona, Spain, 2008b.
19. V. Haarslev, R. M¨oller, Racer system description. In Gor´e, R., Leitsch, A., Nipkow, T., eds.: International Joint Conference on Automated Reasoning, IJCAR' 2001, June 18-23, Siena, Italy, Springer-Verlag (2001) 701–705
20. Z. Pan, Benchmarking DL Reasoners Using Realistic Ontologies. Bell Labs Research and Lehigh University, 2007
21. B. Parsia, E. Sirin, Pellet: An owl dl reasoner. In: Proc. International Semantic Web Conference. (2005)
22. I. Horrocks, U. Sattler, A tableaux decision procedure for SHOIQ. In: Proceedings of Nineteenth International Joint Conference on Artificial Intelligence. (2005)
23. I. Horrocks, The FaCT System. International conference. on Analytic Tableaux and Related Methods (TABLEAUX'98), pp 307-312,vol 1397, Springer-Verlag, 1998

ER2OWL: Generating OWL Ontology from ER Diagram

Muhammad Fahad

Mohammad Ali Jinnah University, Islamabad, Pakistan
mhd.fahad@gmail.com

Abstract. Ontology is the fundamental part of Semantic Web. The goal of W3C is to bring the web into (its full potential) a semantic web with reusing previous systems and artifacts. Most legacy systems have been documented in structural analysis and structured design (SASD), especially in simple or Extended ER Diagram (ERD). Such systems need up-gradation to become the part of semantic web. In this paper, we present ERD to OWL-DL ontology transformation rules at concrete level. These rules facilitate an easy and understandable transformation from ERD to OWL. The set of rules for transformation is tested on a structured analysis and design example. The framework provides OWL ontology for semantic web fundamental. This framework helps software engineers in upgrading the structured analysis and design artifact ERD, to components of semantic web. Moreover our transformation tool, ER2OWL, reduces the cost and time for building OWL ontologies with the reuse of existing entity relationship models.

1 Introduction

Ontology is regarded as the formal specification of the knowledge of concepts and the relationships among them [7]. They require formal syntax and semantics to represent domain concepts. They have played a key role for describing semantics of data not only the applications of semantic web but also revolutionized the traditional knowledge engineering [14]. There are many languages proposed to build ontologies e.g. RDFS, OWL, LOOM, OIL etc. In 2004, W3C has made OWL as a standard to build ontologies [9], because of its decidability and high level of expressivity. OWL describes many types of semantics about terms to facilitate high mechanisms for reasoning; like its hierarchal information, its relation with others and its own description in the form that are machine-interpretable and machine-understandable.

However, many legacy systems have been documented using Structured Analysis and Structured Design (SASD) [1]. The most common artifact of SASD is the

---

Please use the following format when citing this chapter:

Fahad, M., 2008, in IFIP International Federation for Information Processing, Volume 288; *Intelligent Information Processing IV*; Zhongzhi Shi, E. Mercier-Laurent, D. Leake; (Boston: Springer), pp. 28–37.

Entity Relationship (ER) Diagram or Extended ER Diagram. There are many problems in understanding and upgrading a legacy system. To use old system as a component of emerging semantic web, these systems need up-gradation. Software engineers require OWL ontology to aid in the up-gradation of these systems. The new OWL ontology can act as the basis for design and implementation of the new system with in the semantic web. Both ERD and OWL represent entities and their relationships. This provides an intuitive transformation of the ERD to OWL ontology. Translating ERD into OWL is indeed seems like a worthy goal of current model driven architecture, in order to integrate legacy systems into the Semantic Web. Extended ER has a bigger domain then ER, so from now onward we refer ERD formed from Extended ER notations. There are so many conventions and notations used for conceptual modeling of ER, here we are using the notations of Chen [10].

As ontologies have been used by couple of industry applications, our transformation tool will open up a number of advantages. Especially ontologies played an important role for heterogeneous database integration [4]. Heterogeneous databases are represented by the ontologies and can combine together efficiently. As semantic web is emerging, schema integration becomes the main hindrance in achieving its goal. Here we have developed concrete rules that aid in schema integration. We demonstrate an example to facilitate usage of these rules. They also help in mapping between relational database schema and OWL ontologies for deep annotation. "*Deep Annotation means the process of creating ontological instances for the database-based, dynamic contents by reaching out to the 'deep Web' and directly annotating the underlying database of the dynamic Web site*" [3].

Ontology integration is one of the active research areas of present era, as different models are used to build up different domain ontologies such as RDBMS, XML, etc. This framework helps the ontologists to resolve model conflict [7] in ontology integration. Those ontologies that are build-up on RDBMS model are transformed into OWL and then different OWL ontologies are combined together through conventional methods.

Rest of the paper is organized as follows: Section 2 discusses related work. Section 3 presents the framework for transforming ERD to OWL. Section 4 concludes the paper and shows future directions.

2 Related Work

Vasilecas et al. proposed an approach to automatically transform enterprise ontology into conceptual model [6]. They used metamodels of ontology and conceptual model to facilitate transformations from one domain to another. A prototype was developed to show the effectiveness and automation of their proposed technique. They build ontology in Protégé 2000 and Power Designer was used to implement ER model. They transform class of ontology in protégé to entity in ER, and slot (property) to attribute, directed binary relation to inheritance and ontology constraints to entity constraints.

Xu et al. proposed mapping rules between relational database schema and OWL ontology for deep annotation [3]. Ontological annotation is used for dynamic web page contents extracted from the database. Their Framework, DPAnnotator, translate the ER Schema of the relational database into OWL ontology. They provide a D2OMapper tool, which automatically creates the mappings by following their rules.

Colomb et al. discussed the issues in mapping metamodels in the ontology development metamodel using QVT [2]. They suggest many ways to integrate several metamodels in one structure. First approach is to take one metamodel as basic, and represent others by subclasses. Second approach suggests taking one metamodel as basic and translating others into it. Third approach suggests representing the metamodels separate and providing transformation rules from one domain to another using QVT. They gave QVT transformations between UML and DL (Description Logic), ER and DL, and OWL to DL. QVT does not only help in transformation process but also keeps track of the association between source and target model elements.

Kupfer et al. proposed an approach that allows the database schema and the ontology to change and evolve, without breaking their connection with each other during maintenance [4]. They gave the automatic mappings from database schemas to database ontologies, with maintaining connection with each other when one of the artifact changes. They called this process, the Coevolution process that tracks changes of the database schema into related database ontology.

In Ontology Definition Metamodel, researchers provided ER to OWL mappings [5]. They used abstract syntax for representation of mapping specification. Understanding their mapping specification is much tedious task. A new researcher needs much effort to transform ERD to OWL ontology, as they did not provide any explanation, case study or tool support. Furthermore their proposal provides a starting point, but never provides formal rules that could be used to automate the transformation. It also needs further elaboration and examples to help aid in transforming ERD to OWL. While transforming conventional ERD to OWL, we find many inconvenience especially transforming association entity and unary, binary and ternary relationships between entities, as they did not incorporate association entity in their metamodel and differentiate between unary, binary and ternary relationship. Besides these, they did not included ER metamodel and mapping rules in their latest document and thus did not elaborate them further. Thus we feel a need to extend their work and propose a framework, which facilitates an easy and thorough transformation.

A more related work of our domain is done by Upadhyaya et al. He presented the implementation details of their tool, ERONTO, that extracts ontologies from Extended ERD [8]. His proposal provides a good starting point but lack some features, as the tool does not produce complete mappings from ERD to OWL, and user himself has to check the incompleteness and write glue code himself. They call the generated OWL as a "*near-complete ontology*" and conclude that users track the portions that are missing and enhance the generated ontology themselves. They gave an inappropriate mapping of composite attribute to OWL Class, which increases the overhead to produce ObjectProperties that relate OWL Class (corresponding to Entity) to another OWL Class (corresponding to composite attribute), and cardinalities restrictions associated with both the classes. Furthermore they did not tell how the Restriction code is generated that is equivalent to cardinality in conjunction with modalities i.e. cardinality of N represents 1..* or 0..* for mandatory and optional modalities respectively. Ignoring restrictions in the code of generated OWL Class equivalent to associative entity makes the code inconsistent. As associative entity does not exist without the existence of corresponding entities, and the only way to apply this constraint is to produce restrictions in that class. Moreover they did not handle multivalued attributes, unary relationships 1:N or N:M etc. Another serious incompleteness error [11,12,13] that ERONTO produces is the functional property omission error for single valued property (attribute). This type of error creates inconsistencies by allowing attribute to accept many values and create ambiguity.

3. Transformation Framework

SASD uses the Entity Relationship Diagram (ERD) to model data. Both ERD and OWL represent entities and their relationships and this gives an intuitive transformation of the ERD to OWL ontology: ERD entities become OWL classes; ERD attributes become Datatype Properties of corresponding OWL class.

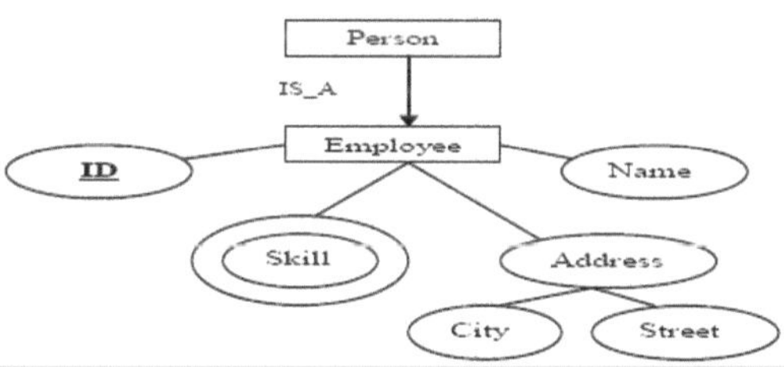


```
<owl:Class rdf:ID="Person"/>
 <owl:Class rdf:ID="Employee">
  <rdfs:subClassOf rdf:resource="#Person"/>
 </owl:Class>
 <owl:InverseFunctionalProperty rdf:ID="ID">
  <rdf:type rdf:resource=" #FunctionalProperty"/>
  <rdfs:range rdf:resource=" #int"/>
  <rdfs:domain rdf:resource="#Employee"/>
  <rdf:type rdf:resource="#DatatypeProperty"/>
 </owl:InverseFunctionalProperty>
```

```
<owl:DatatypeProperty rdf:ID="Skill">
  <rdfs:range rdf:resource="#string"/>
  <rdfs:domain rdf:resource="#Employee"/>
 </owl:DatatypeProperty>
<owl:FunctionalProperty rdf:ID="Name">
  <rdfs:range rdf:resource="#string"/>
  <rdfs:domain rdf:resource="#Employee"/>
  <rdf:type rdf:resource="#DatatypeProperty"/>
 </owl:FunctionalProperty>
```

Fig. 1. ER Entity to OWL Class mapping.

Bidirectional Relationships become two Object Properties. Cardinalities on the ERD can be used in conjunction with modalities to produce restrictions for the OWL class.

3.1 ERD to OWL Mapping Rules

The set of rules to transform an ERD into OWL ontology are outlined below:

Entity. Map each Entity in the ERD into OWL class in the OWL Ontology. In Fig. 1, Person and Employee are entities that are mapped to OWL classes.

Attribute. There are many types of attributes that belong to entity i.e. simple attributes, composite attributes and multi-valued attributes. These require separate ways to map into OWL datatype properties. While transforming attributes to properties, it should be taken care of making local unique names. Incase of two unique names associated with entities, our system appends the entity name with start of attribute like (*Entity: Attribute*). Moreover, Range mapping of values has to take care of mapping the datatypes of the ER domain to *XSD* datatypes.

Simple Attribute. Map Simple Attribute of entity into datatype property of corresponding OWL class. Domain of the datatype property is the Entity, and range is the actual datatype (int, string, etc) of that attribute. Range mapping of values has to take care of mapping the datatypes of the ER domain to XSD datatypes. One important point should be considered here is that as this attribute takes only one value so a special tag "functional" should be tagged with this datatype property, otherwise OWL DL allows datatype property to take many values by default. In Fig. 1, Name of Employee is a simple attribute.

Composite Attribute. There are two ways to map Composite Attribute to OWL datatype property. One is to map only their simple component attributes (city, street, country, etc) of composite attribute (Address) to datatype properties

```
<owl:FunctionalProperty rdf:ID="City">
  <rdfs:range rdf:resource="#string"/>
  <rdf:type rdf:resource="#DatatypeProperty"/>
  <rdfs:domain rdf:resource="#Employee"/>
 </owl:FunctionalProperty>
<owl:FunctionalProperty rdf:ID="Street">
  <rdfs:domain rdf:resource="#Employee"/>
  <rdf:type rdf:resource=" #DatatypeProperty"/>
  <rdfs:range rdf:resource=" #string"/>
 </owl:FunctionalProperty>
```

```
<owl:DatatypeProperty rdf:ID="Address">
  <rdfs:domain rdf:resource="#Employee"/>
  <rdfs:range rdf:resource="#string"/>
</owl:DatatypeProperty>
<owl:DatatypeProperty rdf:ID="street">
  <rdf:type rdf:resource="#FunctionalProperty"/>
  <rdfs:subPropertyOf rdf:resource="#Address"/>
</owl:DatatypeProperty>
<owl:DatatypeProperty rdf:ID="city">
  <rdf:type rdf:resource="#FunctionalProperty"/>
  <rdfs:subPropertyOf rdf:resource="#Address"/>
</owl:DatatypeProperty>
```

Fig. 2. Composite Attribute to Datatype Property Mapping

of corresponding OWL class, and ignore composite attribute (Address) itself. Second is to map composite attribute to datatype property and then map its simple, component attributes to *subproperty* of corresponding datatype property. The first one is more preferred while working with transformation of relational databases because in Relational Schema, we do have only the instances of simple, component attributes and composite attributes are ignored. By using this rule one has not preserved the conceptual modeling of composite attribute and when performing reverse engineering from ontology to ER, we lost composite attributes. If someone wants to preserve such knowledge then second one is used effectively by analyzing datatype property to composite attribute and subproperty-of to its component attribute. All the datatype properties produce should be tagged as "functional" as they all get only one value. Fig. 2 shows both the method of transforming Composite Attribute to OWL ontology.

Multi-valued Attribute. Multi-valued Attribute is mapped to datatype property like simple attribute, but without a "*functional*" tag. For an example, Skill of an employee may have many values, so OWL DL property by default takes *many* values.

Primary Key. An attribute which stands as a primary key, is transformed into datatype property and is tagged with both "*functional*" and "*inverse-functional*". Functional tag restricts object to take only one value for a given subject, and inverse-functional restricts the subject to associate with only one object [9].

Subtype Relations (IS-A). Convert subtype relations in the ERD to subClassOf in the OWL ontology. In OWL ontology, *OWL:subClassOf* represents the generalization hierarchy.

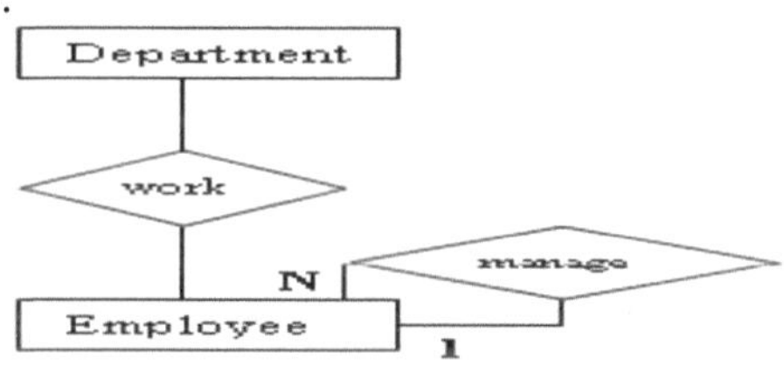


```
<owl:ObjectProperty rdf:ID="work">
  <rdfs:domain rdf:resource="#Employee"/>
  <rdfs:range rdf:resource="#Department"/>
</owl:ObjectProperty>

<owl:ObjectProperty rdf:ID="has_work">
  <owl:inverseOf rdf:resource="#work"/>
</owl:ObjectProperty>
```

```
<owl:Class rdf:ID="Employee">
  <owl:Restriction><owl:someValuesFrom>
    <owl:Class rdf:about="#Employee "/>
  </owl:someValuesFrom>
  <owl:onProperty>
    <owl:ObjectProperty rdf:resourse="#manage"/>
  </owl:onProperty></owl:Restriction>
</owl:Class>
<owl:ObjectProperty rdf:ID="manage">
  <rdfs:domain rdf:resource="#Employee"/>
  <rdfs:range rdf:resource="#Employee"/>
</owl:ObjectProperty>
```

Fig. 3. Bi-Directional Relationship to Object Property Mapping

Bi-Directional Relationship. Every relationship between entities is mapped onto object property between classes. But in ERD it is bi-directional and object property in OWL is uni-directional, so *two* object properties should be generated between those entities having bi-directioanl relationship. One corresponding to the relationship as represented in the ERD, and second as an inverse property of the original object property. For example if a relationship *Work* exists between Employee and Department as shown in Fig. 3, then in OWL two object properties are generated with names Work(domain:Employee and range:Department) and other Has_Work (by default it takes the opposite domain and range values of Work property) as the inverse property of *Work*. Note that the name of second property is generated by preceding the word '*has*' of the actual property and later on can be changed to give meaningful name to it.

Unary (recursive) 1:N Relationship. Unary recursive relation between a person Employee and other worker Employees can exists when one Employee handles/assists many Employees. In Fig. 3, Employee entity with *Manages* relationship is transformed into Employee OWL class and Manages as an Object property with *same* domain and range as employee.

Unary M:N Relationship. When unary relationship exists between M object to N objects then that it is transformed into two OWL classes. For example Many *Items* contain many item-components as shown in Fig. 4. In this case, we transform Item entity to Item OWL class and build another OWL *Contains* class that has some values from item class.

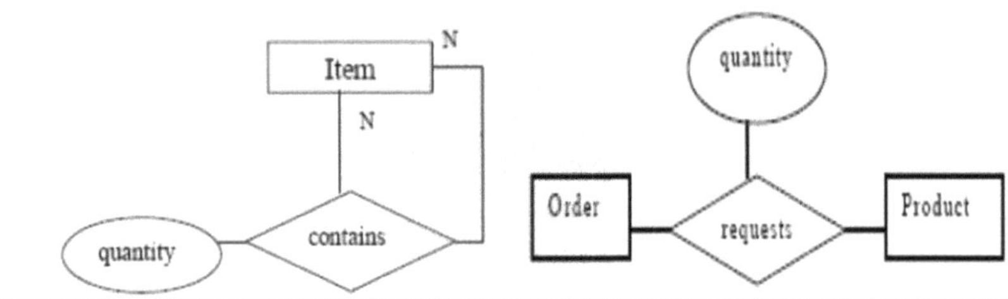


```
<owl:Class rdf:ID="Contains">
  <owl:Restriction><owl:someValuesFrom>
    <owl:Class rdf:ID="Item"/>
  </owl:someValuesFrom><owl:onProperty>
  <owl:ObjectProperty rdf:resourse="#has"/>
  </owl:onProperty></owl:Restriction>
</owl:Class>
<owl:ObjectProperty rdf:ID="has">
  <rdfs:domain rdf:resource="#Contains"/>
  <rdfs:range rdf:resource="#Item"/>
</owl:ObjectProperty>
```

```
<owl:Class rdf:ID="Requests">

<owl:DatatypeProperty rdf:ID="quantity">
  <rdf:type rdf:resource="#FunctionalProperty"/>
  <rdfs:subPropertyOf rdf:resource="#Request"/>
</owl:DatatypeProperty>
```

Fig. 4. Associative Entity and Unary Recursive Mappings

Associative Entity or Relationship having attribute. Associative Entity or Relationship having attribute is also mapped onto OWL class as shown in Fig. 4. Attribute of Relationship or Associative Entity is mapped into datatype property of corresponding OWL class.

1 to Many Relationship (mandatory). Cardinalities and Modalities are transformed into OWL restrictions within corresponding OWL classes. 1 to many relationship is transformed into restrictions as shown in Fig. 5.

1 to Many Relationship (optional). In case of optional, we do not put restrictions in the corresponding class.

Many to Many Relationship. This type of relationship in ERD is transformed into restrictions in OWL classes, and corresponding cardinalities and modalities are split up into two indicating Many to 1 and 1 to Many relationships, their implementation rules are applied accordingly to generate OWL code.

```
<owl:Class rdf:ID="Student">
  <rdfs:subClassOf><owl:Restriction>
    <owl:valuesFrom><owl:Class rdf:ID="Professor"/>
    </owl:valuesFrom><owl:onProperty>
     <owl:ObjectProperty rdf:ID="isTaughtBy"/>
    </owl:onProperty><owl:cardinality
rdf:datatype="#int"> 1</owl:cardinality>
   </owl:Restriction></rdfs:subClassOf>
 </owl:Class>

<owl:ObjectProperty rdf:about="#isTaughtBy">
  <owl:inverseOf rdf:resource="#teaches"/>
 </owl:ObjectProperty>
```

```
<owl:Class rdf:about="#Professor">
  <rdfs:subClassOf>
   <owl:Restriction>
    <owl:someValuesFrom rdf:resource="#Student"/>
    <owl:onProperty>
     <owl:ObjectProperty rdf:about="#teaches"/>
    </owl:onProperty>
   </owl:Restriction>
  </rdfs:subClassOf>
 </owl:Class>
<owl:ObjectProperty rdf:about="#teaches">
  <rdfs:domain rdf:resource="#Professor"/>
  <rdfs:range rdf:resource="#Student"/>
 </owl:ObjectProperty>
```

Fig. 5. 1 to Many Relationship Mappings

3.2 Comparison with ERONTO

We have implemented the above defined rules into a prototype, ER2OWL. It facilitates a quick transformation, and reduces the cost and time for building OWL ontologies with the reuse of existing entity relationship models. As comparison with ERONTO, the generated ontology is more complete and does not have incompleteness errors.

The limitations of ERONTO are addressed by ER2OWL and produce ontologies that serve best when spread out to be used in real world applications. Unlike ERONTO, the system attach the "functional" tag with datatype properties with single valued property, moreover does not create overheads by transforming composite attributes to owl classes and let the application safe from incompleteness and consistency errors [11,12,13]. (Details about these errors are found in individual paper and are out of scope of this paper). Our system asks the user to suggest the direction of relationship between entities, so that valid domain and range of object properties should be generated against each object property.

4 Conclusions and Future Work

This paper presents a framework for transforming the structured analysis and design artifact, ERD, into the OWL ontology. We have provided rules to transform ERD concepts into equivalent OWL ontology for semantic web. The set of mapping rules has been demonstrated with the diagrams to promote understanding. The framework provides OWL ontology for semantic web component from old legacy systems and enable them to upgrade and become a part of emerging semantic web. This proposed framework helps software engineers in upgrading the structured analysis and design artifact ERD, to components of semantic web. Our ongoing research on this topic is to handle other cases of relationships that are not binary, which require reification.

Reference

[1] T. P. Fries. A Framework for Transforming Structured Analysis and Design Artifacts to UML. SIGDOC'06, Myrtle Beach, South Carolina, USA, October 18-20, 2006,

[2] R. M. Colomb, A. Gerber, M. Lawley. Issues in Mapping Metamodels in the Ontology Development Metamodel Using QVT.

[3] Z. Xu, S. Zhang, Y. Dong. Mapping between Relational Database Schema and OWL ontology for Deep Annotation. Proceedings of the 2006 IEEE/WIC/ACM International Conference on Web Intelligence (WI'06), 2006 IEEE

[4] A. Kupfer, S. Eckstein, K. Neumann and B. Mathiak. A Coevolution Approach for Database Schemas and related Ontologies. Proceedings of the 19th IEEE Symposium on Computer-Based Medical Systems (CBMS'06), 2006 IEEE

[5] Ontology Definition Metamodel, second Revised Submission to OMG/RDF ad/2006-04-13

[6] O. Vasilecas, D. Bugaite, J. Trinkunas. On Approach for Enterprise Ontology Transformation into Conceptual Model. International Conference on Computer Systems and Technologies, CompSysTech'06

[7] D. Dou, P. LePendu. Ontology based Integration for Relational Databases. *SAC'06,* April 2327, 2006, Dijon, France.

[8] S. R. Upadhyaya and P. S. Kumar. ERONTO: A Tool for Extracting Ontologies from Extended E/R Diagrams, ACM Symposium on Applied Computing 2005.
[9] OWL Web Ontology Language Guide, W3C Recommendation 10 February 2004. http://www.w3.org/TR/2004/REC-owl-guide-20040210/
[10] P. Chen. The Entity Relationship model towards a unified view of data, ACM Transactions Database Systems., I,1(March 1976),9-36.
[11]. M.A. Qadir, M. Fahad, S.A. Hussain-Shah, Incompleteness Errors in Ontologies. InProc. of International Conference on Granular Computing, Silicon Valley, USA, IEEE Computer Society. pp 279-282
[12]. W. Noshairwan, M.A. Qadir, M. Fahad. Sufficient Knowledge Omission error and Redundant Disjoint Relation in Ontology. InProc. 5th Atlantic Web Intelligence Conference, Fontainebleau, France (June 25-27, 2007)
[13]. M. Fahad, M.A. Qadir, W. Noshairwan. Semantic Inconsistency Errors in Ontologies. In Proc. of InternaQtional Conference on Granular Computing, Silicon Valley, USA, IEEE Computer Society. pp 283-286
[14]. G. Antoniou, and F.V. Harmelen, A Semantic Web Primer. MIT Press Cambridge, ISBN 0-262-01210-3, 2004.

Voice knowledge acquisition system for the management of cultural heritage

Stefan du Château, Danielle Boulanger and Eunika Mercier-Laurent

MODEME, IAE Research Center Lyon University 6, av Albert Thomas F-69008 Lyon

Abstract: This document presents our work on a definition and experimentation of a voice interface for cultural heritage inventory. This hybrid system includes signal processing, natural language techniques and knowledge modeling for future retrieval. We discuss the first results and give some points on future work.

1 Introduction

The inventory of the cultural heritage includes several tasks such as the study, analysis, description of the masterpieces still existing, preserved as vestiges, destroyed or disappeared but known through documents (Verdier and al ., 1999).

All categories of masterpieces are concerned, such as religious, civil, military, in a perimeter as large as are the human activities.

The work of the researchers of the inventory consists partially in collecting the on field information available in the cities, villages and specific places. It can take the form of text files, pictures, drawings, video, or plans. Researchers can also conduct a study about a given place or topic before collecting.

The study documents and the collected information are registered in a data base which could be general or personal.

When back to the office the researcher can improve the gathered information on a given object or add some elements from archives to update the content of the data base. Collecting of information into paper files or recording them on a laptop is demanding and time consuming. The amount of the completed and corrected information is still very large and heterogeneous.

Each masterpiece has its own history, past and present, it can be moved from one historical context to the other or it can be modified. In brief, it can change its spatiotemporal context. This kind of information and related knowledge is impossible to represent just in a classic data base.

Our objective is to design and experiment a new collecting support system to help the cultural heritage inventory researchers to perform their work better and in a more efficient way. It is also to help indexing and retrieving information and

---

Please use the following format when citing this chapter:

du Château, S., Boulanger, D. and Mercier-Laurent, E., 2008, in IFIP International Federation for Information Processing, Volume 288; *Intelligent Information Processing IV*; Zhongzhi Shi, E. Mercier-Laurent, D. Leake; (Boston: Springer), pp. 38–49.

knowledge on a given masterpiece and its context. This paper describes our work on such a hybrid system using a voice interface (signal processing), natural language processing and knowledge modeling for the information gathering, management and retrieval. Sect. 2 presents relative work, Sect. 3 describes our work and in Sect. 4 we discuss directions for future work.

2 State of the art knowledge modeling for cultural heritage

2.1 The inventory of the cultural heritage

Most projects in the field of the inventory of the cultural heritage are based on data bases systems. The structures of these data bases, which correspond with well defined specifications on a given application, are not easily extensible. The relative lack of flexibility of these systems makes them incompatible with the notion of knowledge based systems, which are flexible.

The existing systems contain a lot of incompatible data recorded in various data bases using several languages. In such situations an intelligent system with the ability to manage this huge amount of data effectively will be very useful.

Among the different European projects we can quote MICHAEL[1] the purpose of which is to valorize Europe's cultural heritage. This project provides a multilingual interface to encourage the interoperability of different national heritage data bases.

Other projects such as HEDD[2], a project of the English Heritage committee brings together 22 museums, 3 libraries and deposits of archives and uses ontologies to model common knowledge distributed in heterogeneous data. .

Other projects such as those of the national Gallery of Finland[3], the University of Queensland in Australia[4] and SCULPTOR[5], use the ontology CIDOC-Conceptual Reference Model[6] (CRM) (Doerr, 2006) as a tool for knowledge modeling. They unite big galleries and European cultural institutions.

---

[1] http://www.michael-culture.eu/project.html[2]

[2] http://www.fish-forum.info

[3] http://www.fng.fi/fng/rootnew/en/vtm/etusivu.htm

[4] http://www.metadata.net/harmony/MW2002_paper.pdf

[5] http://www.sculpteurweb.org/html/approach.htm

[6] http://cidoc.ics.forth.gr/index.html

2.2 Automatic knowledge acquisition and speech apprehension

Since the beginning of artificial intelligence many researchers have been working on the topics such as automatic knowledge acquisition and speech apprehension, mainly using signal processing techniques. The first voice interface was probably this of a workstation called Buroviseur, built in INRIA in 1981 (Kayak, 1982 Mercier-Laurent, 1980). The voice interface was also used for knowledge acquisition for expert systems (Balaram, 1988) or for human-machine dialog in machine learning systems (Michalski, 1985). This technology is now mature and can be integrated in applications using a large vocabulary with more than 60 000 words (Haton, 2006)

The quality of voice acquisition systems depends of many parameters such as external acoustic environment (noisy or silent) and the quality of the equipment employed.

The main specialists of the field state that these performances provide 90 % of a correct recognition (Veronis 2000).

This performance can seem insufficient in a system with full automatic transcription; however it is acceptable in the half automatic system, where the results are validated by an expert, especially when it is a question of not validating the whole of the re-transcribed text, but only a part corresponding to the predefined information.

The outlines of the extraction of information systems were defined during several *Message Understanding Conference* (MUC) conferences, which took place between 1987 and 1998. It can be said that between the first conference in 1987 and the last one in 1998, the initial ambitions - the understanding of a text by computers - were revised to finally become systems of information extraction.

The goal of the information extraction is to produce a structured representation of unstructured texts by searching for given patterns in the texts which are relevant to an application (Ibekwe-SanJuan, 2007). Basically, we are looking for the partners of a transaction, the names of the bodies, the transactions (sale, purchase) etc.

The text mining information extraction systems are based mainly on two technologies: the one uses automatic learning, the other one uses natural language processing (NLP).

The techniques of machine learning provide the possibility to automatically extract dictionaries and specialized grammar, as well as annotations. They allow reducing the time needed to construct linguistic resources. Their main disadvantage is that they need an important text corpus for each application domain. Information extraction techniques based on NLP use morphosyntactic analyses of text documents. This technique splits a text in sentences and terms. The tagging is based on external resources and grammar, defined by the user for a given field.

While the voice recognition and text mining are not new, the association of both is, based on our knowledge, not really deployed. Our work links these two domains and applies them to knowledge modeling.

There are only a few publications on knowledge modeling in the field of cultural heritage. The main known contribution is the domain ontology CIDOC-CRM, based on object knowledge representation which is flexible and convertible into various formats such as **RDF**, **XML**, **DAML+OIL**, **OWL**. The CRM covers all information required for the scientific documentation in the field of cultural heritage.

In terms of concepts and relations between concepts and the construction of ontologies, text mining has been described in numerous works. Among them we quote Charlet (Charlet, 2002) and Bourigault (Bourigault, 2003), who work on the construction of ontologies from texts in the medical domain.

3 Our work

Our voice acquisition system is presented in Fig 1.
It follows four steps:

1. Voice acquisition of a given masterpiece description
2. Automatic transcription of the voice file into the text file by Dragon[7],
3. Extraction of concepts and relations between concepts
4. Validation of the extracted concepts found in the previous stage by expert.

The validated descriptors are registered in a data base and will be used to update the existing ontologies. The acquired voice information is distributed in fields of the data base such as: DENOMINATION, CATEGORY, MATERIAL, DESCRIPTION, and INSCRIPTION without constraining the speaker to say the name of the descriptive field. These fields constitute the descriptive system defined by the heritage inventory department (Verdier and al ., 1999). Some of these fields are compulsory, the others optional. The contents of certain fields are defined by a lexicon, the contents of the other fields remaining free.

Usually the acquisition of the data is made using a keyboard and needs to strictly respect a data acquisition model. In the case of a voice acquisition, there is no structure to guide the acquisition. The involved people are specialists in the given field, thus we can expect a coherent and well structured text.

[7] http://www.nuance.fr/naturallyspeaking/

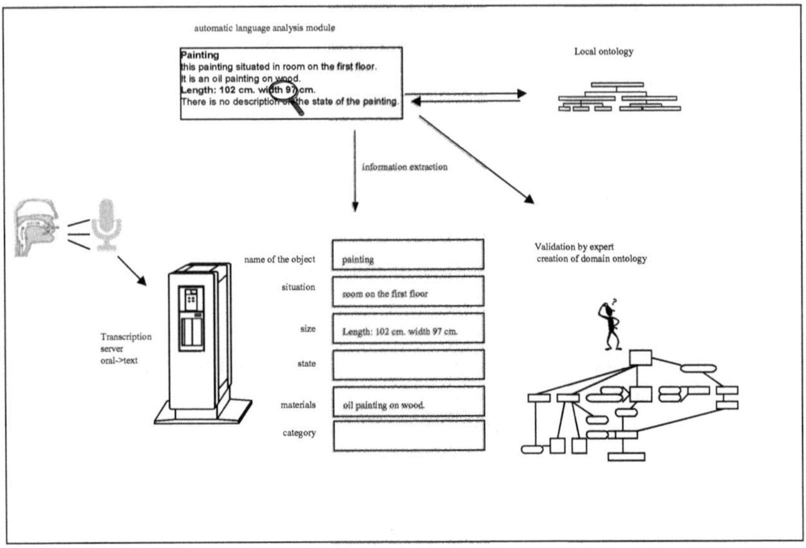

Fig. 1 Voice acquisition system helping assistant in knowledge acquisition.

3.1 *Robust syntactic analysis*

Despite the good performances of the re-transcription software, some syntactical and semantic errors can occur in the re-transcribed files. The origin of its errors can be directly connected to the way the speaker dictates the text (waiting time, hesitation, back on sentences or words). The transcription process itself may also cause errors.

We started the acquisition without any text archives what made the applying of machine learning methods impossible. We have chosen the robust incremental syntactic analyzer (Hagège and al., 2003). Such an analyzer always insures good results even with a badly structured or erroneous input text.

Incremental means that the rules of disambiguation, category, construction of constituents and the extraction of syntactical dependencies are applied one after the other. The specific and reliable rules are first to filter the rare or exceptional configurations, while the more general rules are at the end of grammar. (Hagège and al., 2003).

For our experiments we use the XIP[8] analyzer created by XRCE[9], whose architecture is presented in Fig 2.

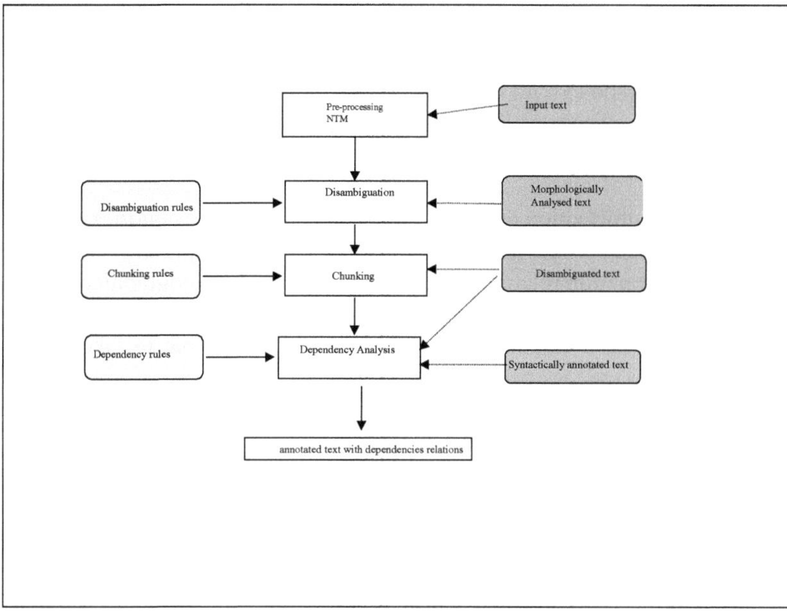

Fig. 2 XIP Architecture

Legend: NTM[10]; Disambiguation[11]; Segmentation[12]; Analysis of the dependences[13].

---

[8] XIP (Xerox Incremental Parser) by AïtMokhtar, Chanod et Roux .

[9] Xerox Research Center Europe

[10] Normalization(Standardization), Tokenisation (Division of a text in words), Morpholgy

[11] Disambiguation: Disambiguation of the categories of the words according to their context of appearance

[12] Segmentation: cut the serial linguistic units (unities) of constituents nucleus(kernel)

[13] Analysis of the dependency: identify syntactical links between the words

3.2 From the data entry form to the extraction patterns[14]

As we mentioned before, the information to find is defined by the descriptive system of the inventory (Verdier and al 1999). It indicates the type of information to be looked for, but also controls, in certain cases, the vocabulary to be used. The terms have to correspond with the entry of a lexicon.

The descriptive system of the inventory will partially guide the conception of the extractions patterns and local grammar.

The collected information on the field can be split in two categories:

- Physical aspects: material of manufacturing, structure, place.
- All the information relative to the historical, social, ethnographical context.

It is the type of information that can be known only by experts of a given domain. Our system of extraction of information has to be able to take it into account.

Two scenarios are possible:

1. The result corresponds exactly to a defined entry of a lexicon. In this case the local grammar must be defined to insure that the analysis and the result of extraction is a word or a constituent, which corresponds exactly to an entry of this lexicon.
2. The result is an incomplete description of a given place, for example:

« ... le retable comprend 4 tableaux : Baptême du Christ, Christ au Jardin des oliviers, la Cène et la Résurrection... ».

The constituent « *Baptême du Christ* » will be tracked down in the text without problem because it exists in the lexicon, then thanks to an analysis of dependence; it can be associated with the representation. The constituent *« Christ au Jardin des oliviers »* will not be recognized as representation because it does not exist in this lexicon. The system has to be able to recognize this entry as a constituent, and to suggest it as a possible entry. A local syntactic analysis must be triggered by one of the words of the constituent because they belong to the lexicon, or because the sentence contains a word or a constituent which is associated with the idea of the representation: *the representation, are represented.*

In our example, the constituent « *Jardin des oliviers* » and the word « *Christ* » exist separately in the lexicon representation, which is the condition to propose the constituent *Christ in the Garden of olive trees* as a possible descriptor of the representation. According to the principle of relations « sort of » the representation of the « *Christ au Jardin des oliviers* » *is* a specific case of a representation of Christ.

The identification of the words or the constituents is not the only difficulty, which we have to face. The language of the cultural heritage is extremely rich and

---

[14] Extraction pattern: set(group) rules allowing to identify the expected, relevant information

words can have multiple meanings, which means that the system has to be able to deal with ambiguities. A word or a constituent can be used in various contexts as well as to describe the representation of a masterpiece or a masterpiece itself. In the example *a picture representing a chalice* the name could be the name of the person represented on the chalice or the artist's name. It frequently happens that the described belongs to a group. The description of this type of objects can hint at the contained or containing elements. We are thus in a situation where several names of a masterpiece are quoted. How can we know which one is the object of the study?

The resolution of ambiguities requires an analysis and the understanding of the local context. Some ambiguities can be decided by using a morphosyntactic analysis of the following or previous words or by searching for linguistic indications according to the given topic.

3.3 The initial position

The study of the organization of descriptors in a text can be of considerable help, notably for the resolution of certain types of ambiguities. The study of the initial position, which leans on the cognitive consideration (Enkvist, 1976), (Ho-Dac, 2007), states that the beginning of a sentence has a great importance, as we place important information in an initial position of sentences.

In this perspective, the extraction of the information from the text:

Musée de la société archéologique de Montpellier.

Panneau de Saint Guilhem et Sainte Apolline (87 x 136) en cours de restauration par Anne Baxter.

C'est une peinture à l'huile de très grande qualité, panneau sur bois représentant deux figures à mi corps sur fond de paysage, saint Guilhem et sainte Apolline, peintures enchâssées sous des architectures à décor polylobés; Saint Guilhem est représenté en abbé bénédictin (alors qu'à sa mort en 812 il n'était que simple moine); sainte Apolline tient l'instrument de son martyre, une longue tenaille.

will prefer the descriptor *Panneau* over the descriptor *Peinture*, to indicate the naming of the studied object.

3.4 Semiautomatic generation of ontology

The collected knowledge on a masterpiece is partial; it is valid only for a lapse of time and cannot be limited to a fix frame defined for a given application.

The knowledge is flexible, the masterpieces of the cultural heritage have a past, a present and maybe a future "life", and they can change in time. As we mentioned before the extraction of information in our case has to correspond to a precise specification.

We have to face two requirements: to fill a data base defined by the descriptive system of the inventory and allow the flexibility of a knowledge management system. For the first the information found by extraction can be adjusted, and validated by an expert if it is necessary. We think that it is also a convenient moment to satisfy the second point; the validated information composed of descriptors and their relation, which describes the material and immaterial aspects of masterpiece, will feed the ontology of a domain in a vaster and more flexible way.

How to define the ontology regarding the problem of modeling, opening, and knowledge sharing?

There is a vast variety of definitions of ontology, and that of Gruber (Gruber, 93) seems to correspond the best in case: *« ontology is an explicit and formal specification of a conceptualization being the object of a consensus ».*

In other words the ontology of a domain is a set of concepts and relations between these concepts defined by means of a formal language by involved actors and for a particular domain.

According to Charlet (Charlet, 2002), in an ontology we represent and classify concepts and their characteristics (properties); we also represent relations between these concepts.

In our case, we have to describe of what material the object of cultural heritage is made, by whom, when, why, what transformations were done, what is its state of preservation as well as the masterpieces movements. We can say that a certain number of concepts is outlined: time, place, actor (person) and state of preservation.

Intuitively, we guess that some of these concepts are connected to each other, as for example the state of preservation and time, transformations and time, movements and place, transformation and person.

The CIDOC-CRM ontology, already quoted in Sect. 2, presents the necessary formalism allowing reporting relations, which an object can have in time and space.

The heart of CRM is constituted by the temporal entity expressing the dependence between time and the various events in the life of the historical object.

If we consider an example of a sculpture described by the inventory system, information such as author, naming, materials (...) are easily expressed. Because this system is not able to model the various movements of a given object, this information is described using free text and mixed with other type of information in the historic field.

The same information can be easily expressed by the CRM ontology, presented in Fig 3.

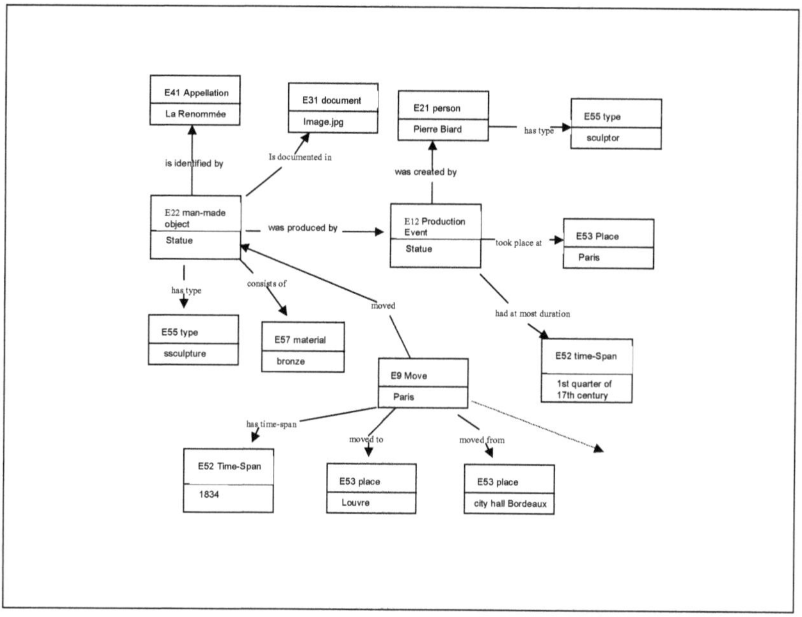

Fig. 3 Example of a sculpture modeling in CIDOC-CRM.

The evolution from the model defined by the inventory descriptive system to the CIDOC-CRM ontology is possible by the search for the correspondences between the fields of the descriptive system, in which the content be considered as the instance of one of the classes of the CRM ontology.

For the cases, in which this correspondence could not be found because the information does not exist in the descriptive system, it will be necessary to extract it from the re-transcribed text, under the condition that the speaker registered it. Otherwise it will be necessary to enter it during the validation of the information extracted automatically by the system.

4 Conclusion and perspectives

This paper presents our work on a voice assistant for knowledge acquisition in the domain of cultural heritage. The originality of our system is the link between three distinctive research domains such as signal processing, ontology and natural language processing. We experimented on field voice knowledge acquisition, "translation" of voice into a text file, the work on text files in order to extract the relative concepts and relation between them in semiautomatic way. The voice interface provides a considerable help and efficiency for an expert working in the

field. The knowledge modeling with ontology adds the flexibility to the classic inventory systems and allows future knowledge retrieval.
We expect to continue this work by incorporating a control of the voice acquisition, in the form of a dialogue human-machine. So the "knowledge collector" would have a real-time feedback on the understanding by the machine of what he dictates. We believe that the implementation of a transcription system and the extraction of information will be shortly possible on mobile devices.

References

Balaram M (1998), PC Version of a Knowledge-Based Expert System with Voice Interface. IEA/AIE (Vol. 2) 1988: 1168-1173
Bourigault D, Aussenac-Gilles N (2003), Construction d'ontologies à partir de textes, TALN 2003, Batz-sur-Mer.
Boufaden N, Bengio Y, Lapalme G (2004), Approche statistique pour le repérage de mots informatifs dans les textes oraux, TALN 2004, Fés, 2004
Boufaden N (2004), Extraction d'information à partir de transcriptions de conversations téléphoniques spécialisées, Thèse de doctorat, Université de Montréal, 2004.
Burns G , Cheng WC (2006), Tools for knowledge acquisition within the NeuroScholar system and their application to anatomical tract-tracing data, Journal of Biomedical Discovery and Collaboration, http://www.j-biomed-discovery.com/content/1/1/10
Charlet J., Zacklad M., Kassel G. & Bourigault D. (eds) (2000), Ingénierie des connaissances, Evolutions récentes et nouveaux défis, Editions Eyrolles et France Télécom-CENT, Paris 2000.
Charlet J. (2002), L'ingénierie des connaissances : résultats, développements et perspectives pour la gestion des connaissances médicales. Mémoire d'habilitation à diriger des recherches, Université Pierre et Marie Curie.
Cole R. A., Hirschman L., et al. (1992), Workshop on spoken language understanding. Technical Report CSE 92-014, Oregon Graduate Institute of Science & Technology, P.O.Box 91000, Portland, OR 97291-1000 USA, September 1992.
Condamines A. et Rebeyrolles J (2000), Construction d'une base de connaissances terminologiques à partir de textes : expérimentation et définition d'une méthode. In Charlet J,
Doerr M, Crofts N, Gill T, Stead S, Stiff M (editors) (2006), Definition of the CIDOC Conceptual Reference Model, October 2006.
Enkvist N.E, (1976), Notes on valency, semantic scope, and thematic perspective as parameters of adverbial placement in English". In: Enkvist, Nils E./Kohonen, Viljo (eds.) (1976): Reports on Text Linguistics: Approaches to Word Order.
GRUBER T. R. (1993). A Translation Approach to Portable Ontology Specifications. Knowledge Acquisition, 5, 199.220
Hagège C, Roux C (2003), Entre syntaxe et sémantique : Normalisation de la sortie de l'analyse syntaxique en vue de l'amélioration de l'extraction d'information à partir de textes, TALN 2003, Batz-sur-Mer, 11–14 juin 2003
Haton J-P, Cerisara C, Fohr D, Laprie Y, Smaïli K (2006), Reconnaissance automatique de la parole, Du signal à son interpétation, Donod.
Hernandez N (2005), Ontologies de domaine pour la modélisation de contexte en recherche d'information, Thèse de doctorat, Université Paul Sabatier, Toulouse,2005.
Ho-Dac L (2007), La position Initiale dans l'organisation du discours : une exploration en corpus. Thèse de doctorat, Université Toulouse le Mirail.

Kaufmann K., Michalski R.S. (1986) EMERALD: An Integrated System of Machine Learning and Discovery Programs to Support AI Education and Experimental Research, Center for Artificial Intelligence George Mason University.
Le Priol F (2000), Extraction et capitalisation automatiques de connaissances à partir de documents textuels.Thèse de doctorat, Université Paris-Sorbonne, 2000.
Mercier-Laurent E,(1980), Réalisation de communications dans un processeur de consultation de données textuelles, Thèse Docteur-Ingénieur, INRIA 1980.
Mercier-Laurent E (2007) Role de l'ordinateur dans le processus global de l'innovation à partir de connaissances, HDR, University Jean-Moulin, Lyon
Mykowiecka A, Kupsc A, Marciniak M (2005), Rule-Based Medical Content Extraction and Classification, Intelligent Information Systems 2005
Pavia N G (2003), Un modèle d'analyseur syntaxique robuste fondé sur la modularité et la lexicalisation de ses grammaires, Thèse de doctorat, Université Paris XI, 2003.
Poibeau T (2003), Extraction automatique d'information, Du texte brut au web sémantique, Hérmes, Paris.
Roche Ch (2003), La Construction d'Ontologies : Quel Constat ?,EGC 2003, Lyon 22-23-24 janvier 2003.
Séguéla P (2001), Construction de modèles de connaissances par analyse linguistique de relations lexicales dans les documents techniques. Thèse de doctorat; Université Toulouse III, 2001.
Troncy R (2004), Formalisation des connaissances documentaires et des connaissances conceptuelles à l'aide d'ontologies : application à la description de documents audiovisuels , Thèse de doctorat, Université Joseph Fourier, 2004.
Verdier H. (1999),- Système descriptif des objets mobiliers. Paris, 1999.- Editions du Patrimoine.
Veronis J (2000), « Annotation automatique de corpus : panorama et état de la technique », Ingénierie des langues, Hermes,2000.
Yangarber R (2001), Scenario Customization for Information Extraction. Thèse de doctorat, New York University, 2001.

Granularity of Knowledge from Different Sources

Maria A. Mach and Mieczyslaw L. Owoc

University of Economics

Komandorska 118/120

53-345 Wroclaw, Poland

maria.mach@ue.wroc.pl

mieczyslaw.owoc@ue.wroc.pl

Abstract: The paper deals with the problem of knowledge granularity in case of building intelligent systems. The origin of the problem is discussed, some knowledge classifications are presented, next the links between types of knowledge and knowledge granularity are shown. In the last part of the paper the question of knowledge granularity types and their usage in intelligent systems is presented and discussed.

Keywords: knowledge based systems, knowledge heterogeneity, knowledge granularity.

Please use the following format when citing this chapter:

Mach, M.A. and Owoc, M.L., 2008, in IFIP International Federation for Information Processing, Volume 288; *Intelligent Information Processing IV*; Zhongzhi Shi, E. Mercier-Laurent, D. Leake; (Boston: Springer), pp. 50–57.

1. Introduction

Knowledge existing in modern information systems usually comes from many sources and is mapped in many ways. There is a real need for representing "knowledge pieces" as rather universal objects that should fit to multi-purpose acting systems. According to great number of information system's tasks, knowledge representation is more or less detailed (e.g. some level of its granularity is assumed). The main goal of this paper is to present chosen aspects of expressing granularity of knowledge implemented in intelligent systems. One of the main reasons of granularity phenomena is diversification of knowledge sources, therefore the next section is devoted to this issue.

2. Heterogeneous Knowledge as a Source for Intelligent Systems

Knowledge, the main element of so-called intelligent applications and systems, is very often heterogeneous. This heterogeneity concerns the origin of knowledge, its sources as well as its final forms of presentation. In this section the selected criteria of knowledge differentiation will be presented, in the context of potential sources of knowledge acquisition. In Fig. 1 an environment of intelligent systems is shown, divided into different knowledge sources for the system.

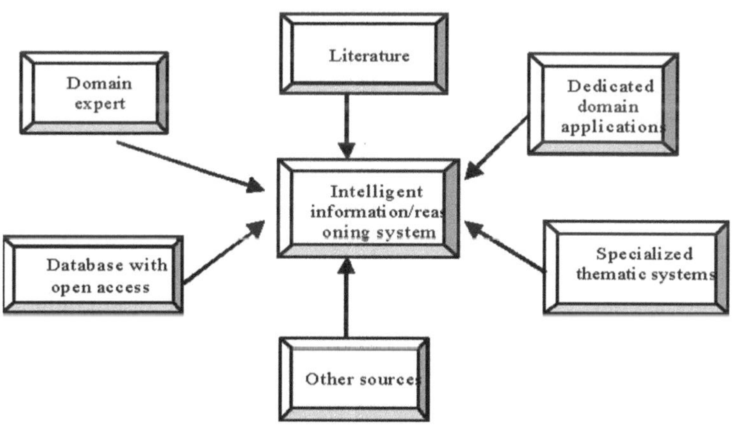

Fig. 1. Potential knowledge sources for intelligent information/reasoning system. Source: own elaboration based on (Mach, 2007) p. 24.

Classical knowledge sources are as follows: literature concerning the problem to be solved; domain experts possessing knowledge on the way of preparing decisions; databases, from which – using appropriate techniques – it is possible to acquire knowledge; specialized knowledge base systems, providing useful intermediate expertise (see Nycz&Smok, 2000). Knowledge gained from each of the above mentioned sources may have a specific form (e.g. report on discussion with an expert, description of a problem solving method or a set of rules generated on the basis of former system's correct reasoning procedures).

The sources pointed out above constitute the main factor, enabling to differentiate the acquired knowledge. Nevertheless, assuming more precise criteria it is possible to obtain different forms of knowledge, taking into account e.g. the domain and type of knowledge application, or the way in which knowledge is transformed during the process of building an intelligent system.

With the first criterion – domain of knowledge application – we may point out the following types of knowledge: the one supporting management (manufacturing and different kinds of business) and other forms of human activity, e.g. medicine or military activity. This criterion is strictly connected to the next one – category of tasks being supported. In this context, we may speak of: knowledge used for classification, for diagnostics, for monitoring etc. Computer applications making use of particular knowledge types, usually concern a concrete domain (or several domains) and generate solutions according to previously defined tasks.

According to the third criterion – the type of domain knowledge – we may mark off several specific forms of knowledge, encompassing among others:

- declarative knowledge – that is knowledge on what is already known about the problem,
- procedural knowledge – stating how the problem may be solved, and finally,
- heuristic knowledge – describing expert's experience, gained during previous problem solving procedures (see e.g. Durkin, 1994).

The type of knowledge is in this case identified according to the source knowledge comes from.

If we use the criterion of knowledge representation form, we have two main classes of solutions: the symbolic and non-symbolic knowledge (see Durkin, 1994). In case of symbolic representation, we deal with so called explicit representation (it will be discussed below), while non-symbolic representation concerns such representations, as neural networks, genetic algorithms, or algorithms of inductive training.

The next criterion concerns the way knowledge is represented: knowledge representation techniques. It leads to a more detailed diversification, because it is strictly connected with the previous classification (symbolic and non-symbolic representations). According to the classical depictions of the topic, one may speak about knowledge expressed in the form of:

- propositional logic,
- semantic networks,
- rules,
- mixed techniques (hybrid knowledge, e.g. frames).

The last criterion – method of knowledge creation – allows for denoting knowledge represented according to the selected methodology, and knowledge generated with the aid of selected tools. The first type of knowledge (bases) is built in three main steps: knowledge acquisition from an expert, knowledge representation using one of the above mentioned techniques, and knowledge implementation. It may be therefore said that this type corresponds with symbolic representations. On the other hand, generated knowledge bases correspond generally with non-symbolic representations and are built up automatically.

Summing up, we have to deal with so-called multi-sourced knowledge, which in intelligent systems may be represented using different methods, may have different forms and different structures. In particular, these structures may have a different level of details, which in turn is connected with the phenomenon of knowledge granularity.

3. Granularity Concepts in Information Technologies

One of the crucial aspects of information architecture is how to define data structures for multi-purpose usage and to process it effectively. Some of these data structures can include repeatable elements while some cover different levels of data details. At least two main trends in information technologies touch such issues (see: BitsOfPower, 2007) :

1. increasing recognition of the importance of standards and
2. growing acceptance of a need for cooperation in monitoring and controlling network.

In both cases a concept of creation universal data "storages" seems to be a potential solution.

In practice such approach is typical for two advanced technologies: object-oriented (in databases, programming languages, knowledge representation techniques) and distance learning (e.g. in formulation of learning units, sharing common "knowledge pieces"). Modeling information and knowledge architecture in such a context a category of an object or a learning object are defined respectively in mentioned technologies.

Nevertheless of data/information/knowledge unit's content the problem of its range and level of details is fundamental for encapsulation of data collections. In other words, granularity phenomena in informational infrastructures can be observed and investigated.

Granularity is a term used in photography to describe accuracy or measure of pictorial presentation on film (the higher level means more details). There are several interpretations of this category in physics, computing and risk management for example. Granularity of information resources refers to size, decomposability and the extent to which a resource is intended to be used as part of a larger resource (see: Wagner, 2002).

It should be stressed certain aspects of "sizing" or "dimensioning" that are present in particular definitions of granularity.

First, granularity refers to **temporal** context of a defined object e.g. provides service of an acting objects across the time. Sometime we need to gather and to process information structures daily, weekly, monthly and the like. Smaller time units allow to represent more details of the investigated phenomena.

Second, granularity relates to **spatial** dimension of a determined entity e.g. cover its functioning in a particular space. Again, the smaller space unit the more details can be achieved.

Third, granularity considers ways of **assuring consistency** of objects belonging to information architecture. Two approaches represent this type of granularity: abstraction and aggregation. In a case of abstraction generated objects are a result of generalization procedures while aggregation deals with defining conditioning of joint objects.

More detailed taxonomy of granularity including formal interpretation of interrelated objects is presented by C.M. Keet – see (Keet, 2006).

General concepts of granularity implemented in IT sector very often are oriented at intelligent systems. The process starts with representation of knowledge pieces in targeted applications. Of course solutions based on particular granularity concept allow (or not) to obtain defined goals of such systems.

4. Granularity and Ontology

In Section 3 some concepts of granularity have been briefly outlined. The question is, where these granularities come from. In our opinion, granularity is strictly connected with the notion of ontology. Therefore, let us now investigate different granularities in context of different ontologies, as suggested in previous section.

First, the temporal ontology typically concerns ontology of time, that is, what is time composed of: points, intervals or both, as basic temporal entities. But in more common, everyday context, ontology of time concerns calendar units, and here one deals with such units as e.g. years, quarters, months, days, referred to as time granularities (Goralwalla et al., 2001). Granularities are unanchored durations, which can be used as units of time (ibidem). The most complete formal framework for manipulating temporal granularities was described by (Bettini et al., 2000).

Spatial ontology strictly depends on the definition of space adopted. For example, if one assumes a metric space, that is a generalization of n-dimensional Euclidean space, the only ontological elements of this space are points and there is no granularity problem. However, this is of course not the only model of space possible.

In the field of artificial intelligence, where time and space are often considered together, the region-based theory of space is often assumed and employed (see e.g. Bennett, 2001). It is a theory of spatial regions based on parthood relation P(r1, r2), and the sphere predicate S(r). If we adopt the RGB theory of space, every region may be treated as a granule in space and the problem here is whether these granules may be compared or not. If so, what conditions have to be fulfilled by the space granules to compared them?

Information architecture ontology deals with objects considered as primitive units of information architecture. They depend on the level of architecture that are considered as a basic one, e.g. logical and physical one.

Granularity phenomena can be defined including many purposes. One of the most demanding approaches comes from the e-learning area. Learning courses can be divided into "knowledge pieces" according to audience familiarization with presented topics or aims of the course. Therefore from logical point of view we may separate knowledge presenting definition of some phenomena, put some procedures how to classify some objects or give examples of this sort procedural knowledge. Of course ontologies mentioned before (spatial or temporal) are actual in may respects e.g. a definition of a database can be detailed for particular users taking into account their properties and ways of applications. On the other hand physical "pieces of knowledge" can be identified as different files or cluster of some media aggregations.

Nowadays knowledge granularity is strictly connected to knowledge grid ideas. Any concept of knowledge grid acquires resolving problems with knowledge aggregation and its distribution. In every case we are obliged to divide the whole domain knowledge into units sometimes at many levels.

Granularity concepts presented earlier can be applied in different areas. Let's try to investigate their usability in the knowledge acquisition process.

One of the mentioned granularity types stressed importance of time category. This type of knowledge granularity is connected with the question of representing knowledge about dynamic heterogeneous environment in the intelligent system's knowledge base. In this case, it may happen, that particular elements of the environment present different pace of changes. This leads to the need of representing temporal knowledge that is heterogeneous in the temporal context: each part of knowledge (concerning a particular environment element) may have a different time granularity. In this situation a solution may consist of using different temporal formalisms for knowledge representation, which in turn leads to the problem of representation integration. This question is beyond the scope of this paper, more details may be found in (Mach, 2005).

Spatial aspect of knowledge granularity refers to gathering domain knowledge from many sources. They can represent different subjects allocated in separated sites. The main problem is how to implement standards of knowledge representation that will lead to universal form of knowledge mapping in case of diversification of sourced data. This is a typical challenge for hybrid intelligent systems.

Procedures of knowledge refinement use the third type of the mentioned phenomena, namely abstraction and aggregation. Looking for more efficient knowledge bases we try to discover new knowledge pieces to generalize initially introduced information or to elaborate useful extended “knowledge grains”.

5. Conclusions

Aspects of knowledge granularity presented in this paper refer to rather specific way of information processing called granular computing. In a more philosophical sense, granular computing can describe an approach that relies on the human and computer ability to perceive the real world under different levels of granularity (i.e., abstraction). In order to abstract and consider useful from the defined goals knowledge pieces should be represent and switch among different granularities. Focusing on different levels of granularity, one can obtain various levels of knowledge, as well as a greater understanding of the inherent knowledge structure. Granular computing can be treated as an essential way of human problem solving and hence should have a very significant impact on the design and implementation of intelligent systems.

In order to establish a proper granularity, one has to investigate the context of the problem and the ontology of the domain. In our opinion ontology plays the decisive role in establishing knowledge granularity. In case of ontology and/or knowledge sources heterogeneity, there is the need of unification before establishing the final granularity. These problems are discussed e.g. in (Mach, 2003).

References

Bennett B., Space, Time, Matter and Things. Proc. FOIS’01. ACM, USA, 2001.

Bettini, C., Jajodia, S. & Wang, S. X. (2000). Time Granularities in Databases, Data Mining, and Temporal Reasoning. Berlin Heidelberg: Springer-Verlag.

www.nap.edu/readingroom/books/BitsOfPower/2.html; 2007

Durkin J.: Expert Systems: Design and Development. Prentice Hall, Enlewood Cliffs 1994.

Goralwalla, I. A., Leontiev, Y., Ozsu, T. M. & Szafron, D. (2001). Temporal Granularity: Completing the Puzzle. Journal of Intelligent Information Systems, 16, 41-46.

Keet, C.M. A taxonomy of types of granularity. IEEE Conference in Granular Computing (GrC06). 10-12 May 2006, Atlanta, USA.

Mach M., Integrating Knowledge from Heterogeneous Sources. “Argumenta Oeconomica”, No. 1-2(14) 2003, University of Economics, Poland Publishing House, PL ISSN 1233-5835, pp. 189-210.

Mach M., Analysing Economic Environment with Temporal Intelligent Systems: the Union of Economic and Technical Perspectives, [in:] Tadeusiewicz R., Ligeza A., Szymkat M. (eds.), Computer Methods and Systems, Volume I, Kraków 2005, ISBN 83-916420-3-8, p. 355-366.

Mach M. : Temporalna analiza otoczenia przedsiebiorstwa. Techniki i narzedzia inteligentne. [Temporal analysis of enterprise's environment. Intelligent tools and techniques]. Wydawnictwo Akademii Ekonomicznej Wroclaw, 2007 (in Polish).
Nycz M., Smok B.: Knowledge Sources for Expert Systems. Transactions in International Information Systems. Systems Analysis and Development Theory and Practice. Nowicki A. and Unold J. (eds.) Wroclaw university if Economics
Wagner, E.: Steps to Creating a Content Strategy for Your Organization. eLearning Developers' Journal. eLearning Guild. October 29, 2002. Retrieved from http://www.elearningguild.com/pdf/2/102902MGT -H.pdf on 12/07/2007

Fuzzy Ontology Models Based on Fuzzy Linguistic Variable for Knowledge Management and Information Retrieval

Jun Zhai, Yiduo Liang, Jiatao Jiang and Yi Yu

School of Economics and Managemen, Dalian Maritime University, Dalian, 116026, China

Abstract: Ontology is the basis of sharing and reusing knowledge on the Semantic Web, and ontology-based semantic retrieval is a hotspot of current research. Fuzzy ontology is an extension of domain ontology for solving the uncertainty problems. To represent fuzzy knowledge more effectively, this paper presents a new series of fuzzy ontology models that consists of fuzzy domain ontology and fuzzy linguistic variable ontologies, considering semantic relationships of concepts, including set relation, order relation, equivalence relation and semantic association relation etc. The process to construct linguistic variables ontology is discussed. Using ontology and RDFS, the knowledge model for product information is created. To achieve semantic retrieval, the semantic query expansion in SeRQL is constructed by semantic relations between fuzzy concepts. The application shows that these models can overcome the localization of other fuzzy ontology models, and this research facilitates the fuzzy knowledge sharing and semantic retrieval on the Semantic Web.

1. Introduction

Ontology is a conceptualization of a domain into a human understandable, machine-readable format consisting of entities, attributes, relationships, and axioms [1].It is used as a standard knowledge representation for the Semantic Web. However, the conceptual formalism supported by typical ontology may not be sufficient to represent uncertainty information commonly found in many application domains due to the lack of clear-cut boundaries between concepts of the domains. Moreover, fuzzy knowledge plays an important role in many domains that face a huge amount of imprecise and vague knowledge and information, such as text mining, multimedia information system, medical informatics, machine learning, and human natural language processing.

Please use the following format when citing this chapter:

Zhai, J., Liang, Y., Jiang, J. and Yu, Y., 2008, in IFIP International Federation for Information Processing, Volume 288; *Intelligent Information Processing IV*; Zhongzhi Shi, E. Mercier-Laurent, D. Leake; (Boston: Springer), pp. 58–67.

To handle uncertainty of information and knowledge, one possible solution is to incorporate fuzzy theory into ontology. Then we can generate fuzzy ontologies, which contain fuzzy concepts and fuzzy memberships. The fuzzy ontologies are capable of dealing with fuzzy knowledge [2], and are efficient in text and multimedia object representation and retrieval.

Lee et al. proposed an algorithm to create fuzzy ontology and applied it to news summarization [3]. This work is based on their previous work on ontology-based fuzzy event extraction agents for Chinese news summarization. Tho et al. proposed a Fuzzy Ontology Generation Framework (FOGA) for fuzzy ontology generation on uncertainty information [4]. This framework is based on the idea of fuzzy theory and Formal Concept Analysis (FCA). Abulaish et al. proposed a fuzzy ontology framework in which a concept descriptor is represented as a fuzzy relation which encodes the degree of a property value using a fuzzy membership function [5]. To enable representation and reasoning for fuzzy ontologies, Kang et al. proposed a new fuzzy extension of description logics called the fuzzy description logics with comparison expressions (FCDLs) [6]. Calegari et al. presented the fuzzy OWL language [7]. Zhai et al. studied the fuzzy ontology using intuitionistic fuzzy set [8].

But, current fuzzy ontology models have localization in fuzzy semantic retrieval. To represent formally the fuzzy knowledge more effectively, this paper presents a new kind of fuzzy ontology models. The rest of this paper is organized as follows: Section 2 introduces fuzzy domain ontology model. Section 3 presents fuzzy linguistic variable ontology models. Section 4 applies fuzzy ontology to knowledge modeling and section 5 studies information retrieval based on SeRQL. Finally, section 6 concludes the paper.

2. Fuzzy domain ontology model

An ontology organizes domain knowledge in terms of concepts, properties, relations and axioms, and the fuzzy ontology is created as an extension to the standard ontology.

Definition 1 (Fuzzy domain ontology) – A fuzzy domain ontology is a 6-tuple $O_F = (I, C, P^C, R, P^R, A_F)$, where:

(1) I is the set of individuals, also called instances of the concepts.

(2) C is a set of concepts. A concept is often considered as a class in an ontology. Every concept here has some properties whose value is fuzzy concept or fuzzy set. And, every concept can have the degree of membership $\mu_C(i): I \rightarrow [0,1]$ and the degree of non-membership $\nu_C(i): I \rightarrow [0,1]$ of the $i \in I$ in C.

(3) P^C is a set of concepts properties. A property $p^C \in P^C$ is defined as a 5-tuple of the form $p^C(c, v_F, q_F, f, U)$, where $c \in C$ is an ontology concept, v_F represents property values , q_F models linguistic qualifiers, which can control or alter the strength of a property value v_F, f is the restriction facets on v_F, and U is the universe of discourse. Both v_F and q_F are the fuzzy concepts on U, but q_F changes the fuzzy degree of v_F. For example, "price" is a property of concept "product". The value of "price" may be either fuzzy concept "cheap" or fuzzy number "around 50", and the linguistic qualifiers may be "very", "little", "close to" etc. Therefore, the final value of "price" may be "very cheap" or "little expensive". At the same time, the property $p^C \in P^C$ has also the non-fuzzy form $p^C(c, v, f)$.

(4) R is a set of inter-concept relations between concepts. The relation type is not only the ordinary binary relation of $r \subseteq C \times C$, but also is the fuzzy relation and the intuitionistic fuzzy relation from C to C.

(5) P^R is a set of relations properties. Like concept properties, $p^R \in P^R$ is defined as a 4-tuple of the form $p^R(c_1, c_2, r, s_F)$, where $c_1, c_2 \in C$ are ontology concepts, r represents relation, and $s_F \in [0,1]$ or $s_F \subseteq [0,1]$ models relation strengths and has meaning of fuzzy set or intuitionistic fuzzy set on $C \times C$, which can represent the strength of association between concept-pairs $< c_1, c_2 >$. For instance, there is a relation of "loyalty" between "customer" and "brand". The strength of "loyalty" can be 0.7, a fuzzy value, and can be [0.6,0.8], a interval value, i.e. intuitionistic fuzzy value, which express more abundant information about uncertainty. On the other hand, s_F can also be fuzzy linguistic value, i.e. fuzzy concept.

(6) A_F is a set of fuzzy rules. In a fuzzy system the set of fuzzy rules is used as knowledge base.

The fuzzy domain ontology is used to model domain expert knowledge. But, due to the lack of relationships between fuzzy concepts that can be the value of properties, it is difficult to integrate diverse ontology systems. For example, in an ontology the set of property "price" value is {cheap, appropriate, expensive, ...}, and in other ontology the same set is {high, low, middle, ...}. To map these ontologies, it is necessary to define the semantic relationship between fuzzy concepts, e.g. "cheap" and "expensive" have the relation of disjointness, and "low" and "high" have the same relation of disjointness etc.

Consequently, we propose the fuzzy linguistic variables ontology models.

3. Fuzzy linguistic variable ontology

The fuzzy linguistic variables proposed by Zadeh are the basic of fuzzy knowledge and fuzzy system. To achieve the knowledge share and reuse for fuzzy systems on the Semantic Web, it is necessary to represent the fuzzy linguistic variables with ontology.

Definition 2 (Fuzzy linguistic variable) – Fuzzy linguistic variable is the variable whose value is term or concept in natural language. A fuzzy linguistic variable is a 4-tuple (X, T, M, U), where:

(1) X is the name of fuzzy linguistic variable, e.g. "price" or "speed" etc.

(2) T is the set of terms which is the value of fuzzy linguistic variable, e.g. T ={ cheap, appropriate, expensive, ...} or T ={fast, middle, slow,...}.

(3) M is the mapping rules which map every term of T to fuzzy set at U.

(4) U is the universe of discourse.

Introducing semantic relationships between concepts, we obtain the ontology model.

Definition 3 (Fuzzy linguistic variable ontology) – A fuzzy linguistic variable ontology is a 6-tuple $O_F = (c_a, C_F, R, F, S, U)$, where:

(1) c_a is a concept on the abstract level, e.g. "price", "speed" etc. The corresponding element of c_a is X in definition 2.

(2) C_F is the set of fuzzy concepts which describes all values of c_a. The corresponding element of C_F is T in definition 2, but C_F has certain structure or relations R.

(3) $R = \{r \mid r \subseteq C_F \times C_F\}$ is a set of binary relations between concepts in C_F. A kind of relation is set relation R_S = {inclusion (i.e. $\subseteq$), intersection, disjointness, complement (i.e. $\neg$)}, and the other relations are the order relation and equivalence relation $R_O = \{\leq, \geq, =\}$. C_F and an order relation r compose the ordered structure $< C_F, r >$. There are other semantic relations between concepts, such as semantic distance relation, semantic proximity relation and semantic association relation etc.

(4) F is the set of membership functions at U, which is isomorphic to C_F. The corresponding element of F is M in definition 2, but F has also certain structure or relations.

(5) $S = \{s \mid s : C_F \times C_F \to C_F\}$ is a set of binary operators at C_F. These binary operators form the mechanism of generating new fuzzy concepts. Basic operators are the "union", "intersection" and "complement" etc., i.e. $S = \{\vee, \wedge, \neg, \Lambda\}$. C_F and S compose the algebra structure $< C_F, S >$.

(6) U is the universe of discourse.

Definition 3 is more complex than definition 2 in order to describe the semantic information.

Modeling the linguistic qualifiers, we extend the fuzzy linguistic variable ontology as follows.

Definition 4 (Extended fuzzy ontology) – An extended fuzzy ontology is a 8-tuple $O_F = (c_a, C_F, R, F, S, Q, O, U)$, where:

(1) c_a, C_F, R, F, S, U have same interpretations as defined in definition 3.

(2) Q is the set of the linguistic qualifiers, e.g. Q={very, little, close to, …}. An qualifier $q \in Q$ and a fuzzy concept $c_F \in C_F$ compose a composition fuzzy concept that can be the value of c_a, e.g. "very cheap".

(3) O is the set of fuzzy operators at U, which is isomorphic to Q.

To simplify the transform from fuzzy linguistic variables to fuzzy ontology, we introduce the basic fuzzy ontology model as follows.

Definition 5 (Basic fuzzy ontology) –A basic fuzzy ontology is a 4-tuple $O_F = (c_a, C_F, F, U)$, where c_a, C_F, F, U have same interpretations as defined in definition 5, which satisfy the following conditions:

(1) $C_F = \{c_1, c_2, \Lambda, c_n\}$ is a limited set.

(2) Only one relation of set, the relation of disjointness, exists in C_F, and C_F is complete at U. In the other words, C_F is a fuzzy partition of U.

(3) C_F has an ordered relation $\leq$, and $< C_F, \leq >$ is a complete ordered set, i.e. all concepts in C_F constitute a chain $c_1 \leq c_2 \leq \Lambda \leq c_n$.

(4) F is optional element of ontology.

An example of basic fuzzy ontology is O_F = (c_a = price of product, C_F = {very cheap, cheap, appropriate, expensive, very expensive}, $U = [0,100]$) , where "very cheap" ≤ "cheap" ≤ "appropriate" ≤ "expensive" ≤ "very expensive" .

The process to construct fuzzy linguistic variables ontology is as following:

1. Extracting linguistic variables from application domain.
2. Naming the linguistic variables based on domain ontology.
3. Specifying the fuzzy concepts which are the value of fuzzy linguistic variable.
4. (Analyzing the semantic relation between fuzzy concepts.
5. Mapping these fuzzy concepts and their relations to space of membership functions.

For instance, industrial washing machine is used in a variety of domain, but it consumes a mass of water and electricity. Using fuzzy control, the optimal washing strategy which is determined by fuzzy inference can save water and electricity effectively. Fuzzy inference depends on fuzzy knowledge base, i.e. the set of fuzzy rules, which are summarized from human experiences expressed by fuzzy linguistic variables.

Therefore, definition of fuzzy linguistic variables is the basic of construction of fuzzy rules. To share and reuse fuzzy knowledge, it is necessary to represent formally the fuzzy linguistic variables through ontology. Representing input variables in fuzzy control system for industrial washing machine, there are three basic fuzzy ontologies defined in definition 5 as following:

(1) $O_1 =$ ($c_a =$ quality of cloth, $C_F =$ {chemical fiber, textile, cotton}, $U = [0,100]$), where "chemical fiber" $\leq$ "textile" $\leq$ "cotton" from point of view of cotton content, and the membership functions are shown in Fig 1.

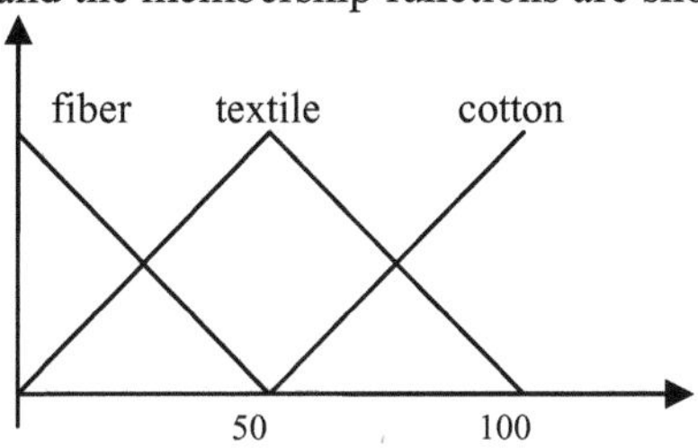

Fig. 1. Membership functions for quality of cloth

(2) $O_2 =$ ($c_a =$ quantity of cloth, $C_F =$ {little, middle, much, very much}, $U = [0,25]$), where "little" $\leq$ "middle" $\leq$ "much" $\leq$ "very much" , and the membership functions are shown in Fig 2.

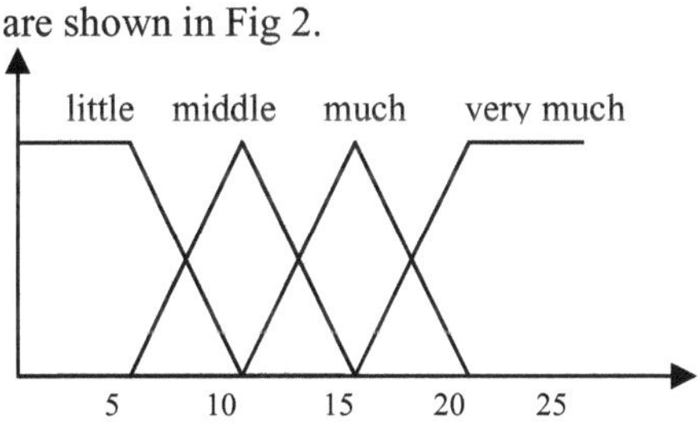

Fig. 2. Membership functions for quantity of cloth

(3) $O_3 =$ ($c_a =$ degree of squalidity, $C_F =$ {clean, dirtish, dirty, filthy}, $U = [0,100]$), where "clean" $\leq$ "dirtish" $\leq$ "dirty" $\leq$ "filthy" , and the membership functions are shown in Fig 3.

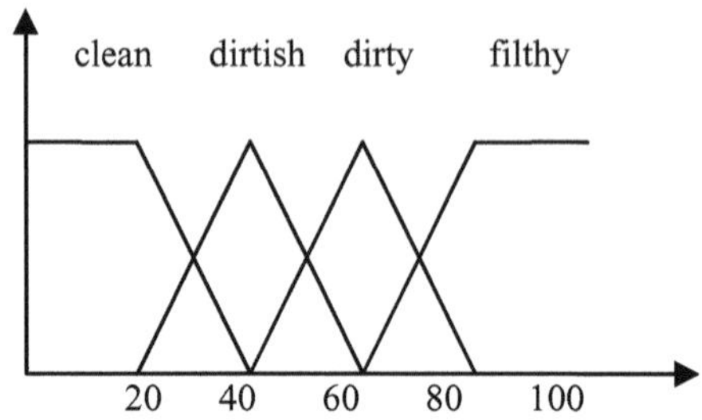

Fig. 3. Membership functions for degree of squalidity

4. Knowledge modeling

In the open and distributed environments of WWW, in order to integrate and reuse information and knowledge in supply chain, ontology becomes the means to model knowledge for customer and product [9]. But the standard ontology is not able to handle fuzzy phenomenon and uncertainty of information and knowledge. It is sufficient for managers and customers to obtain some message in linguistic values rather than in accurate numeric values, such as customer information, product information etc. For instance, the linguistic values for customer income include “low”, “middle”, “high” etc, and linguistic values for product price include “cheap”, “appropriate”, “expensive” etc. These linguistic values have uncertainty and are fuzzy concepts.

The idea of Semantic Web came from Tim Bemers-Lee in his vision to move the web into a new generation, where the web resources are annotated with meaning in a form that machines can understand. This will open up vast opportunities for automated processing of the rich knowledge resources available on the web to applications in information search and filtering, knowledge mining, coordination and collaborative processing by intelligent agents. The Semantic Web is to be realized through a shared infrastructure consisting of languages and tools for knowledge representation and processing. The basic knowledge representation format is the Resource Description Framework (RDF) and RDF Schema (RDFS) [10].

Using RDF and RDFS, we construct the ontology structure for customer and product knowledge shown in Fig. 4, in which the linguistic values are represented formally through fuzzy linguistic variable ontologies. The main fuzzy linguistic variable ontologies are as following:

O1=(age, {old, youth, middle-aged, …});

O2=(income, {little, low, middle, high, …});

O3=(customer type, {new customer, loyalty customer, gold customer, big customer, lost customer, switched customer …});

O4=(price, {very cheap, cheap, appropriate, expensive, very expensive});

O5=(zone of influence, {regional, national, international, …});…… ……
There is a lot of semantic relation between fuzzy concepts. For instance, “gold customer”= “big customer”, “switched customer” ⊆ “lost customer”, “youth” ≤ “middle-aged” ≤ “old” etc.

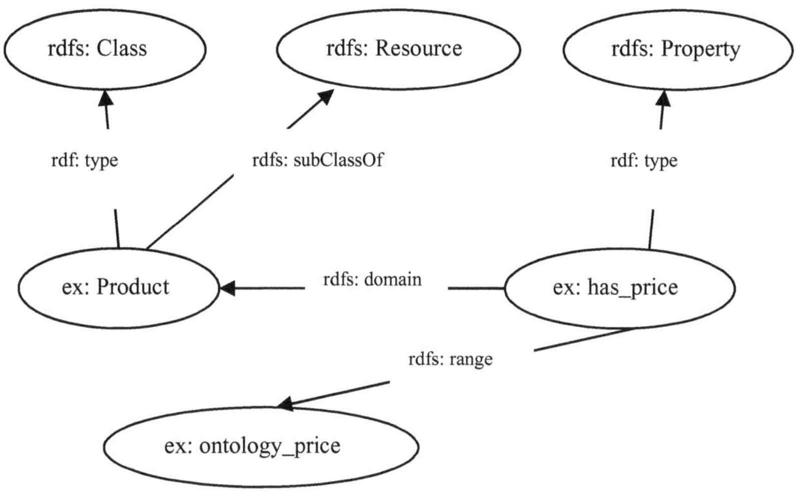

Fig. 4. Ontology structure for product knowledge (portion)

5. Semantic information retrieval

Since the process for information retrieval is based on the knowledge ontology, the semantic and concept research can be achieved. Especially, using linguistic value of fuzzy concept, we can construct the research pattern in SeRQL (Sesame RDF Query Language) [11] such as:

SELECT instance of concept **FROM** {concept} has_property {property} **WHERE** (property of concept) <comparison operator> “Linguistic value of fuzzy concept”, in which the comparison operators includes: equal comparison (=), less than or equal (≤) and greater than or equal (≥) etc.

For instance, we can retrieve “product” information through “price” of property, using the search statement such as: **SELECT** Product **FROM** {product} has_price {price} **WHERE** price ≤ “ expensive”. The standard ontology and other fuzzy ontology are not able to handle the search condition at semantic level, which includes fuzzy concept and semantic relation between them.

Using the “order relation” defined in fuzzy linguistic variable ontology : “very cheap” ≤ “cheap” ≤ “appropriate” ≤ “expensive” ≤ “very expensive” , we can transform the search statement to: **SELECT** Product **FROM** {product} has_price

{price} **WHERE** price = "very cheap" or price = "cheap" or price = "appropriate" or price = "expensive", in which every sub-condition is ordinary and can be completed easily in SeRQL engine.

When retrieving the information about gold customer by the statement: **SELECT** Customer **FROM** {customer} has_type {type} **WHERE** type="gold customer", we can obtain the information about big customer using equivalence relation: "gold customer"= "big customer".

When retrieving the information about lost customer by the statement: **SELECT** Customer **FROM** {customer} has_type {type} **WHERE** type="lost customer", we can obtain the information about switched customer using inclusion relation: "switched customer" $\subseteq$ "lost customer".

Based on other semantic relations defined in fuzzy ontology, we can create and complete more complex semantic retrieval, which will be described in future work.

6. Conclusion

In this paper we have proposed the fuzzy domain ontology model and the fuzzy linguistic variables ontology model to represent fuzzy knowledge. The fuzzy linguistic variables ontology models focus on essential semantic relationships between fuzzy concepts, which facilitates the information retrieval at semantic level. The semantic query expansion in SeRQL query language is constructed by semantic relations between fuzzy concepts.

Our further researches lay on the automatic construction of fuzzy ontology and the integration among standard ontology and fuzzy ontology.

Acknowledgments

This work was supported in part by the Research Project of the Educational Department of Liaoning Province (Leading Laboratory Project) under Grant 20060083.

References

[1] Fensel D., F. van Harmelen, Horrocks I., D.L.McGuinness, and Patel-Schneider P. F., "OIL: an ontology infrastructure for the semantic web", IEEE Intelligent Systems, vol. 16 , no. 2, 2001, p. 38-45.

[2] Widyantoro D. H., Yen J., "A fuzzy ontology-based abstract search engine and its user studies", in: Proceedings of the 10th IEEE International Conference on Fuzzy Systems, Melbourne, Australia, 2001, p. 1291- 1294.
[3] Lee C. S., Jian Z. W., and Huang L. K., "A fuzzy ontology and its application to news summarization", IEEE Transactions on Systems, Man and Cybernetics (Part B), vol. 35, no. 5, 2005, p. 859- 880.
[4] Tho Q. T., Hui S. C., Fong A. C. M., and Cao T. H., "Automatic fuzzy ontology generation for semantic web", IEEE Transactions on Knowledge and Data Engineering, vol. 18, no. 6, 2006, p. 842- 856.
[5] Abulaish M., Dey L., "A fuzzy ontology generation framework for handling uncertainties and nonuniformity in domain knowledge description", in: Proceedings of 2007 International Conference on Computing: Theory and Applications, Kolkata, 2007, p. 287-293.
[6] Kang D. Z., Xu B. W., Lu J. J., Li Y. H., "Description logics for fuzzy ontologies on semantic web", Journal of Southeast University (English Edition), vol. 22, no. 3, 2006, p. 343 – 347.
[7] Calegari S., Ciucci D., "Fuzzy ontology and fuzzy-OWL in the KAON project", in: Proceedings of 2007 IEEE International Conference on Fuzzy Systems Conference, London, UK, 2007, p.1-6.
[8] Jun Zhai, Yan Chen, Qinglian Wang, and Miao Lv, "Fuzzy Ontology Models Using Intuitionistic Fuzzy Set for Knowledge Sharing on the Semantic Web", in: Proceedings of the 12th International Conference on Computer Supported Cooperative Work in Design (CSCWD 2008)(volume 1), 2008, IEEE Press, p.465-469.
[9] Lu X. W., Jiang F., Hou L. W., "Customer features extraction based on customer ontology", Computer Engineering, vol. 31, no. 5, 2005, p. 31-33. (in Chinese)
[10] John W.T. Lee, Alex K.S. Wong, "Information retrieval based on semantic query on RDF annotated resources", in Proceedings of the 2004 IEEE International Conference on Systems, Man and Cybernetics, 2004, p. 3220-3225.
[11] .B. V. Aduna, "The SeRQL query language," http: //www.openrdf.org/doc/sesame/users/ch06.html#d0e1977, 2002.

Blog Classification: Adding Linguistic Knowledge to Improve the K-NN Algorithm

Ines Bayoudh [1,2], Nicolas Bechet [2] and Mathieu Roche [2]

[1] INSAT
Université du 7 Novembre à Carthage
Centre Urbain Nord, Tunis
Tunisie
Ines.Bayoudh@lirmm

[2] LIRMM
UMR 5506, CNRS
Université Montpellier 2, France
Nicolas.Bechet @lirmm.fr, Mathieu.Roche@lirmm.fr

ABSTRACT: Blogs are interactive and regularly updated websites which can be seen as diaries. These websites are composed by articles based on distinct topics. Thus, it is necessary to develop Information Retrieval approaches for this new web knowledge. The first important step of this process is the categorization of the articles. The paper above compares several methods using linguistic knowledge with k-NN algorithm for automatic categorization of weblogs articles.

KEYWORDS: blog, categorization, linguistic knowledge, K-NN

1. Introduction

The work presented in this paper has been made with the collaboration of PaperBlog Company. This company hosts a website that proposes blog indexing, taken from partner websites. Blogs are similar to websites composed by articles chronologically or ante chronologically ranked. Each article is written like a log book which can be commented. This new type of websites, illustrating the concepts of Web 2.0, became very popular these last years due to its easiness of publication and its interactivity. However, blogs can be written in various ways of expression which constitute the main problem for information searching.

Please use the following format when citing this chapter:

Bayoudh, I., Bechet, N. and Roche, M., 2008, in IFIP International Federation for Information Processing, Volume 288; *Intelligent Information Processing IV*; Zhongzhi Shi, E. Mercier-Laurent, D. Leake; (Boston: Springer), pp. 68–77.

The main purpose of the Paperblog Company is to answer to the question: How to find an article of a specific theme from blogs? Thus, blog articles are evaluated according to their relevance and then associated to a category such as culture, computers, unusual, etc. This approach helps to retrieve information of a specific theme contained in blogs. The purpose of our work is to find a method which can automatically classify articles which is currently, manually done.

For this task, we chose to implement a classic algorithm of text classification: the K-Nearest Neighbor (K-NN). This classifier will be first implemented in a standard form then will be associated to different approaches by using Part-Of-Speech (POS) knowledge. Thus, we will be able to evaluate different data representations in order to determinate the most suitable one. We used a 3.4 Mb corpus of 2520 articles, written in French and composed by more than 400 000 words. This corpus is divided into 5 classes: food, talent, people, cooking, and market.

The following section introduces the state of the art of text classification and the K-NN algorithm, while the 3rd one will describe the grammatically-based approaches. Finally, the 4th section will describe the approach based on weighting of Tf-Idf matrices and will analyze the obtained results.

2. The state of the art of text classification

Our paper is based on a supervised approach with the automatic classification of blog articles in defined classes. We worked on manually classified articles provided by PaperBlog Company thus it is necessary to automate the categorization process. The purpose of this procedure is gathering articles which have the same thematic.

The learning process consists in realizing an automatic classifier which considers the characteristics of preordered examples. This classifier allows to add new articles and to find out their belonging category. The second part of our article presents two methods currently used in our categorization process.

– **The Support Vector Machine (SVM)**

Many methods use the SVM concept on multi-classes problem. However, they need several stages and everyone creates a new binary classification. The order of class processing has an influence on classification results. It was shown that SVM method needs more learning time (Joachim (1998)) than Naive Bayes or K-NN (described in the following section). The SVMs are more accurate when applied on text classification (Lewis et al. (2004)). A detailed description of SVM is introduced by (Burges (1998)).

– **Naive Bayes classifier**

These classifiers, based on the Bayes theorem, are defined as follows:

$$[1]\ P(h|D) = \frac{P(D|h) \times P(h)}{P(D)}$$

- P (h|D) = probability of h hypotesis given D (post probability),
- P (h) =H probability that h is independently verified of D (ex-ante probability),
- P (D) = Probability of observing D data regardless of h,
- P (D|h) = Probability of observing D knowing that H is verified.

This theorem supposes that the solutions can be found from probability distributions contained in the hypothesis and data. In case of texts classification, a Naive Bayesian classifier helps to determine the class of a specified document assuming that the documents are independent. This hypothesis of independence does not reflect the reality hence the name Naive. The class of a new object is determined after combining the predictions of all hypotheses by weighting them by their ex-ante probabilities. For a group of classes C and a set of attributes A, the value of c naive Bayesian classification is defined as follows:

$$[2]\ c = \operatorname{argmax} P(c_j)_{c_j \in C} \prod_{a_i \in A} P(a_i|c_j)$$

This classification has been less efficient for text classification then the other methods (Weiss et al. (2005)). Nevertheless, it remains efficient when applied on incomplete data and can be used in many areas (legal, medical, economic, etc.).

These two methods are commonly employed in classification of texts containing a comparison (with opinion's comments) such as (Chen and al. (2006)).

There are other approaches for text categorization such as Decision Trees or DTree (Quinlan (1986)) or C4.5 (Quinlan (1993)). These trees determine rules (or terms) to separate and to classify texts according to their common attributes. We can also mention Artificial Neural Networks (NNet) which simulate the functioning of human neurons (Mcculloch et Pitts (1943)). The main inconvenience of this approach is the growth of calculating time with the size of learning corpus.

Finally, we introduce the K Nearest Neighbors (K-NN) which has been applied in our work. In fact, this method is very simple, quick to implement and provides satisfactory results (Yang (1999)). In addition, this method is still robust in case of incomplete data, which is quite common for blog articles. This approach will be detailed in the following section.

– **The K-NN algorithm**

The principle of K-NN algorithm (Cover et Hart (on 1967)) is to measure the similarity between a new document and all the documents already ordered. These documents can be considered as a learning dataset even if there is no learning phase in the K-NN algorithm.

This algorithm means constituting a vector space in which each document is represented by a vector of words. The dimension of a vector is the number of words it contains. Each element of this vector is constituted by the number of words occurrences came from the learning set. The classified documents are decreasingly ordered so that the first document is the one with the highest score of similarity with the document to classify. Then, they are ordered according to the value of k, this made a classification of k closest documents. The measure of similarity usually used is the calculation of the cosine of the angle formed by both vectors of documents. The cosine between two vectors A and B is the scalar product of vectors A and B divided by the product of the norm of A and B. Having identified the k nearest neighbors, we have to define a methodology to assign a class to the new document. The second phase calculates the number of documents belonging to every category among the k closest one.

Let us take for example a document d to classify among four classes, C1, C2, C3 and C4. Let us define k = 6 and consider the following classification of dnew with the set of learning documents D containing documents di:

Table 1. Example of text classification using K-NN

Documents	Documents class
d1	C2
d2	C2
d3	C4
d4	C4
d5	C1
d6	C4

By using our approach, we would attribute the class C4 in dnew. Indeed, the class C4 is the one who possesses most documents among the k nearest neighbors (three documents).

In our experiments, we used two parameters:

- The threshold of class that fixes a minimal number of terms that must belong to a class so that a new document is assigned to this class,
- The threshold of similarity below which the new document will not be anymore allowed among the k nearest neighbors.

3. The used approaches

We propose in this paper, approaches establishing new representations of original corpus by using grammatical knowledge. To obtain such knowledge, we use a Part-Of-Speech Tagger.

3.1. The Part-Of-Speech TreeTagger

We chose the TreeTagger (Schmid (1995)), which allows texts labeling in several languages such us French. The step of TreeTagger is based on a set of trigrams, constituted by three consecutive Part-Of-Speech labels. For example, TreeTagger proposes the following results for the sentence: *The authors added linguistic information*

The	DT	the
authors	NNS	author
added	VVD	add
linguistic	JJ	linguistic
information	NN	information

The first column corresponds to the words of the sentence; the second one informs on the word category and the last one gives the lemmatized form. We propose to use these different information on various approaches presented in the following section.

3.2. The experimental approaches

We suggest using combinations of words with the categories: Noun (N), Verb (V) and Adjective (A). This approach consists in reconstituting a corpus which contains only the words belonging to the defined combination. Let us take for example the combination V_N: such a corpus will contain only verbs and nouns. The used combinations are: N, V, A, N_V, N_A, V_A, and N_V_A. We also define respectively the methods F and L for the corpus with inflected forms and the corpus in lemmatized form1.

The following section presents the experimental protocol and the results obtained with our various approaches.

4. Experiments

---

[1] Using the TreeTagger

4.1. *Steps of the experimental protocol*

For our experiments, we compared the performances of the algorithm of k-NN by using different methods. This evaluation includes several stages:

- Deletion of the Html tags and the stop words (generic words often coming back in the text as "thus", "someone", etc.) from the corpus.
- Application of one of the presented methods.
- Application of crossed validation by segmenting the data in five groups.
- Calculation of the rate of error.

The rate of error, which measures the rate of badly classified articles, is defined as following:

$$[3]\ \text{Rate of error} = \frac{\text{Number of badly classified articles}}{\text{Total number of articles}}$$

4.2 Normalization of the corpus

The normalization of our corpus was obtained by calculating the Tf-Idf (Term Frequency x Inverse Document Frequency) which is a statistical measure used to evaluate the importance of a word in a corpus. The Term frequency measures the importance of the term Ti within the particular document Dj. The Inverse document frequency measures the general importance of the term. The measure of Tf-Idf is defined as follows:

$$[4]\ Wij = Tfij \,.\log2\,(N/n)$$

With:

- Wij = weight of the term Tj in the document Di,
- Tfij = frequency of the term Tj in the document Di,
- N = number of documents in the collection,
- n = number of documents where the term Tj appears at least once.

We used a value of 2 for the threshold of class and 0.2 for the threshold of similarity because these values were experimentally considered as the most suited to our works. Consequently, these measures imply that certain articles can be considered as not classified.

4.3 Results

First of all, we measured the contribution of normalization (Tf-Idf) and lemmatization on our corpus by using the approaches L (lemmatized form) and C (original corpus). The table 1 presents the rate of error obtained with the application of these approaches. It shows that the lemmatization of the corpus tends to degrade the results in terms of error rate. However, by applying Tf-Idf, this tendency is reversed with better results for the lemmatized from (method L), which obtained the lowest rate of error.

Table 2. Evaluation of the advantages of lemmatization and normalizing

Approach	Error rate
C	0,39
C and Tf-Idf	0,25
L	0,42
L and Tf-Idf	0,21

The table shows that the N-V method (nouns and verbs) gives good results by considering the application of Tf-Idf. However, it equals the method L. These experiments show that verbs and adjectives contain less useful information compared with nouns.

Table 3. Table of error rate obtained for different approaches

Approach	Error rate	
	without Tf-Idf	with Tf-Idf
L	0,42	0,21
N	0,33	0,27
V	0,58	0,47
A	0,51	0,44
N_V	0,27	0,21
N_A	0,36	0,27
V_A	0,34	0,29
N_V_A	0,36	0,27

According to the experiments that we made, we can conclude that certain grammatical combinations brought more information than others and can improve the process of blogs classification. We wanted to exploit this point by granting more importance for these words and affecting them a more important weight than for the others. This weighting consists in the multiplication of the Tf-Idf of the word, which has a certain category, by a factor of weight.

Table 4. Table estimating the influence of the weight of 2 on the Tf-Idf matrix of a lemmatized corpus

Noun	Verb	Adjective	Error rate
1	2	1	0.31
1	1	2	0.30
2	1	1	0.31
2	2	1	0.29
1	2	2	0.31
2	1	2	0.23

The tables 5 and 6 present the results obtained with two values of weight (2 and 3). For example Noun: 3, Verb: 3, and Adjective: 1 corresponds respectively to a multiplication by 3, 3 and 1, in the Tf-Idf matrix.

According to the rate of error, we can notice an improvement of the obtained results for all the grammatical combinations and with the weight of 3. These results confirm that the combination of nouns and verbs realizes a finer classification with a very weak rate of error (0.06).

These results show that it is important to take into account all grammatical information (nouns, verbs, but also adjectives) giving different weights to the types of words to improve the classification tasks.

Table 5. Table estimating the influence of the weight of 3 on the Tf-Idf matrix of a lemmatized corpus

Noun	Verb	Adjective	Error rate
1	3	1	0.10
1	1	3	0.29
3	1	1	0.11
3	3	1	0.06
1	3	3	0.10
3	1	3	0.09

5. Conclusion

In this article, we presented an automatic categorization of blogs articles of the PaperBlog Company. We have used the algorithm of k Nearest Neighbors than we have compared with different approaches using Part-Of-Speech information. These experiments showed the advantages within the application of normalization. Then an important weight was assigned to the words which have a specific Part-Of-Speech tag (in our experiments, Nouns and Verbs). This improves the results of the categorization task.

In our future work, we will apply a machine learning approach to calculate the optimal weight to assign to the types of words. Moreover, we will experiment our approach with other categorization algorithms.

Acknowledgement

We are grateful to the PaperBlog Company (http://www.paperblog.fr/) for providing access to the Blog data, and to Nicolas Verdier and Maxime Biais in particular for their participation in this work.

References

Bergo, A. (2001). Text categorization and prototypes. Technical report.

Borko, H. et M. Bernick (1963). Automatic document classification. J. ACM 10(2), 151–162.

Burges, C. J. C. (1998). A tutorial on support vector machines for pattern recognition. Data Mining and Knowledge Discovery 2(2), 121–167.

Chen, C., F. Ibekwe-SanJuan, E. SanJuan, et C. Weaver (2006). Visual analysis of conflicting opinions. vast 0, 59–66.

Cormack, R. M. (1971). “A review of classification” (with discussion). the Royal Statistical Society 3, 321–367.

Cornuéjols, A. et L. Miclet (2002). “Apprentissage artificiel, Concepts et algorithme”s. Eyrolles.

Cover, T. et P. Hart (1967). Nearest neighbor pattern classification. Information Theory, IEEE Transactions on 13(1), 21–27.

Joachims, T. (1998). “Text categorization with support vector machines: learning with many relevant features”. In Proc. 10th European Conference on Machine Learning ECML-98, pp. 137–142.

Johnson, S. C. (1967). “Hierarchical clustering schemes”. Psychometrika 32, 241–254.

Lewis, D. D., Y. Yang, T. G. Rose, et F. Li (2004). “Rcv1 : A new benchmark collection for text categorization research”. Journal of Machine Learning Research 5(Apr), 361–397.

Mcculloch, W. et W. Pitts (1943). “A logical calculus of the ideas immanent in nervous activity”. Bulletin of Mathematical Biophysics 5, 115–133.

Moulinier, I., G. Raskinis, et J. Ganascia (1996). “Text categorization : a symbolic approach”. In In Proceedings of the Fifth Annual Symposium on Document Analysis and Information Retrieval, pp. 87–99.

Quinlan, J. R. (1986). Induction of decision trees. Mach. Learn. 1(1), 81–106.

Quinlan, J. R. (1993). C4.5 : programs for machine learning. San Francisco, CA, USA : Morgan Kaufmann Publishers Inc.

Schmid, H. (1995). “Improvements in part-of-speech tagging with an application to german”. In Proceedings of the ACL SIGDAT-Workshop, Dublin.

Vapnik, V. (1995). The Nature of Statistical Learning Theory. Springer, N.Y.

Weiss, S. M., N. Indurkhya, T. Zhang, et F. Damerau (2005). Text Mining : Predictive Methods for Analyzing Unstructured Information. Springer.

Yang, Y. (1999). An Evaluation of Statistical Approaches to Text Categorization. Information Retrieval 1(1-2), 69–90.

Yang, Y. et X. Liu (1999). “A re-examination of text categorization methods”. In SIGIR ’99: Proceedings of the 22nd annual international ACM SIGIR conference on Research and development in information retrieval, New York, NY, USA, pp. 42–49. ACM Press.

A Modified Clustering Method with Fuzzy Ants

Jianbin Chen, Deying Fang and Yun Xue

Business College, Beijing Union University, Beijing, 100025

Abstract: Ant-based clustering due to its flexibility, stigmergic and self-organization has been applied in variety areas from problems arising in commerce, to circuit design, and to text-mining, etc. A modified clustering method with fuzzy ants has been presented in this paper. Firstly, fuzzy ants and its behavior are defined; secondly, the new clustering algorithm has been constructed based on fuzzy ants. In this algorithm, we consider multiple ants based on Schockaert's algorithm. This algorithm can be accelerated by the use of parallel ants, global memory banks and density-based 'look ahead' method. Experimental results show that this algorithm is more efficient to other ant clustering methods.

Keywords: Data mining, Fuzzy ants, clustering, algorithm

1.Introduction

Clustering has been widely studied since the early 60's. Some classic approaches include hierarchical algorithms, partitioning method such as K-means, Fuzzy C-means, graph theoretic clustering, neural networks clustering, and statistical mechanics based techniques. Recently, several papers have highlighted the efficiency of stochastic approaches based on ant colonies for data clustering [1,2,3,4].

While the behavior of individual ants is very primitive, the resulting behavior on the colony-level can be quite complex. A particularly interesting example is the clustering of dead nestmates, as observed with several ant species under laboratory conditions. By exhibiting only simple basic actions and without negotiating about where to gather the corpses, ants manage to cluster all corpses into 1or 2 piles. The conceptual simplicity of this phenomenon, together with the lack of centralized control and a priori information, are the main motivations for designing a clustering algorithm inspired by this behaviorLorem; sed ipsum?

Please use the following format when citing this chapter:

Chen, J., Fang, D. and Xue, Y., 2008, in IFIP International Federation for Information Processing, Volume 288; *Intelligent Information Processing IV*; Zhongzhi Shi, E. Mercier-Laurent, D. Leake; (Boston: Springer), pp. 78–85.

2.Related Work

Ant-based clustering and sorting was originally introduced for tasks in robotics by Deneubourg [3]. This paper has proposed a basic model that explains the spatial structure of cemetery forms as a result of simple, local interactions without any centralized control or global representation of the environment. Holland et al. applied related model to robotics to accomplish complex tasks by several simple robots [5]. Lumer and Faieta modified the algorithm to extend to numerical data analysis by introducing a measure of dissimilarity between data objects [3].Kuntz et al. applied it to graph-partitioning[6], text-mining[7] and VLSI circuit design[8].Wu and shi applied Deneubourg's model in clustering to derive (Clustering based on Swarm Intelligence) CSI model and some important concepts, such as swarm similarity, swarm similarity coefficient and probability conversion function.

Monmarché[1] proposed an algorithm in which several items are allowed to be on the same cell. Each cell with a nonzero number of items corresponds to a cluster. Each ant *a* is endowed with a certain capacity *c(a)* . Instead of carrying one item at a time, an ant *a* can carry a heap of *c(a)* items. Probabilities for picking up, at most *c(a)* items from a heap and for dropping the load on a heap are based on characteristics of the heap, such as the average dissimilarity between items of the heap. When an ant decides go pick up items, the *c(a)* items whose dissimilarity to the centre of the heap under consideration is highest, are chosen. Two particularly interesting values for the capacity of an ant *a* are $c(a)=1$ and $c(a)=\infty$. Monmarché proposes to apply this algorithm twice. The first time, the capacity of all ants is 1, which results in a high number of tight clusters. Subsequently the algorithm is repeated with the clusters of the first pass as atomic objects and ants with infinite capacity. After each pass k-means clustering is applied for handling small classification errors. Inspired by Monmarché's paper, Schockaert *et al.* proposed a clustering method with only one fuzzy ant since the use of multiple ants on a non-parallel implementation has no advantage[9].

3.Fuzzy Ants

In papers[9,10,11,12,13], fuzzy ants have been discussed more than ones. Our algorithm is based on Schockaert's method. Because of the limited space we do not go into detail about the algorithm based on fuzzy ants. We only give same basic concept and focus on the optimization.

First we introduce some notations, and then give some definition.

Let E be a fuzzy relation in X, *i.e.* a fuzzy set in X^2, which is reflexive and T_W-transitive(*i.e.* $T_W(E(x,y),E(y,z)\leq E(x,z))$, for all x,y and z in X) where X in the set of items to be clustered and T_W the Lukasiewicz triangular norm defined by

$T_W(x,y)=max(0,x+y-1)$, for all x and y in [0,1]. For x and y in X, $E(x,y)$ denotes the degree of similarity between the items x and y. For a heap $H \not\subset X$ with centre c in X, we define $avg(H)=\frac{1}{|H|}\sum_{h\in H}E(h,c)$ and $min(H)=min_{h\in H}E(h,c)$. Let $E^*(H_1,H_2)$be the similarity between the centres of the heap H_1 and the heap H_2. Because of the limited space we do not go into the detail about how to define and /or compute the centre of a heap, as this can be dependent on the kind of the data that needs to be clustered.

Definition1 A heap is defined as a collection of 2 or more data items. A heap is spatially located in a single cell and has unique ID in this algorithm.

Definition2 The probability that an ant starts performing a task with stimulus s and response threshold value θ is given by

$$T_n(s;\theta)=\frac{s^n}{s^n+\theta^n} \tag{1}$$

Where n is a positive integer.

Definition 3 The probability of dropping the load is given by

$$P_{drop}=T_{n_i}(s_{drop};\theta_{drop}) \tag{2}$$

Where $i\in\{1,2\}$ and n_1,n_2 positive integers.

Dfinition4 The probabilities for picking up one item and picking up all the items are given by

$$P_{pickup\_one}=\frac{s_{one}}{s_{one}+s_{all}}\cdot T_{m1}(s_{one};\theta_{one}) \tag{3}$$

$$P_{pickup\_all}=\frac{s_{all}}{s_{one}+s_{all}}\cdot T_{m2}(s_{all};\theta_{all}) \tag{4}$$

Where m_1 and m_2 are positive integers, s_{one} and s_{all} are the respective stimuli , θ_{one} andθ_{all} the response threshold values.

The values of the stimuli are calculated by evaluating fuzzy if-then rules as explained in paper[9]. Compared with those algorithms such as FCM, this algorithm has several advantages. Firstly, it is the first time for the fuzzy rules to be used in clustering algorithm. Secondly, it is not sensitive with the initial value of cluster center. Thirdly, it is robust and efficiently. But it is not so perfect and can be optimized on several points.

4.ALGORITHM OPTIMIZATION

Contrasting with those traditional clustering methods, ant-clustering boasts a number of advantages due to the use of mobile agents, which are autonomous entities, both proactive and reactive, and have the capability to adapt, cooperate and move intelligently from one location to the other in the bi-dimensional grid space. Generally said that an ant-based algorithm should be autonomy, flexibility and parallelism. But with the fuzzy ants clustering algorithm discussed in paper[9], there are several drawbacks. Firstly, used only one ant, this method has loosen the parallel characteristic of ants colony. Second, it is too complex to calculate the similarity based on rough set theory. Thirdly, there may be some data objects which have never been assigned to an ant when the algorithm is terminate. Fuzzy ants clustering method needs to be improved in these aspects.

4.1parallelize algorithm

Ant based clustering have some advantages, such as

Autonomy: Not any prior knowledge (like initial partition or number of classes) about the future classification of the data set is required. Clusters are formed naturally through ant's collective actions.

Flexibility: Rather than deterministic search, a stochastic one is used to avoid locally optimal.

Parallelism: Agent operations are inherently parallel.

But if we have only one ants in algorithm, it is not a real ant colony method. So, we preserve multi-ants to perform parallel clustering. There are *n/3* ants, where *n* is the number of data items.

4.2memory bank

The clustering process on the grid can be accelerated significantly by the use of a device of memory bank for the fuzzy ant, a modified version of the 'short-term memory' introduced by Lumer and Faieta[3].

No like Lumer and Faieta's approach that there are ant agents and data items respectively in the system, we have only ant agents. To bias the direction of the agent's random walk, we keep a global memory to store the ever-moved cells for each ant. In the algorithm iteration, the loaded ants can referentially search their memory banks for a best direction to move. The best cell *i*, defined by a pair of coordinate *(x,y)*, is a cell with heap *H* that the load *L* was most similar to.

The decision whether drop its load at cell *i* still be taken probabilistically with the threshold IF-THEN rules defined in paper[9]. Memory bank brings forth heuristic knowledge guiding ants' moving in the bi-dimensional grid space. So the randomness of ants' motion decreases, meanwhile the algorithm's convergence speeds up.

4.3density-based 'look ahead' method

Depending on the definition of items and heap/clusters similarity, we can decide whether a item belongs to a cluster or not. According the idea in DBSCAN that a cluster can be looked as a neighborhood of a given radius which contains at least a minimum number of points, i.e. the density in the neighborhood has to exceed a threshold [14]. So after a few iterations of clustering, the data objects in a high density cell can be approximately classified into the same cluster. Thus these itmes have no need to be visit frequently. The main job is to survey those items in less density cells and determine where to move. Then those items which belong to a cluster already will be resting for a long time, and has lower probability to be moved again. This method will not lead to high misclassification error rate.

Definition: A cell is '***dense-cell***' if the data item number, *Pts*, exceed a certain threshold, *MinPts*. Else if *Pts* less than *MinPts* but bigger than zero, we call this cell as '*sparse-cell*'. Else *Pts=0*, i.e. there is no any items in this cell, we call it "*empty-cell*".

MinPts can be defined as follows:

$$MinPts = k \times \frac{N_{item}}{N_{cell}} \tag{5}$$

Where k is an adjusting coefficient, $k>1$.

We propose here a **'look ahead'** strategy: Before an ant moved to cell, it firstly estimates the cell's density into three types. If the cell is a *dense-cell*, it will go to next position. If the cell is a *sparse-cell*, it will drop a item based on IF-THRN rules. If the cell is *empty-cell*, i.e. there is no data item at all, then the ant agent will moving directly.

5.ALGORITHM IMPLEMENTATION

In our algorithm, there are n data items, and n/3 ants. Initially the items are scattered randomly on a discrete 2D board, the board can be considered a matrix of m×m cells, and m2=4n. We maintained a cell list, each cell has five parameters.

$$U = \{X_1, X_2, \ldots\ldots, X_{m\times m}\}, \text{ and}$$

$$X_i = \{s, t, O, C, Pts\}, i = 1,2,\ldots, m\times m$$

Where s and t are the position parameter, O is a binary value to identify if an ant is visiting this cell, C is the center of heap in this cell, and Pts is number items in it.

There are also a cell list for each ant to save its visit history, which is a memory bank discussed above.

$MB_i = \{X_j| \}$, where $i=1,..., n/3$, and $j=1,......, m \times m$.

The algorithm is given as follows.

```
Initialize {Cell list, data items, ants, NumberOfIteration=0}
Parallel for each ant ()
While NumberOfIteration<NumberOfIteration_max
Get a random heap from cell list and check the Pts
Let O_i=1
If the current ant load a heap
    Check whether to unload the loaded item
    Unload and form a new heap
    Calculate the center C and Pts for this heap
    Update the memory bank of this ant
Let O_i=0
  Return
End if
Else if the current ant is unloaded
    Check whether to load the whole heap or the dissimilar item
  Load the whole heap or the dissimilar item
    If the dissimilar item is taken away
      Calculate the center C and Pts for this heap
Check the memory bank to decide next position
Return
    End if
End Else if
NumberOfIteration++
End While
Wait for ending of each task and merge heaps
Display the clustering result
```

Figure1:Tthe modified algorithm

6.EXPERIMENT RESULTS AND ANALYSIS

We have applied our new algorithm to several numerical databases including synthetic ones and real databases from the Machine Learning repository（Machine Learning Repository, http://www.ics.uci.edu/~mlearn/MLRepository .html）.

We have used 4 evaluation measures to evaluate the resulting partition obtained by the three clustering algorithms. They are the number of identified clusters(#Clusters)、Inner Cluster Variance(Variance)， Classification Error Rate

(Cl.Err) [2] and the overall running time of the algorithm(Runtime). Table 1 gives the parts of experiment results.

Table 1: Results for k-means, CSI and AMC on three synthetic data sets: ant1 ~ant3, and two real data sets: Iris, Soybean.

ANT1	k-means	CSI	Ours
#Clusters	4	4	4
Variance	0.408532	0.331668	0.332412
Cl.Err	2.15%	3.02%	1.26%
Runtime	6.0	10.2	6.3
IRIS	k-means	CSI	Ours
#Clusters	3	3	3
Variance	0.531222	0.411138	0.412018
Cl.Err	5.28%	5.66%	3.37%
Runtime	10.4	13.4	9.8

The results demonstrate that, if clear cluster structures exist within the data, the ant clustering algorithm including: CSI and Ours, is quite reliable at identifying the correct number of clusters. In contrast with the *k*-means, Our algorithm shows its strength in its ability to automatically determine the number of clusters within the data.

Compare the runtimes of the three algorithms, we can see our algorithm is the fastest algorithms and its time consumer changes little with the scale of data set. So it is a fast clustering algorithm with prefect scalability.

7.CONCLUSION

In this paper, we have proposed a modified clustering algorithm with fuzzy ants. With the use of IF-THEN rules, it can be simplify the calculating in clustering. Based on the single fuzzy ant algorithm, we extended it to parallel ants, added a memory bank for each ant, and proposed a density-based method permits each ant to "look ahead", which reduces the times of cell-inquiry. Consequently the clustering time gets saved. We made some experiments on real data sets and synthetic data sets. Compared with other classical clustering algorithm, our algorithm is a viable and effective clustering algorithm.

REFERENCE

[1] Nicolas Monmarché, Mohamed Slimane, Gilles Venturini. AntClass: discovery of clusters in numeric data by an hybridization of an ant colony with the Kmeans algorithm, Internal Rep-port No 213,E3i,January 1999

[2] Deneubourg J L , Goss S , Frank N , Sendova-hanks A ,Detrain C ,Chrerien L. The dynamics of collective sorting : robot-like ants and ant-like robots. In : Proceedings of the 1st International Conference on Simulation of Adaptive Behavior : From Animals to Animats , MIT Press/ Bradford Books , Cambridge , MA , 1991. 356~363

[3] E. Lumer and B. Faieta. Diversity and adaption in populations of clustering ants. In Proceedings of the Third International Conference on Simulation of Adaptive Behaviour: From Animals to Animats 3, pages . 501–508. MIT Press, Cambridge, MA, 1994.

[4]B.wu,Y.zheng,S.liu and Z.shi, SIM:A Document Clustering Algorithm Based on Swarm Intelligence. IEEE World Congress on Computational Intelligence,Hawaiian,PP.477-482.2002

[5] O.E.Holland and C.Melhuish. Stigmergy, self-organization, and sorting in collective robotics, Artificial Life,5,1999,pp.173-202

[6] P. Kuntz, D. Snyers, and P. Layzell. A stochastic heuristic for visualizing graph clusters in a bi-dimensional space prior to partitioning. Journal of Heuristics, 5(3):327–351, 1998.

[7] K. Hoe, W. Lai, and T. Tai. Homogenous ants for web document similarity modeling and categorization. In Proceedings of the Third International Workshop on Ant Algorithms (ANTS 2002), volume 2463 of LNCS, pages 256–261. Springer-Verlag, Berlin, Germany, 2002.

[8] P.Kuntz,P.Layzell,D.Snyers. A colony of ant-like agents for partitioning in VLSI technology, in: P.Husbans,I.Harvey(Eds.), Proceeding of the Fourth European Conference on Artificial Life, MIT Press, Cambridege,MA,1997,pp.417-424

[9] S. Schockaert, M. De Cock, C. Cornelis, E. E. Kerre. Efficient Clustering with Fuzzy Ants [A]. Applied Computational Intelligence[C] (D. Ruan, P. D'hondt, M. De Cock, M. Nachtegael, E. E. Kerre, eds.), World Scientific,2004. P. 195-200.

[10] P. Kanade. Fuzzy ants as a clustering concept[D]. M.S dissertation. University of South Florida, Tampa, FL.2004.

[11] P. M. Kanade and L. O. hall. Fuzzy ants clustering with centroids[A]. FUZZ-IEEE'04[C], 2004.

[12] S. Schockaert, M. De Cock, C. Cornelis, E. E. Kerre. Fuzzy Ant Based Clustering[A]. Ant Colony Optimization and Swarm Intelligence, 4th International Workshop (ANTS 2004)[C], LNCS 3172. P. 342-349.

[13] Valeri Rozin, Michael Margaliot .The Fuzzy Ant[A]. IEEE International Conference on Fuzzy Systems Sheraton Vancouver Wall Centre Hotel, Vancouver, BC, Canada July 16-21[C], 2006. P.1679-1686

[14] M.Ester, H.-P.Kriegel, J.Sander and X.Xu. A density-based algorithm for discovering clusters in large spatial databases. In Proc.1996 Int.Conf. Knowledge Discovery and Data Mining (KDD'96), page 226-231, Portland, OR, Aug.1996

An New Algorithm for Modeling Regression Curve

JiSheng Hao, LeRong Ma and WenDong Wang

College of Computer Science, Yanan University, Shanxi Yanan, China 716000,Email:yadxhjs1963@163.com

Abstract: A new algorithm for modeling regression curve is put forward in the paper, it combines the B-spline network with improved support vector regression. Our experimental results on simulated data demonstrate that it is feasible and effective.

Keywords: Support vector machines; support vector regression; B-spline network; regression curve;

1 introduction

Support vector machines (SVM) is a new method of machine learning from statistical learning theory, which is a fresh tool of solving machine learning problem in virtue of optimization. It was first put forward by Vapnik in the 1990s [1]. In recent years, it have made breakthrough progress in its theoretical research, applied research and algorithm implementation that become a good way of overcoming traditional difficulty for dimension of the disaster and overfitting [2]. SVM uses structural risk minimization principle that has the promotion of good performance because it is considered the fitting and complexity for training samples. SVM can solve pattern classification and regression problems.

B-spline network is the lattice three-tier structure of associative memory networks [3][5], its structure is illustrated in Figure.1. B-spline function in latent layer is used as the basic function that is defined in input space of lattice. For a random input, a few B-spline functions in latent layer is activated and the network output is a linear combination of these active basic function. Since the support set of the basic function is limited, the network has the following features:

Please use the following format when citing this chapter:

Hao, J., Ma, L. and Wang, W., 2008, in IFIP International Federation for Information Processing, Volume 288; *Intelligent Information Processing IV*; Zhongzhi Shi, E. Mercier-Laurent, D. Leake; (Boston: Springer), pp. 86–91.

a) The knowledge in the network is locally stored without global distributed storing, and learning is local. Therefore the learning from a part in input space isn't influence the learning results in other part.

b) The learning algorithm converges fast, and the network is convenient for real time online applications.

c) The network has the good expressing capacity for fuzzy knowledge.

Thereby this kind network becomes more and more important, and widely used in control, modeling and pattern recognition, and other fields [5]

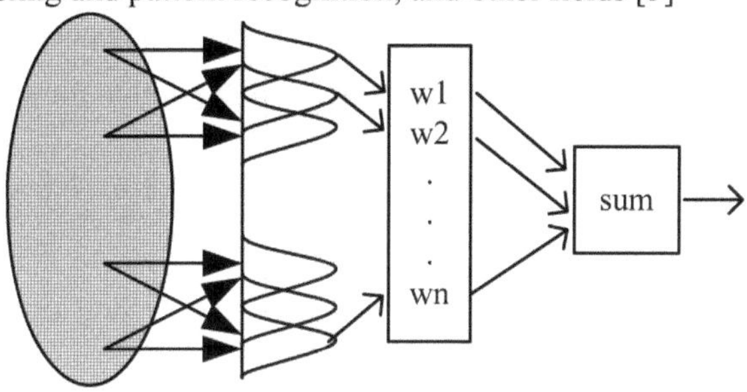

Fig.1. B-spline network structure

In the paper, a new algorithm for Modeling Regression Curve is put forward. Firstly, we obtain the support vectors from input sample set by an improved support vectors regression algorithm [2][4][6].Then, we train the B-spline network with these support vectors as training sample set. Thus, we can quickly create the model of regression curve with this method because the B-spline network is characterized by short training period, fast convergence. Moreover, the regression curve that is created is smoothing curve as the basis functions for B-spline network are continuous functions.

2 ε—Support Vectors Regression Algorithm

The basic problem of Regression is to find $f \in F$,where F is function set, such that

$$R(f) = \int l(y - f(\vec{x}))dP(\vec{x}, y)\text{ , } \vec{x} \in R^n, y \in R$$

minimizes, where $l(\bullet)$ is loss function that denotes the deviation between y and $f(\vec{x})$ which always is defined to be

$$l(\bullet) = |y - f(\vec{x})|^m$$

where m is a positive integer, and $P(\vec{x}, y)$ is a Probability distribution function. Since we don't prior know $P(\vec{x}, y)$, we can't calculate the $R(f)$ directly. According to structural risk minimization principle we have

$$R(f) \le R_{emp} + R_{gen}$$

where $R_{emp} = \frac{1}{l}\sum_{i=1}^{l} l(y_i - f(\vec{x}_i))$ is empirical risk, and R_{gen} is a measure of the complexity for $f(\vec{x})$.Hence, $R_{emp} + R_{gen}$ can be a upper bound of $R(f)$.

The core of ε—Support Vectors Regression Algorithm for solving the regression problem is the following:

Given a sample set $\{(\vec{x}_i, y_i) | (\vec{x}_i, y_i) \in R^n \times R, i = 1,2,\Lambda, l\}$ which probability distribution function is $P(\vec{x}, y)$, assumed that $F = \{f | f(\vec{x}) = \vec{\omega}^T \Phi(\vec{x}) + b, \vec{\omega}^T \in R^n\}$ is a regression fuction set.

Introduced structural risk function

$$R_{reg} = \frac{1}{2}\|\vec{\omega}\|^2 + C \bullet R_{emp}^{\varepsilon}[f] \qquad (1)$$

where $\|\vec{\omega}\|^2$ is the complexity of $f(\vec{x})$, and c is punishment coefficient, $R_{emp}^{\varepsilon}[f]$ is the empirical risk which role is a tradeoff between the model complexity and the empirical risk.

Introduced ε-insensitive loss function

$$|y - f(\vec{x})|_{\varepsilon} = \begin{cases} 0 & |y - f(\vec{x})| \le \varepsilon \\ |y - f(\vec{x})| - \varepsilon & other \end{cases} . \qquad (2)$$

Its meaning don't punish the item which deviation is less than ε,thus can increase the robustness of regression.

According to (2) we can define $R_{emp}^{\varepsilon}[f] = \frac{1}{l}\sum_{i=1}^{l} |y_i - f(\vec{x}_i)|_{\varepsilon}$。

In order to make the mean risk minimize we not only control training error but also control the model complexity, thus can improve the generalized ability of the model. Hence, (1)minimized is the core idea of statistic learning theory.

The above regression problem is equal to

$$\min \frac{1}{2}\vec{\omega}^T \vec{\omega} + C\sum_{i=1}^{l}(\zeta_i + \zeta_i^*) \qquad (3)$$

$$s.t. \quad y_i - \vec{\omega}^T \vec{x}_i - b \le \varepsilon + \zeta_i \quad ; \quad \vec{\omega}^T \vec{x}_i + b - y_i \le \varepsilon + \zeta_i^* \quad ;$$

$$\zeta_i, \zeta_i^* \ge 0, i = 1,2,\Lambda, l$$

Where ζ_i, ζ_i^* are introduced relaxation variables which intent are made(3)solution exist。

We can obtain the following dual problem by Lagrangian and dual theorem:

$$\min_{\alpha,\alpha^*}\{\frac{1}{2}[\vec{\alpha},(\vec{\alpha}^*)^T]\begin{bmatrix}\vec{Q} & -\vec{Q}\\ -\vec{Q} & \vec{Q}\end{bmatrix}\begin{bmatrix}\vec{\alpha}\\ \vec{\alpha}^*\end{bmatrix}+\left[\varepsilon\vec{I}^T+\vec{y}^T,\varepsilon\vec{I}^T-\vec{y}^T\right]\begin{bmatrix}\vec{\alpha}\\ \vec{\alpha}^*\end{bmatrix} \quad (4)$$

$$s.t.\ \left[\vec{I}^T,-\vec{I}^T\right]\begin{bmatrix}\vec{\alpha}\\ \vec{\alpha}^T\end{bmatrix}=0,\alpha_i,\alpha_i^*\in[0,C]$$

where $Q_{i,j}=\Phi^T(\vec{x}_i)\Phi(\vec{x}_j)$; $I=[1,1,\Lambda,1]^T$; $\vec{\alpha},\vec{\alpha}^*$ are Lagrange multiplier。

We can get the value of $\vec{\alpha}$ by solving this quadratic programming problem, and obtain

$$\vec{\omega}=\sum_{i=1}^{l}(\alpha_i-\alpha_i^*)\Phi(\vec{x}_i) \quad (5)$$

With KKT condition we can calculate b as the following

$$\begin{cases} b=y_j-\varepsilon-\sum_{i=1}^{l}(\alpha_i-\alpha_i^*)K(x_j,x_i);\alpha_i,\alpha_i^*\in[0,C] \\ b=y_j+\varepsilon-\sum_{i=1}^{l}(\alpha_i-\alpha_i^*)K(x_j,x_i);\alpha_i,\alpha_i^*\in[0,C] \end{cases} \quad (6)$$

so we can obtain

$$f(\vec{x})=\sum_{i=1}^{l}(\alpha_i-\alpha_i^*)K(\vec{x},\vec{x}_i)+b \quad (7)$$

Where $K(\vec{x},\vec{x}_i)=\Phi^T(\vec{x})\Phi(\vec{x}_i)$ is the kernel function that satisfy Mercer's condition。Without knowing the Φ this function achieves the nonlinear transform between the input space and feature Space, it is an important feature for SVM.

The common kernel functions are the following:

Polynomial function: $K(\vec{x}_i,\vec{x}_j)=((\vec{x}_i\bullet\vec{x}_j)+c)^d$

Gaussian radial basis kernel function:

$K(\vec{x}_i,\vec{x}_j)=\exp(-\|\vec{x}_i-\vec{x}_j\|^2/\sigma^2)^d$

Sigmoid kernel function: $K(\vec{x}_i,\vec{x}_j)=\tanh(c_1(\vec{x}_i\bullet\vec{x}_j)+c_2)$

3 The improved support vectors regression machines

In [6] the author put forwards an improved support vectors regression machine, which modifies (3) the following:

$$\min(\frac{1}{2}\vec{\omega}^T\vec{\omega}+b^2)+C\sum_{i=1}^{l}(\zeta_i+\zeta_i^{*2}) \qquad (8)$$

$$s.t.\quad y_i-\vec{\omega}^T\vec{x}_i-b\le\varepsilon+\zeta_i\ ;\quad \vec{\omega}^T\vec{x}_i+b-y_i\le\varepsilon+\zeta_i^*\ ;$$

$$\zeta_i,\zeta_i^*\ge 0, i=1,2,\Lambda\ ,l$$

With the similar approach like the second section we can obtain the regression function for the improved support vectors regression machines

$$f(\vec{x})=\sum_{i=1}^{l}(\alpha_i-\alpha_i^*)(K(\vec{x},\vec{x}_i)+1) \qquad (9)$$

Obviously, this improved support vectors regression machines simplify the constraints of optimization, which have no equality constraints and the constraints of rectangular and there only have nonnegative constraints [6]. In addition, it has a more concise dual expression than standard SVM because there is no parameter b in (9).

4 The Algorithm of Regression Curve based the improved support vectors regression machines and B-spline netowork

Given a training sample set $\{(\vec{x}_i,y_i)|(\vec{x}_i,y_i)\in R^n\times R, i=1,2,\Lambda\ ,l\ \}$, and assumed that the sample points are independence with the same probability distribution $P(\vec{x},y)$ in $R^n\times R$, and also given ε-insensitive loss function (2),thus the regression problem is to find a $f(\vec{x})$ such that

$$R(f)=\int l(y-f(\vec{x}))dP(\vec{x},y)$$

minimizes. The Algorithm of Regression Curve based the improved support vectors regression machines and the B-spline network is the following:

By selecting the proper kernel function and C 、ε in (1) we can obtain the support vectors for input sample points with the support vectors regression algorithm in the third section.

We train the B-spline network with the get support vectors.

Since the basis functions for the B-spline network are continuous functions and this network can approximate a random functional with arbitrary precision,we can create the model of smoothing regeression curve.

Let the training set $T=\{(x_i,y_i)|i=1,2,\Lambda\ ,65\}$ from $y=f(x)=\sin x$ that has the noise. Namely, $x_1,x_2,\Lambda\ ,x_{65}$ are the points that are *subject to* uniform distribution in [-3.2, 3.2],and $y_i=\sin x_i+\xi_i\ i=1,2,\Lambda\ ,65$, where the noise ξ_i is subject to normal distribution,and $E\xi_i = 0, E\xi_i^2 = \sigma^2, \sigma = 0.5$. With the algorithm that we put forward in the paper we finally create the model of regression curve as the Figure 2.

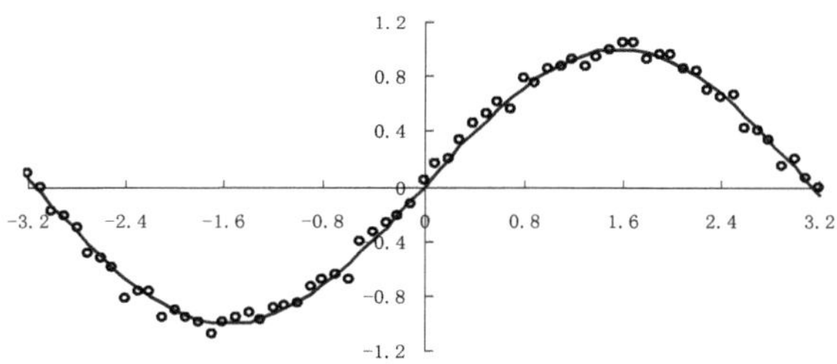

Fig. 2 The regression curve model

6 Conclusion

The Algorithm of Regression Curve based the improved support vectors regression machines and B-spline netowork is put forward in this paper. With this algorithm we can create the model of smoothing regression curve. The algorithm is very feasible and effective that can be showed the above simulation.

References

[1] Vapnik V. Statistical learning theory[M]. New York: John Wiley& Sons, 1998.
[2] Deng NaiYang,Tian YingJie.A New Method in Data Mining—Support Vector Machine [M]. Science Press,2004.6,224-273.
[3] Moody J. Fastlearning in multi-resolution hierarchies[J]. Advances in Neural information Processing System, vol.1, 1989:29-39.
[4] Scholkopf B, Smola A J. Learning with Kernels Support Vector Machines, Regularization, Optimization, and Beyond[M].The MIT Press,2002.
[5] Martin Brown, Chris Harris. Neurofuzzy adaptive modeling and control [M]. Prentice Hall International (UK) Limited, 1994: 89-100 .
[6] Zhang HaoRan, Learing Algorithm for a New Regression SVM[J] .Journal of Test and Measurement Technology, Vol.20 No.2 2006

Enhancing Web Search with Heterogeneous Semantic Knowledge

Rui Huang [1,2] and Zhongzhi Shi [1]

[1]Key Laboratory of Intelligent Information Processing

Institute of Computing Technology, Chinese Academy of Sciences

Beijing100190, China

[2]Graduate University of the Chinese Academy of Sciences

Beijing100049, China

huangr@ics.ict.ac.cn, shizz@ics.ict.ac.cn

Abstract: This paper explores four kinds of semantic knowledge to improve keyword-based Web search, including thesauruses, categories, ontologies, and social annotations. These heterogeneous semantic knowledge represent meanings of Web information, thus they can be used to improve search results in respect of semantic relevance. Currently, different semantic search paradigms have been developed for different kind of semantic knowledge respectively. However, how to make the most of all heterogeneous semantic knowledge to optimize Web search is still a big challenge in practice. To these ends, this paper proposes an integrated semantic search mechanism to incorporate textual information and keyword search with heterogeneous semantic knowledge and semantic search. Experiments show that the proposed mechanism effectively integrates heterogeneous semantic knowledge to improve Web search.
Keywords: Web search, semantic search, semantic Web, Web 2.0, ontology, social annotation

1. INTRODUCTION

Nowadays, search engines have been heavily relied on to retrieve information on the Web. Relevance ranking is vital to Web search paradigms, according to which potentially related Web documents with respect to the user's query are retrieved and ordered. As keyword-based Web search does not guarantee relevance in meanings, semantic search has recently attracted enormous and growing research focuses [1-5].

Please use the following format when citing this chapter:

Huang, R. and Shi, Z., 2008, in IFIP International Federation for Information Processing, Volume 288; *Intelligent Information Processing IV*; Zhongzhi Shi, E. Mercier-Laurent, D. Leake; (Boston: Springer), pp. 92–101.

Heterogeneous semantic models have been introduced to represent the knowledge of interpreting the semantics of Web information and adopted for semantic search. Latent semantic models are induced from statistics of terms in documents, and used for semantic similarity computing [6]. Thesauruses (e.g. WordNet[1]) provide explanations of words and phrases as well as their synonyms and antonyms, which can be used for query expansion [7], similarity computing [8], etc. Categories (e.g. ODP[2]) include manually created classifications of Web documents according to their contents, with which to support category search. Ontologies [9] are manually formalized with commonly recognized knowledge in a certain domain, which can be used to understand data (semantic markups) on the Semantic Web [10]. They well support logical inference of semantic relations to obtain more exact semantic search results [11, 12], and can be combined to improve keyword-based search [2-4, 13]. Recent Web 2.0 [14] introduces social semantic annotations (e.g. social bookmarks on Del.icio.us[3]) assigned by common users to Web documents, which can be used to optimize search [15, 16, 5].

As all kinds of these semantic knowledge can help to interpret the meanings of Web information, to incorporate more of them would logically improve keyword search in respect of semantic relevance. However, to the best of our knowledge, no current search paradigm achieves such expected integration of heterogeneous semantic knowledge.

This paper proposes an integrated search mechanism to explore four kinds of semantic knowledge for keyword-based Web search, including thesauruses, categories, ontologies (and semantic markups), and social annotations. A statistical based measurement of semantic relevance, defined as semantic probabilities, is introduced to integrate heterogeneous semantic knowledge. It is calculated with all textual information and heterogeneous semantic knowledge, and stored in a newly proposed index structure called semantic-keyword dual index. Based on this uniform measurement, the search mechanism is developed to incorporate heterogeneous semantic knowledge for crawling, meta search and query expansion. Experiments show that the proposed mechanism can effectively integrate heterogeneous semantic knowledge to enhance Web Search in terms of semantic relevance.

Our work is among to first to improve Web search with heterogeneous semantic knowledge of all four mainstream semantic models. Two kinds of most related works are ontology and semantic markup based semantic search [2-4] and social annotation based search [15, 16, 5].

Mayfield et al. [2] propose to tightly integrate semantic inference and text retrieval, which is followed by works as [3] and [4] besides ours. [2] accepts keyword and semantic web queries separately, integrating only in retrieved results and through feedback mechanisms. Zhang et al. [3] use fuzzy description logic (DL) to integrate inference and retrieval, and thus accepts mainly formal DL queries. Tran

---

[1] http://wordnet.princeton.edu/

[2] http://dmoz.org/

[3] http://del.icio.us

et al. [4] present an ontology based approach to translate keyword queries to semantic web queries. Wu et al. [15] enlighten our statistical semantic relationship measurement, yet their work mainly focuses on social relationships of users. Dmitriev et al. [16] explore semantic relationships for enterprise search in which annotations are used as feedbacks. Bao et al. [5] improve Web search with social annotations and social page ranks. Our approach is designed for the open Web with different kinds of semantic knowledge. Statistical computing is adopted to integrate heterogeneous semantic knowledge throughout the whole process of crawling, indexing, query expansion and relevance ranking for Web search.

Rest of the paper is organized as follows. Section 2 describes the proposed semantic search mechanism, including overall framework, integration approach and search paradigm. Section 3 presents the experimental data and results and Section 4 concludes the paper.

2. SEMANTIC SEARCH MECHANISM

2.1 Overview

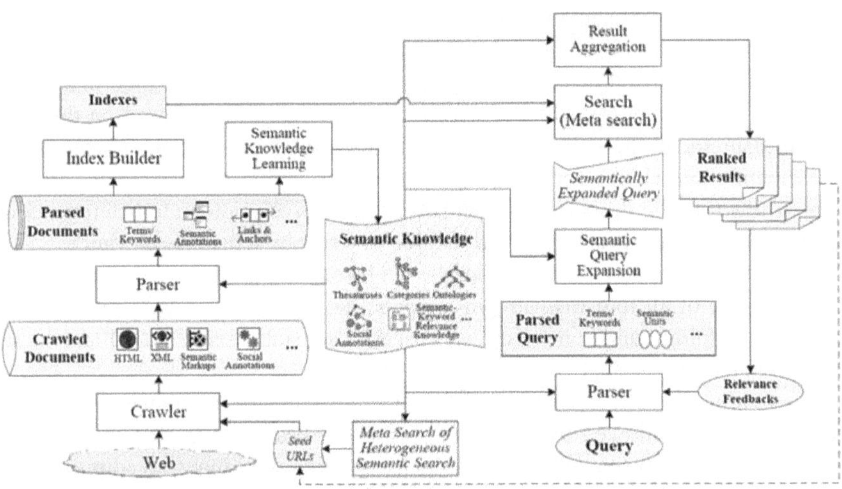

Fig. 1. Integrated Heterogeneous Semantic Search Framework

Fig. 1 illustrates the integrated heterogeneous semantic search framework. The knowledge base contains thesauruses, categories, ontologies, social annotations, and the automatically calculated semantic-keyword dual index (Section 2.2.3).

Based on semantic knowledge, related documents are crawled from the Web and parsed for the document corpus. The crawler and the parser can also use such domain knowledge for topical crawling (Section 2.3.1). The parsed document base includes not only keywords and links, but also semantic annotations (e.g. semantic markups, social annotations). When a new query is issued or relevance feedbacks are given, they are parsed and expanded with both keywords and heterogeneous semantic knowledge in the knowledge base (Section 2.3.2). Search (or meta-search) results are ranked and aggregated based on the semantic knowledge base and presented for the user (Section 2.3.3 & 2.3.4). For those URLs which are relevant to the query, yet not included in the crawling list, crawl them to update the document corpus, semantic knowledge base and index base.

2.2 Integration of heterogeneous semantic knowledge

2.2.1 Definition: semantic probabilities

Heterogeneous semantic knowledge are integrated with a uniform measure of semantic probabilities. Since not all semantic models involved are easily formalized (e.g. social annotations), we propose to adopt statistical computing in completion, and recast the definitions of traditional probabilities to represent both keyword based textual information and heterogeneous semantic knowledge.

Each keyword based textual (Web) document and its corresponding semantic knowledge is represented with a semantic annotation $sa = [T, S]$, where T is the list of all keyword based terms in the document, and S is the list of all semantic unit in the semantic knowledge. Here, semantic unit defines the minimum unit that represents certain complete and clear semantics, such as a phrase in the thesaurus, a category name, a concept in the ontology, or a social annotation.

In a semantic annotation $sa = [T, S]$, $\forall t_i \in T$ is called semantically occur in sa, represented as $t_i \vdash^T_{sa}$. $\forall s_j \in S$ is called semantically occur in sa, represented as $s_j \vdash^S_{sa}$. If $t_i \vdash^T_{sa} \wedge s_j \vdash^S_{sa}$, then t_i and s_j are called semantically cooccur in sa, represented as $< t_i, s_j > \vdash_{sa}$.

All Web documents and semantic information construct the semantic annotation space $SA = (sa_1, ..., sa_n)$, in which semantic occurrence probability, semantic cooccurrence probability and semantic conditional probability are defined.

Definition 1 (Semantic Occurrence Probability)

$\forall(t_i \vdash^T_{sa}) \wedge (sa \in SA)$, $P(t_i) \in [0,1]$ denotes the semantic occurrence probability that term t_i semantically occurs in SA. $\forall(s_j \vdash_{sa}^{S}) \wedge (sa \in SA)$, $P(s_j) \in [0,1]$ denotes the semantic occurrence probability that semantic unit s_j semantically occurs in SA.

Definition 2 (Semantic Cooccurrence Probability)
$\forall(<t_i, s_j> \vdash_{sa}) \wedge (sa \in SA)$, $P(<t_i, s_j>) \in [0,1]$ denotes the probability that term t_i semantically cooccurs with semantic unit s_j in SA.

Definition 3 (Semantic Conditional Probability)
$P(t_i / s_j) = P(<t_i, s_j>) / P(s_j) \in [0,1]$ denotes the semantic conditional probability of term t_i given semantic unit s_j, $P(s_j / t_i) = P(<t_i, s_j>) / P(t_i) \in [0,1]$ denotes the semantic conditional probability of semantic unit s_j given term t_i.

2.2.2 Computation model

In order to compute the above defined semantic probabilities, traditional TF-IDF computation model is extended to cover both terms and semantic units, represented with formulae (1)-(4).

$$P(t_i) = \left(\sum_{sa=[T,S]\in SA, t_i \vdash_{sa}^{T}} \left(\ln \frac{\|SA\| - df(t_i) + 0.5}{df(t_i) + 0.5} * \frac{1 + \ln(1 + \ln tf(t_i, T))}{(1-\gamma) + \gamma \frac{\|T\|}{avTl}}\right)\right) / \|SA\| \quad (1)$$

$$P(s_j) = \left(\sum_{sa=[T,S]\in SA, s_j \vdash_{sa}^{S}} \left(\ln \frac{\|SA\| - df(s_j) + 0.5}{df(s_j) + 0.5} * \frac{1 + \ln(1 + \ln tf(s_j, S))}{(1-\delta) + \delta \frac{\|S\|}{avSl}}\right)\right) / \|SA\| \quad (2)$$

$$P(<t_i, s_j>) = \left(\sum_{sa=[T,S]\in SA, t_i \vdash_{sa}^{T} \wedge s_j \vdash_{sa}^{S}} \left(\ln \frac{\|SA\| - df(t_i) + 0.5}{df(t_i) + 0.5} * \ln \frac{\|SA\| - df(s_j) + 0.5}{df(s_j) + 0.5} * \frac{1 + \ln(1 + \ln tf(t_i, T))}{(1-\gamma) + \gamma \frac{\|T\|}{avTl}} * \frac{1 + \ln(1 + \ln tf(s_j, S))}{(1-\delta) + \delta \frac{\|S\|}{avSl}}\right)\right) / \|SA\| \quad (3)$$

$$P(t_i / s_j) = P(<t_i, s_j>) / P(s_j), \quad P(s_j / t_i) = P(<t_i, s_j>) / P(t_i) \quad (4)$$

where $df(t_i)$ is the document frequency of term t_i in the semantic space SA, $tf(t_i, T)$ is the term frequency of t_i in a semantic annotation $sa = [T, S]$, $df(s_j)$ is the document frequency of semantic unit s_j in SA, $tf(s_j, S)$ is the term frequency of s_j in sa. $avTl$ is the average length of the list of terms, $avSl$ is the average length of the list of semantic units, γ and δ are used to balance the length.

The semantic occurrence probability of each term (or semantic unit) is calculated as the arithmetic average of the TF-IDF of the term (or semantic unit) in each semantic annotation in the semantic space. The semantic cooccurrence probability of a term and a semantic unit is calculated as the arithmetic average of the product of TF-IDF of the term and that of the semantic unit in each semantic annotation in the semantic space. The semantic conditional probability is calculated with semantic occurrence and cooccurrence probability according to its definition.

2.2.3 Storage: semantic-keyword dual index

To effectively retrieve the semantic relevance between all terms and semantic units, semantic-keyword dual index structure is proposed which consist of a pair of interrelated indexes: a term-semantic inverted index and a semantic-term inverted index (shown in Fig. 2).

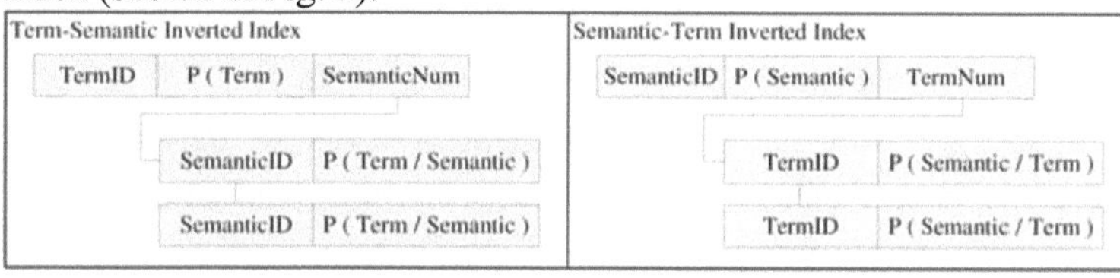

Fig. 2. Semantic-keyword dual index structure

Term-semantic inverted index is ordered by *TermID* unique to each term. $P(Term)$ is the semantic occurrence probabilities of Term. *SemanticNum* stores the length of SemanticID links, indicating the total number of related semantic units. $P(Term\,/\,Semantic)$ is the semantic conditional probability of the term *Term* given the semantic unit *Semantic*. Similar structure holds for semantic-term inverted index. The two interrelated inverted indexes compose the semantic-keyword dual index of statistical semantic relevance knowledge.

2.3 Search with heterogeneous semantic knowledge

2.3.1 Semantic knowledge based crawling

At the beginning of crawling, domain specific semantic knowledge are specified, which are used for meta-search to find seed URLs for both textual documents and semantic information.

A piece of crawled Web document (e.g. an XML document or an HTML webpage) along with its related semantic information (e.g. ontology based semantic markups or semantic annotations) is represented as a semantic annotation $sa_{crawled} = [T_{crawled}, S_{crawled}]$. The specified domain is represented as the whole semantic space SA. Then the semantic relevance of the crawled semantic annotation with the specified domain is represented as $SR(sa_{crawled}/SA)$.

$$SR(sa_{crawled}/SA = (sa_1,..., sa_p)) = \left(\sum_{i=1}^{\|SA\|} SR(sa_{crawled}/sa_i)^2 \Big/ \|SA\| - 1 \right)^{\frac{1}{2}} \tag{5}$$

where $SR(sa_{crawled}/sa_i) =$

$$\frac{\sum_{tcj \in Tsa_{crawled}} \sum_{tj \in Tsa_i} \sum_{sck \in Ssa_{crawled}} \sum_{sk \in Ssa_i} Max(P(t_{cj}/t_j), P(s_{ck}/t_j), P(t_{cj}/s_k), P(s_{ck}/s_k))}{\|Tsa_{new}\| \cdot \|Tsa_i\| \cdot \|Ssa_{crawled}\| \cdot \|Ssa_i\|} \quad (6)$$

As formulae (5)-(6) shows, the similarity of the crawled $sa_{crawled}$ with the specified domain (semantic annotation space SA) is the geometric average of the similarities of $sa_{crawled}$ with each semantic annotation sa_i in SA. The semantic similarity of $sa_{crawled}$ with sa_i is the arithmetic average of the max conditional probability of all terms and semantic units in $sa_{crawled}$ given all terms and semantic unites in sa_i. If the $SR(sa_{new}/SA)$ falls above a minimum relevance threshold, then the document and semantic information is considered relevant to the specified domain, and will be parsed and indexed.

2.3.2 Semantic query expansion

To semantically expand the queries based on statistical semantic similarities among both keywords ant semantic units, three steps of semantic computing, semantic inference and query expansion are involved.

In semantic computing, the semantic-keyword dual index is iteratively searched to find all possible keywords and semantic units of the user specified query (either in the form of traditional keyword query, semantic web query or combination of both). This process of iterative search adopts theories of spread activation [17]. It starts with the original query. For each keyword and semantic unit or, newly found keyword and semantic unit, find its related keywords and semantic units along with their relevance. Termination control is achieved with a decay factor (weighted less after each iteration) and a minimum threshold (terminate when semantic probability is below the threshold). Semantic inference uses ontologies in the semantic knowledge base to infer more semantically related semantic units. Weight of the inferred semantic unit is calculated as the product of the weight of inference and the weight of original semantic unit. Query expansion includes all computed and inferred keywords and semantic unites to expand the original query.

2.3.3 Semantic relevance ranking

Let T be the set of all terms and S be the set of all semantic units. A document and semantic information is represented as $D = [d_T \quad d_S]^T$, where d_T is the term frequency of all terms in D, and d_S is the term frequency of all semantic units in D. The expanded query is represented as $Q' = [q_T \quad q_S]^T$, where q_T is the calculated weight of all terms, and q_S is the calculated weight of all semantic units.

Similarity of D w.r.t. Q' in T and S is represented as $Sim(Q'/D)\big|_{T\cup S}$, which can be calculated as the arithmetic average of the semantic conditional probabilities of each keyword or semantic unit in Q' given each keyword or semantic unit in D (shown in formula (7)).

$$Sim(Q'/D)\big|_{T\cup S} = \sum_{i=1}^{\|T\cup S\|}\sum_{j=1}^{\|T\cup S\|} P(q_i/d_j) \Big/ \|T\cup S\|\cdot\|T\cup S\| \tag{7}$$

2.3.4 Meta search of heterogeneous search engines

The proposed semantic search mechanism also supports meta-search of current heterogeneous search engines. If a domain is specified for the search engine (so called topical search or vertical search engine), then meta-search can be employed to obtain better related seed URLs.

Top search results of each search engine are included (top 500 in this paper). To integrate meta-search results, joint relevance scores are computed according to formula (7). Rank based merge does not fit for heterogeneous semantic search that adopt quite different ranking criteria respectively. The joint relevance ranking take into consideration possible semantic relevance among all keywords and semantic units, even if different result documents are found in different search engines.

3. RESULTS AND DISCUSSIONS

3.1 Datasets

The WordNet thesaurus[4] is used both for stemming and as prior knowledge. ODP data of 730,416 categories obtained May, 2007[5] are included. Three domains of computer, sports and entertainment are experimented. For semantic web data, we use the 10,429,951 RDF triples extracted from Swoogle cache June, 2005[6] and 347 ontologies crawled from the Web. We also crawled a sample of Del.icio.us data during May, 2007, consisting of 459,143 social annotations covering 28,704 different links, 184,136 different users and 54,460 different tags.

4. http://wordnet.princeton.edu/obtain
5. http://rdf.dmoz.org/rdf/
6. http://ebiquity.umbc.edu/resource/html/id/126/10M-RDF-triples

3.2 Preliminary Results

With heterogeneous semantic knowledge, queries are expanded with both keywords and semantic units. For the query "semantic web", the top 10 related keywords are web, semantic, rdf, ontology, xml, w3c, research, data, owl, and knowledge. The top 10 related semantic units are *semantic*, *rdf*, *web*, *reference*, *category:topic*, *ontology*, *owl*, *rdfs:comment*, *web2.0*, and *srwc:isworkedonby*.

For each domain of computer, sports and entertainment, we specify an ontology and a wordlist of related keywords. Then related documents are crawled, parsed and indexed. Breath first strategy is used by the crawler. Results in Table 1 show that the crawlers are effective in topical crawling.

Table 1. Semantic knowledge based crawling statistics

Topic	Visited URLs	Analyzed URLs	Related URLs	Harvest Rate
Computer	16,703	232,991	11,965	71.63%
Sports	19,996	399,110	14,208	71.05%
Entertainment	14,375	303,744	8,964	62.36%

To test the effectiveness of semantic relevance ranking, 3000 web pages are crawled and selected from the corresponding category in Yahoo for each topic to see whether our relevance ranking algorithm takes it as semantically relevant. Table 2 proves the correctness of our proposed algorithm.

Table 2. Semantic relevance ranking correctness

Topic	Related in Yahoo	Related in our algorithm	Correctness
Computer	3000	2,654	88.48%
Sports	3000	2,955	98.50%
Entertainment	3000	2,791	93.03%

4. CONCLUSIONS

This paper proposes to improve Web search with both keyword-based textual information and heterogeneous semantic knowledge. A uniform statistical semantic measure along with its computation model and storage structure is proposed to represent semantic relevance of all keywords and heterogeneous semantic models. Based on this uniform measure, the proposed mechanism well supports semantic knowledge based crawling, query expansion, relevance ranking and meta search. Experimental results prove the effectiveness of the proposed mechanism.

In the future, we will focus on evaluation and optimization of semantic crawling, relevance ranking and heterogeneous result aggregation algorithms. Moreover, we will improve the system for public use.

ACKNOWLEDGEMENTS

This work is supported by the 973 National Basic Research Programme (No.2007CB311004), the 863 National High-Tech Program (No.2006AA01Z128), and the National Natural Science Foundation of China (No.90604017, No.60435010, No.60775035).

REFERENCES

1. Guha R., Mccool, R., and Miller. E. "Semantic search", In Proceedings of WWW '03, pp.700-709, 2003.
2. Mayfield, J., and Finin T. "Information retrieval on the semantic web: Integrating inference and retrieval", In SIGIR 2003 Semantic Web Workshop, 2003.
3. Zhang, L., Yu, Y., Zhou, J., Lin, C., and Yang, Y., "An enhanced model for searching in semantic portals", In Proceedings of WWW '05, pp.453-462, 2005.
4. Tran, T., Cimiano, P., Rudolph, S., and Studer, R., "Ontology-Based Interpretation of Keywords for Semantic Search", In Proceedings of ISWC '07, pp.523–536, 2007.
5. Bao, S., Wu, X., Fei, B., Xue, G., Su, Z., and Yu, Y., "Optimizing web search using social annotations", In Proceedings of WWW '07, pp.501-510, 2007.
6. Furnas, G.W., Deerwester, S., Dumais, S.T., Landauer, T.K., Harshman, R.A., Streeter, L.A., and Lochbaum, K.E., "Information retrieval using a singular value decomposition model of latent semantic structure", In Proceedings of SIGIR '88, pp.465-480, 1988.
7. Voorhees, E.M., "Query expansion using lexical semantic relations", In Proceedings of SIGIR '94, pp.61-69, 1994.
8. Tollari, S., Glotin, H., and Maitre, J.L., "Enhancement of textual images classification using segmented visual contents for image search engine", Multimedia Tools and Applications, vol.25, No.3, pp.405-417, 2005.
9. Studer, R., Benjamins, V.R., and Fensel, D., "Knowledge engineering: principles and methods", Data and Knowledge Engineering, vol.25, No.1-2, pp.161-197, 1998.
10. Berners-Lee, T., Hendler, J., and Lassila, O., "The semantic web", Scientific American, vol.284, No.5, pp.34-43, 2001.
11. Cohen, S., Mamou, J., Kanza, Y., and Sagiv, Y., "Xsearch: A semantic search engine for xml", In Proceedings of VLDB '03, pp.45-56, 2003.
12. Ding, L., Finin, T., Joshi, A., Peng, Y., Pan, R., and Reddivari, P., "Search on the semantic web", IEEE Computer, vol.10, No.38, pp.62-69, 2005.
13. Rocha, C., Schwabe, D., and de Aragao, M.P., "A hybrid approach for searching in the semantic web", In Proceedings of WWW '04, pp.374-383, 2004.
14. O'Reilly, T., "What is web 2.0: Design patterns and business models for the next generation of software", O'Reilly (http://www.oreilly.com/), September 2005.
15. Wu, X., Zhang, L., and Yu, Y., "Exploring social annotations for the semantic web", In Proceedings of WWW '06, pp.417-426, 2006.
16. Dmitriev, D.A., Eiron, N., Fontoura, M., and Shekita, E., "Using annotations in enterprise search", In Proceedings of WWW '06, pp.811-817, 2006.
17. Crestani, F., "Application of spreading activation techniques in information retrieval" Artificial Intelligence Review, vol.11, No.6, pp.453-482, 1997.

ACKNOWLEDGMENTS

[illegible]

[illegible]

Exploring Words with Semantic Correlations from Chinese Wikipedia

Yun Li, Kaiyan Huang, Seiji Tsuchiya, Fuji Ren and Yixin Zhong

Abstract In this paper, we work on semantic correlation between Chinese words based on Wikipedia documents. A corpus with about 50,000 structured documents is generated from Wikipedia pages. Then considering of hyper-links, text overlaps and word frequency, about 300,000 word pairs with semantic correlations are explored from these documents. We roughly measure the degree of semantic correlations and find groups with tight semantic correlations by self clustering.

1 Introduction

Semantic information and semantic relations are more and more important in natural language processing (NLP), being applied in applications such as text retrieval, information extraction etc. For semantic computing, semantic knowledge-base is created. For the complexity of semantic relations, majority of them like WordNet are constructed artificially, which is a time-consuming work. Automatic acquisition of semantic knowledge is important for research.

Wikipedia is an open encyclopedia with hyper-linked documents written cooperate by Internet users. In NLP applications, it could not only act as a huge corpus, but also a knowledge base or a semantic resource comparable to artificial constructed ones. It has been evaluated in the researches of Zesch&Gurevych (2007) etc. Someone explored Wikipedia for semantic relatedness computing (Strube&Ponzetto, 2007), name entity disambiguation (Bunescu&Pasca, 2006), automatic question answering (Ahn, 2004), etc.

Yun Li, Yixin Zhong
Beijing University of Posts and Telecommunications, 310#, BUPT, 10 Xitucheng Road, Haidian, Beijing, 100876, China, e-mail: liyun@is.tokushima-u.ac.jp; yxzhong@ieee.org

Yun Li, Kaiyan Huang, Seiji Tsuchiya, Fuji Ren
The University of Tokushima, Ren Lab,2-1 Minamijosanjima-cho,Tokushima,770-8506 e-mail: (liyun,huangky,tsuchiya,ren)@is.tokushima-u.ac.jp

---

Please use the following format when citing this chapter:

Li, Y., Huang, K., Tsuchiya, S., Ren, F. and Zhong, Y., 2008, in IFIP International Federation for Information Processing, Volume 288; *Intelligent Information Processing IV*; Zhongzhi Shi, E. Mercier-Laurent, D. Leake; (Boston: Springer), pp. 103–108.

In this paper, we work on word semantic correlation with Chinese Wikipedia documents. A structured Wikipedia document corpus is firstly generated from Wikipedia pages. Considering of hyper-links between documents, as well as text overlaps and the location information, pairs with semantic correlations are selected. Semantic relatedness is calculated from the paragraph locations and word frequency information in the Wikipedia documents. Finally we roughly measure the degree of semantic correlations and find groups with semantic correlations by self clustering.

2 Generate Wikipedia Document Corpus

Totally 322,121 Wikipedia words with hyper-links to pages are selected from Wikipedia. Given that the majority of professional terms have low frequency in normal text, words are filtered according to frequency in two Internet word-lists, one of which created by the search engine Sogou, the other with 800,000 words and frequencies of Google&Baidu collected by Internet users. Entries in corpus of People's Daily 2001 are also selected as candidates.

For the selected 66,725 of Wikipedia words with URLs, we download the pages from Chinese Wikipedia.In other works, the source extracted from image package with Wiki format documents is mainly applied. But for Chinese, the source is a mixture with simplified Chinese and traditional Chinese. In order to get localized documents, it is necessary to use the Html pages instead of the source files, as a localization translation services are called automatically in web pages. As redirect pages exist, we actually get 54,745 pages.

In Wikipedia documents, the basic text part is usually the most fundamental and important explanation for a word, located before the outline with less than 3 paragraphs of a document. Other paragraphs are detailed information with less importance. Some table or lists with manually grouped words are shared among some documents. The three kinds of text parts are not equally related to the topic word. In generating structured document, they are separately saved in different fields of the text corpus. As hyper-links in document are important for our research, meeting a hyper-link to another document, we get the word, URL keyword and count in each document parts. Other information is also collected like the length of raw text and html-text, total count of links and duplicated links, keyword and hyper-links to the category graph etc.

For synonyms, a page redirection is used to access the same document. In the following tests, synonyms should be seen as one word in computing of semantic relatedness. Synonyms could be found from the title word and the keyword following a mark of "Redirected From" in the redirected Wikipedia documents. More are collected from paragraphs such as "China Central Television commonly abbreviated as CCTV", "An astronaut or cosmonaut". Taking account of synonyms, the amount of words in the corpus is raised to 89,994, following with 54,745 XML formatted structured documents generated from Wikipedia pages. As synonyms and redirection exists, one page is statistically shared by 1.6 Wikipedia words. There are totally 1,823,883 hyper-links found from all the pages, averagely 33.3 in one page. 411,402 pairs of pages are hyper-linked to each other, with more relatedness and being considered more useful in our works.

3 Exploring Words with Semantic Correlations

Many researches on NLP refer to the semantic relations.Comparing to semantic similarity which shows only the “kind-of” semantic relation, semantic correlation is broad and comprehensive. Different researchers applied their own interpretations. Algorithms on WordNet, Hownet could be found from many related works.

In Wikipedia documents, semantic correlations between the title word and paragraphs are higher than other documents from web. In one view, the text was usually seen as the representation for the title keyword. In our corpus, 1,823,883 hyper-links between lines are explored, which are linked to the corresponding Wikipedia documents, showing relations on semantic meaning of the text lines. We pay more attention on the 411,402 page pairs with hyper-links to each other. By studying some pairs, we found most of them being semantically correlated, at least sharing some topics or events. As relatedness is a kind of importance, if something is noticed easily and usually, the importance should be higher, and their may some semantic relations exists. As correlations are for both sides, the relatedness between each other should be exists. From this view we design our way of finding semantically related words and calculating relatedness from the hyper-linked documents.

Experiments are done using the information of document hyper-links. Firstly Experiment 1 is to find the most word pairs with semantic relations. This time only the Wikipedia basic definition and description part is employed. As during the structure work, we separately saved the main part of text and hyper-link information, we directly used the data. For the document with title word A, we get hyper-linked groups (B, C, F, G), then search for hyper-linked A from each linked documents in this group. If C and G match the rule, two result of (A, C) and (A, G) are selected as candidate pairs. The experiment is done using a C++ program on a data set of word and links with integers IDs. From Experiment 1, 15,512 word pairs were found. It covers 14,290 words that are only 26% of the selected Wikipedia words. During artificial review, most pairs could be accepted by human understanding of semantic correlations. Some of which were listed in Table 1 in the form of (A, B) with English translations.

In Experiment 2, we extend the scope of search to the whole Wikipedia document. As the basic definition or introduction refer only a little part of a topic word, the most related materials exist in other paragraphs. The aim is to find a semantic correlated word set of a bigger coverage of correlates. For word pair (A,B), if each could be find in any position from the other’s document as a hyper-link, it is selected as a candidate pair of Set A, and if one noticed in the main part of the other, which is more reliable, we select the pair to Set B. So the rule of Set B is more strict than Set A but being looser than that of Experiment I. We get the result in Table 2. Generally

Table 1 Semantic Correlated Word Pairs.

A(CN)	A(EN)	B(CN)	B(EN)	A(CN)	A(EN)	B(CN)	B(EN)
信号	Signals	交通	Traffic	按钮	Button	人机交互	HCI
椅子	Chair	轮椅	Wheelchair	彩蛋	EasterEgg	复活节	Easter
棒球	Baseball	球棒	Bat	筷子	Chopsticks	中国烹饪	ChineseCook
赌博	Gambling	赌徒	Gamblers	行动党	ActionParty	马来西亚	Malaysia
专科	College	教育	Educate	演化	Evolutionary	博弈论	GameTheory
软件	Software	许可证	License	阪神	Hanshin	甲子园	Koshien

Table 2 Result with Manual Evaluation.

ID	Word Pair Count	Coverage	Reviews
1	15,512	26%	Correlated
2(A)	79,150	65%	Most correlated
2(B)	411,402	73%	Some unrelated

speaking, the result is reliable with semantic correlations. For some pairs in Set A, the importance is different from each other. Such as "春节(Spring Festival)", "拜年(Say Happy New Year) ", "鞭炮(Firecrackers) ", "年画(New Year Pictures) ".,the "Spring Festival" is more important for "New Year Pictures", but "Spring Festival" could have relatedness with more other than "New Year Pictures".

For Set B the coverage is changed to 73% with 39,925 words, but the accuracy is not very good. A refine work should be down relies on more information not limited to the word frequency, document frequency etc. Among most un-related pairs, a common result is that at least one word in a pair has a high document frequency. Such as "中国(China)", "公司(Company)", "地区(Regions)", "英语(English)" are selected related to many keywords. The mistakes appear because these words easily appear in everyday text files with a high document frequency.

In Experiment 3 document frequency and word frequency are used as filter on Set B. By accessing the documents, we get the count of document containing a word as hyper-linked text for all the selected Wikipedia keywords. Document frequency are calculated with the count divided by total count of documents in corpus. Only the pairs not in Set A are filtered. Several tests are done to find a proper threshold leading to more correlated word pairs and less unnecessary ones. Our result set is finally cut to 360,304 semantic related pairs. Here we employ a way of roughly measuring semantic relatedness. We give each part of the Wikipedia document a score: 4 for the main part, 2 for other part of the document text, and 1 for shared tables and text. During the creating of our Wikipedia corpus, hyper linked words and paragraph information have been extracted, which are used directly. For both words in a pair, we add the score in the document of the other's.

4 Self Clustering for Semantic Related Words

In Experiment 3, taking one word as a center word, we could find an average of 7.3 semantic related words. Small group of words sharing a common topic are easy to group together with more correlations among each other. Taking “北京(Beijing)” for example, 242 words are found covering several aspects, from which smaller groups with tight semantic correlations can be found. Such as “奥运会(Olympics)”, “福娃(Fuwa)”, “鸟巢(Bird Nest)” etc form a cluster of the 2008 Olympics, and “天安门(Tiananmen)”, “西单(Xidan)”, “王府井(Wangfujing)” are grouped as famous places of Beijing.

In our experiment, we make a larger group by adding new nodes into a smaller group. If pairs of (AB, AC, BC) could be found in the semantic related word set, a new group of (ABC) are created. Then a candidate group (ABCD) could be extended to if exist the pairs of (AD, BD, CD). Finally a small group should be removed if being sub set of a larger group. In this way, the fully connected word groups are found with semantic correlations. There are still lots of candidate groups with strong correlations but without full node connections. Take the example of (ABCD) and (ABCE), as missing correlations between D and E, they are considered as two small groups with similar topics. The result means that our method is too strict. Wikipedia documents are not able to cover all related words, missing links may exist. In addition during the selection of semantic related pairs, we only pay attention to those appears in documents of each other and the single way links are ignored. A further work is done on the fully connected nod groups. We find groups with one or two different nodes then try to find more information to combine them together. Take D and E in last example, if we can get a single way hyper link from the Wikipedia document, the candidate group of (ABCDE) is accepted. For a group with more words, more missed relations are allowed.

Finally we get a result set with 87,100 groups. For about 1/3 of the groups, the word count is from 3 to 4. Figure 1(a) shows that large groups with more than 5 words cover only 7%, as for more words being difficult to have correlations to each other. As selected by authors for same topics, they are reliable but not so valuable. There are still more than half (59%) of the result being pairs, but not showing a bad result. Considering of the 360,304 semantic related pairs before the experiment, it is only 14.3%. The 3-word groups combine 3 pairs as a unique result, and other large groups with more. There are also some result with more than 10 related words exist in the result set. As being selected from shared tables of Wikipedia meaningfully related to a topic, these result are reliable, though not with such high relatedness. Calculation of degree of semantic correlations is almost the same for a group with more than 2 words. For a m-word group (m¿2), it could also be calculated by summarizing all the part scores in each documents, then divided by $m \times (m-1)/2$ as the result value. Seeing from Figure 1(b), the groups are almost evenly distributed in the range from 2 to 8.

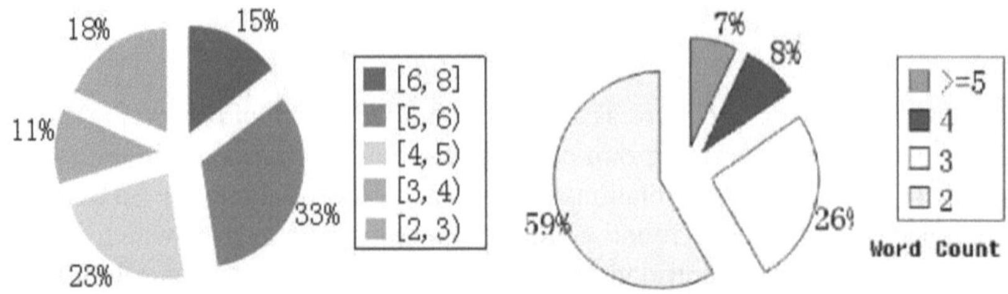

Fig. 1 (a)Groups with Semantic Correlations(b)Distribution of Average Relatedness of Groups.

5 Conclusion and Future Works

In this paper, the Chinese Wikipedia pages are used for semantic related word searching. Considering of hyper-links, text overlaps and word frequency, 360,304 word pairs with semantic correlations are explored from 54,745 structured documents from Wikipedia. We also roughly measured semantic correlations, analyzed the reliability of our measures.

As with similar hierarchical structure, algorithms and applications for WordNet, Hownet may be transplanted to Wikipedia. Semantic Relatedness is used to measuring the degree of semantic correlations, not considering of the difference of relation types. By analyzing the properties of different algorithms based on text overlap or information contents, we are hoping to find a reliable way of searching for groups with semantic correlations and compute the semantic relatedness. For research on semantic relations in NLP, Wikipedia could be employed more in future works.

Acknowledgements This research has been partially supported by the Ministry of Education, Science, Sports and Culture, Grant-in-Aid for Scientific Research (B), 19300029. Thanks to Associate Professor Suzuki, and Doctor Matsumoto from The University of Tokushima for instructions.

References

1. D. Ahn, V. Jijkoun etc.: Using Wikipedia at the TREC QA track. In Proc. of TREC-13 (2004)
2. S. Banerjee, T. Pedersen: Extended gloss overlap as a measure of semantic relatedness. In Proc. of IJCAI-03 (2003)
3. M. Strube, SP. Ponzetto: WikiRelate! Computing semantic relatedness using Wikipedia Proc. of AAAI (2006)
4. R. Bunescu ,M. Pasca: Using Encyclopedic Knowledge for Named Entity Disambiguation Proceedings of the 11th Conference of the European Chapter (2006)
5. SP. Ponzetto, M. Strube: Deriving a Large Scale Taxonomy from Wikipedia ,Proceedings of the 22nd National Conference on Artificial (2007)

A Heuristic Knowledge Reduction Algorithm Based on Partition Subdivision and Consistent Degree

Wen Huo and Xiaoguang Hong

College of Computer Science and Technology,Shandong University,
hw112200@hotmail.com

Abstract: In this paper, a new knowledge reduction definition based on partition subdivision is proposed, its equivalence to the classic attribute reduction definition based on positive region is proved, and a consistent degree is introduced to evaluate the importance of condition attribute for decision attribute. Based on the above results, a heuristic knowledge reduction algorithm is designed.

Keywords: data mining, knowledge reduction, rough set, decision table, positive region, partition subdivision, consistent degree

1. Introduction

Knowledge reduction is one of the key problems of knowledge discovery in data mining. There are two classical definitions of knowledge reduction in rough set theory: one is based on positive region, the other is based on condition information entropy, but they are not equivalent when they deal with inconsistent decision table. In 2005 a definition based on the new condition information entropy was proposed [1], and its equivalence to the definition based on positive region was explained by a knowledge reduction algorithm. In 2006 a definition based on the average decision power was proposed [2]. Afterwards, the average decision power was amended to the decision power [3] in 2007, but the definition based on the decision power is not equivalent to the classical definition based on positive region.

Being illuminated by all the above research, this paper proposed a new knowledge reduction definition based on partition subdivision, and its equivalence to the classical definition based on positive region is proved. Furthermore, a consistent degree is introduced to evaluate the importance of condition attribute for decision attribute. Based on the above results, a heuristic knowledge reduction algorithm based on partition subdivision and consistent degree is designed.

Please use the following format when citing this chapter:

Huo, W. and Hong, X., 2008, in IFIP International Federation for Information Processing, Volume 288; *Intelligent Information Processing IV*; Zhongzhi Shi, E. Mercier-Laurent, D. Leake; (Boston: Springer), pp. 109–117.

2. Basic Notations and Definitions

[Definition 1][4,5] The notion of *information system* is formally defined as S=(U,A,V,f) ,and U,A,V,f is defined as follows: U: nonempty set of objects, called universe; A: nonempty set of attributes; $V=\bigcup_{a\in A} Va$, Va is the range of attribute a; f:U×A→V is an information function, $\forall x\in U$, $a\in A$, $f(x,a)\in Va$.

$\forall P\subseteq A$, IND(P)={(x,y)|(x,y)∈U×U and ∀a∈P, f(x,a)=f(y,a)} is an equivalence relation on U, so U/IND(P), shortly written as U/P, forms an partition on U.

If attribute set A can be divided into condition attribute set C and decision attribute set D, namely, $C\cup D=A$, $C\cap D=\varnothing$, then S is termed decision table, shortly written as S=(U,C,D).

[Definition 2] [4,5] In decision table T=(U,C,D), $P\subseteq C\cup D$, $\forall X\subseteq U$, $\underline{P}X=\cup\{Y|Y\in U/P \text{ and } Y\subseteq X\}$ is termed the lower approximation of X. $POS_P(D)=\bigcup_{X\in U/D}\underline{P}X$ is termed the P positive region of D.

3. The Classical Knowledge Reduction Definition Based on Positive Region

[Definition 3] [4, 5] In decision table T=(U,C,D),$A\subseteq C$, if $POS_A(D)=POS_C(D)$, and $\forall a\in A$, $POS_{A-\{a\}}\neq POS_C(D)$, then A is termed a knowledge reduction of C with respect to D.

4. The Knowledge Reduction Definition Based on Partition Subdivision

[Definition 4][1] In decision table T=(U,C,D),U/D={Y_1, Y_2,..., Y_m},$A\subseteq C$, let $Y_0=U-POS_A(D)$, then the set cluster $R_A=\{\underline{A}Y_0,\underline{A}Y_1,\underline{A}Y_2,\ldots,\underline{A}Y_m\}$ is termed a partition on U educed by A.

Definition 4 is explained as follows: $\underline{A}Y_0=Y_0=U-POS_A(D)$ can be proved easily, and $\bigcup_{i=1}^{m}\underline{A}Y_i=POS_A(D)$, if ∅ exists in R_A, then R_A is still a partition on U after delete the ∅, so we can suppose there is no ∅ in R_A.

[Definition 5] U/P={P_1, P_2,..., P_m},U/Q={Q_1, Q_2,..., Q_n}, if $\forall Q_i\in U/Q$, $\exists P_k\in U/P$, $Q_i\subseteq P_k$, then we say U/Q is a partition subdivision of U/P.

Based on *Definition 4* and *Definition 5,* we propose a new knowledge reduction definition based on partition subdivision as follows:

[Definition 6] In decision table $T=(U,C,D), U/D=\{Y_1,Y_2,\ldots,Y_m\}$, $R_C=\{\underline{C}Y_0,\underline{C}Y_1,\underline{C}Y_2,\ldots,\underline{C}Y_m\}$, $A\subseteq C$, if U/A is a partition subdivision of R_C, and $\forall a\in A, U/(A-\{a\})$ is not the partition subdivision of R_C, then A is termed a knowledge reduction of C with respect to D.

5 The Equivalence between Definition 6 and Definition 3

[Lemma 1][1] In decision table $T=(U,C,D), U/D=\{Y_1, Y_2,\ldots, Y_m\}, A\subseteq C$, then $POS_A(D)=POS_C(D)\Leftrightarrow \underline{A}Y_i=\underline{C}Y_i, \forall i\in\{0,1,2,\ldots,m\}$.

[Lemma 2] In decision table $T=(U,C,D), A\subseteq C, R_A=\{\underline{A}Y_0,\underline{A}Y_1,\underline{A}Y_2,\ldots,\underline{A}Y_m\}$, then U/A is a partition subdivision of R_A.

Proof: Suppose $U/A=\{A1, A2,\ldots, A\ n\}, U/D=\{Y_1, Y_2,\ldots, Y_m\}$, because of $\underline{A}Y_j=\cup\{A_i|A_i\subseteq Y_j\}, j=1,2\ldots,m$, some partition blocks should be a subdivision of $\{\underline{A}Y_0,\underline{A}Y_1,\underline{A}Y_2,\ldots,\underline{A}Y_m\}$, and the other partition blocks should be a subdivision of $\underline{A}Y_0=U-POS_A(D)$, so U/A is a subdivision of R_A.

[Theorem 1] In decision table $T=(U,C,D)$, $U/D=\{Y_1, Y_2,\ldots, Y_m\}$, $A\subseteq C$, $R_C=\{\underline{C}Y_0,\underline{C}Y_1,\underline{C}Y_2,\ldots,\underline{C}Y_m\}$, then $POS_A(D)=POS_C(D)\Leftrightarrow$ U/A is a partition subdivision of R_C.

Proof: 1) First, we prove "$\Rightarrow$": If $POS_A(D)=POS_C(D)$, then according to *Lemma 1* we can get $\underline{A}Y_i=\underline{C}Y_i$, $\forall i\in\{0,1,2,\ldots,m\}$, namely, $R_A=R_C$. Moreover, U/A is a partition subdivision of R_A according to *Lemma 2,* so U/A is a partition subdivision of R_C too.

2) Second, we prove "$\Leftarrow$": If U/A is a partition subdivision of R_C, let $U/A=\{A_1, A_2,\ldots, A_n\}$, and

$\bigcup_{i=1}^{k_1} A_i=\underline{C}Y_0$, $\bigcup_{i=k_1+1}^{k_2} A_i=\underline{C}Y_1,\ldots,$ $\bigcup_{i=k_m+1}^{n} A_i=\underline{C}Y_m$.(*) Then we can get the following conclusions:

Conclusion 1: $\forall i\in\{k_1+1,k_1+2,\ldots,n\}, \exists j\in\{1,2,\ldots,m\}, A_i\subseteq Y_j$.

Conclusion 2: $\forall i\in\{1,2,\ldots,k_1\}, \forall j\in\{1,2,\ldots,m\}, A_i\not\subset Y_j$.

Proof of Conclusion 1: For $\forall i\in\{k_1+1,k_1+2,\ldots,n\}$,according to (*) we can get that $\exists j\in\{1,2,\ldots,m\}, A_i\subseteq\underline{C}Y_j$, because of $\underline{C}Y_j\subseteq Y_j$, so $A_i\subseteq Y_j$.

Proof of Conclusion 2: Suppose $U/C=\{C_1,C_2,\ldots, Cs\}$, $\underline{C}Y_0=\bigcup_{k=1}^{q} C_k$, $q\le s$, and $\forall k\in\{1,2,\ldots,q\}, \forall j\in\{1,2,\ldots,m\}, C_k\not\subset Y_j$ (**), thus $\bigcup_{i=1}^{k_1} A_i=\bigcup_{k=1}^{q} C_k$. Because of U/C is a partition subdivision of U/A [7],$\{C_1,C_2,\ldots,C_q\}$ is definitely a partition subdivision of$\{A_1,A_2,\ldots,A_{k1}\}$,so $\forall$ i $\in \{1,2,\ldots, k_1\}$, A_i is the union of some $C_k(k\in\{1,2,\ldots,q\})$, then we can get that $\forall$ j$\in\{1,2,\ldots,m\}$, $A_i \not\subset Y_j$ due to (**), otherwise, suppose that $\exists$ j$\in\{1,2,\ldots,m\}$, $A_i \subseteq Y_j$, thus $C_k \subseteq Y_j$, which is inconsistent with (**).

According to *Conclusion 1*, *Conclusion 2* and the definition of *A positive region of D*, we can get that

$$U-POS_A(D)= \bigcup_{i=1}^{k_1} A_i=\underline{C}Y_0=U-POS_C(D),\ \text{namely, } POS_A(D)=POS_C(D).$$

From *Theorem 1* we can easily get the conclusion that *Definition 6* is equivalent to *Definition 3.*

Now we validate it by the following examples [2]:

Table 1. Decision Table1.

U	a	b	c	d
1	1	0	0	1
2	2	1	1	3
3	3	1	2	0
4	3	1	2	0
5	3	1	2	1
6	3	1	2	1
7	3	1	1	0
8	3	1	1	0
9	3	1	1	1
10	3	1	1	1

Table 2. Decision Table2.

U	a	b	c	d
1	1	1	0	1
2	3	1	2	0
3	3	1	2	0
4	3	1	2	0
5	3	1	2	0
6	3	1	2	1
7	3	3	0	0
8	3	3	0	0
9	3	3	0	0
10	3	3	0	1

Table 3. Decision Table3.

U	a	b	c	d
1	1	1	0	1
2	3	1	2	0
3	3	1	2	0
4	3	1	2	0
5	3	1	2	0
6	3	1	2	3
7	3	3	0	2
8	3	3	0	2
9	3	3	0	3
10	3	3	0	3

Table 1, *Table 2*and *Table 3* are all inconsistent decision table, we reduce the condition attribute set by Definition 3 and Definition 6, the reductive results list in the following table:

Table 4. Reductive Results of *Table 1, Table 2* and *Table 3.*

	Table 1	Table 2	Table 3
Definition 3	{a}	{a},{b,c}	{a},{b,c}
Definition 6	{a}	{a},{b,c}	{a},{b,c}

If we restrict to get the minimal reduction, which contains attributes the least, then {b,c} should be removed.

6. The Consistent Degree of Condition Attribute Subset Relative to R_C

From *Theorem 1* and *Definition 6* we can get that if condition attribute subset A and B are not reduction, then they are not the partition subdivision of R_C, now, how can we decide which one between A and B is more important for decision attribute? Therefore, we introduce the following definition to evaluate the importance of condition attribute subset for decision attribute.

[Definition 7]In decision table $T=(U,C,D), A \subseteq C, U/D=\{Y_1, Y_2,\ldots,Y_m\}$, $U/A=\{A_1, A_2,\ldots, A_n\}, Y_0=U-POS_C(D)$, $R_C=\{\underline{C}Y_0,\underline{C}Y_1,\underline{C}Y_2,\ldots,\underline{C}Y_m\}$, then $\sigma_A=\sum_{i=1}^{n}\sum_{j=0}^{m}\frac{|\underline{C}Y_j \cap A_i|}{|A_i|}\times\frac{|\underline{C}Y_j \cap A_i|}{|U|}$ is called *the consistent degree of A with respect to R_C.*
(It is obvious that $0<\sigma_A\le 1$.)

Before we clarify the significance of consistent degree, we firstly prove that $\sigma_A=1 \Leftrightarrow$ U/A is a partition subdivision of R_C.

[Lemma 3] let $U/P=\{P_1, P_2,\ldots, P_m\}$, $U/Q=\{Q_1, Q_2,\ldots, Q_n\}$, then $\sum_{i=1}^{n}\sum_{j=1}^{m}\frac{|P_j \cap Q_i|}{|Q_i|}\times\frac{|P_j \cap Q_i|}{|U|}=1 \Leftrightarrow$ U/Q is a partition subdivision of U/P.

Proof: 1) First, we prove "$\Leftarrow$": If U/Q is a partition subdivision of U/P, then $\forall Q_i \in U/Q, \exists P_k \in U/P, Q_i \subseteq P_k$, thus $P_k \cap Q_i = Q_i$, and for the other $P_j \in U/P$, $j \ne k$, $P_j \cap Q_i = \varnothing$. So

$$\sum_{i=1}^{n}\sum_{j=1}^{m}\frac{|P_j \cap Q_i|}{|Q_i|}\times\frac{|P_j \cap Q_i|}{|U|}=\sum_{i=1}^{n}\left(\frac{|P_k \cap Q_i|}{|Q_i|}\times\frac{|P_k \cap Q_i|}{|U|}+\sum_{j\ne k}\frac{|P_j \cap Q_i|}{|Q_i|}\times\frac{|P_j \cap Q_i|}{|U|}\right)=\sum_{i=1}^{n}\left(\frac{|Q_i|}{|U|}+0\right)=1$$

2) Second, we prove "$\Rightarrow$": If U/Q is a partition subdivision of U/P, then $\exists Q_s \in U/Q$, that the elements of Q_s come from different P_j, suppose that there are x_1 elements come from P_{j1}, x_2 elements come from P_{j2},…, x_k elements come from P_{jk}, $x_1+x_2+\ldots+x_k=|Q_s|$, thus $\sum_{j=1}^{m}\frac{|P_j \cap Q_s|}{|Q_s|}\times\frac{|P_j \cap Q_s|}{|U|}=\frac{x_1^2+x_2^2+\ldots+x_k^2}{|Q_s|\times|U|}$,

because of $x_1,x_2,\ldots,x_k>0$, it is obvious that $x_1^2+x_2^2+\ldots+x_k^2<(x_1+x_2+\ldots+x_k)^2=|Q_s|^2$,

thus $\sum_{j=1}^{m}\frac{|P_j \cap Q_s|}{|Q_s|}\times\frac{|P_j \cap Q_s|}{|U|}<\frac{|Q_s|^2}{|Q_s|\times|U|}=\frac{|Q_s|}{|U|}$. Moreover, $\forall Q_i \in U/Q, |P_j \cap Q_i|\le|Q_i|$, thus

$\sum_{j=1}^{m}\frac{|P_j \cap Q_i|}{|Q_i|}\times\frac{|P_j \cap Q_i|}{|U|}\le\frac{|Q_i|}{|U|}$. So $\sum_{i=1}^{n}\sum_{j=1}^{m}\frac{|P_j \cap Q_i|}{|Q_i|}\times\frac{|P_j \cap Q_i|}{|U|}=\sum_{j=1}^{m}\frac{|P_j \cap Q_s|}{|Q_s|}\times\frac{|P_j \cap Q_s|}{|U|}+\sum_{i\ne s}\sum_{j=1}^{m}\frac{|P_j \cap Q_i|}{|Q_i|}\times\frac{|P_j \cap Q_i|}{|U|}$

$<\frac{|Q_s|}{|U|}+\sum_{i\ne s}\frac{|Q_i|}{|U|}<\sum_{i=1}^{n}\frac{|Q_i|}{|U|}=1$.

According to *Lemma3* and *Definition 3* we can easily get the following theorem:

[Theorem 2] $\sigma_A=1 \Leftrightarrow$ U/A is a partition subdivision of R_C.

Now we come to the significance of consistent degree σ_A : $Rc=\{\underline{C}Y_0,\underline{C}Y_1,\underline{C}Y_2,\ldots,\underline{C}Y_m\}$ not only divide the consistent objects belong to different decision class $Y_1,Y_2,\ldots,Y_m$ into different partition blocks $\underline{C}Y_1,\underline{C}Y_2,\ldots,\underline{C}Y_m$, but also put all the inconsistent objects in one partition block $\underline{C}Y_0$ .Therefore, when U/A is not a partition subdivision of R_C, it is positive that the consistent objects belong to different decision class are mixed in one partition block, or the consistent objects and the inconsistent objects are mixed in one partition block. From the proof of *Theorem 2* we can see that the more of these mixtures, the smaller of σ_A, and the less importance of A for decision attribute.

7. A Heuristic Knowledge Reduction Algorithm Based on Partition Subdivision and Consistent Degree

Searching for all reduction or minimal reduction of a decision table was already proved to be a NP-hard problem [6, 7]; therefore, making use of some heuristic information to reduce the searching space is the main idea in most of the algorithms, which can get a minimal reduction or a suboptimal reduction. An algorithm is designed in this paper as follows: Taking the consistent degree of every condition attribute with respect to R_C as the heuristic information, the condition attribute set is presented in the consistent degree's descending order, then we begin to search from the first attribute of this set until the searching result is a partition subdivision of R_C, which is the minimal reduction.

[Algorithm 1] Input: decision table T=(U,C,D)

Output: a minimal reduction of T

Initialize REDU=$\varnothing$.

①Compute U/C, U/D, R_C;

②for each Ci$\in$C, compute U/Ci, if U/Ci is a partition subdivision of R_C, then REDU={Ci} and go to ⑧;
If every U/Ci is not the partition subdivision R_C, then go to ③;

③for each Ci$\in$C, calculate the consistent degree σ_{C_i} , and C is presented in the consistent degree's descending order as C= {A1,A2,…,An};

④REDU={A1,A2}, i=2; If U/REDU is a partition subdivision of R_C, then go to⑧. Else, go to ⑤;

⑤i=i+1, REDU=REDU$\cup${Ai};

⑥If U/REDU is a partition subdivision of R_C, then go to ⑦. Else, go to ⑤;

⑦for(k=i-1;k>=1;k--)
If U/(REDU-{Ak}) is a partition subdivision of R_C, then REDU = REDU-{Ak} and go to ⑧。

⑧Output REDU。

Supplementary explanation: Compute U/C, U/D, U/Ci and U/REDU by Algorithm 1 in reference [10];Compute $POS_C(D)$ by Algorithm 2 in reference[11], so R_C is obtained simultaneously.

We analyze *the time complexity of Algorithm 1* as follows: The time complexity of ① is $O(|C||U|)$[10,11]. In the worst circumstance, the whole C is minimal reduction, then the time complexity of ② is $O(|C|^2|U|)$,③ is $O(|C|^2|U|)$, ④⑤⑥ is $O(|C|^2|U|)$, ⑦ is $O(|C|^2|U|)$.Therefore, the time complexity of *Algorithm 1* is $O(|C|^2|U|)$, which is lower than the time complexity $O(|C|^2|U||\log|U||)$ of Algorithm 2 in reference[1].

The advantage of Algorithm 1:

1) There is no computation for $CORE_D(C)$.
2) Judging if REDU is a subdivision of R_C instead of judging if $POS_{REDU}(D)=POS_C(D)$, the calculation amount shrink evidently.
3) Even in the worst circumstance we only calculate the importance of each single condition attribute for decision attribute, so the calculation amount is less than calculating the importance of some attributes' combination. The calculation of consistent degree is easier than the calculation of condition information entropy too.

Now we clarify *Algorithm 1* by the following example[1] :

Table 5. Decision Table 4.

U	a	b	c	e	f	d
1	0	0	0	0	1	0
2	0	1	1	1	0	1
3	1	1	0	1	1	1
4	0	1	1	1	0	0
5	0	0	1	0	1	0
6	1	1	0	1	0	1
7	0	1	1	1	1	1
8	1	1	1	0	1	1
9	1	1	0	1	1	0
10	0	1	1	1	1	0

①U/D={{1,4,5,9,10},{2,3,6,7,8}},U/C={{1},{2,4},{3,9},{5},{6},{7,10},{8}}, R_C ={{1,5},{6,8},{2,3,4,7,9,10}}.

②U/{a}={{1,2,4,5,7,10},{3,6,8,9}},U/{b}={{1,5},{2,3,4,6,7,8,9,10}}, U/{c}={{1,3,6,9},{2,4,5,7,8,10}},U/{e}={{1,5,8},{2,3,4,6,7,9,10}}, U/{f}={{2,4,6},{1,3,5,7,8,9,10}}.

None of them is the partition subdivision of R_C.

③ $\sigma_{\{a\}}$=0.533, $\sigma_{\{b\}}$=0.7, $\sigma_{\{c\}}$=0.4, $\sigma_{\{e\}}$=0.695, $\sigma_{\{f\}}$=0.467, then C is presented in the consistent degree's descending order as C={b,e,a,f,c}.

④⑤⑥U/{b,e},U/{b,e,a} are not the partition subdivision of R_C, U/{b,e,a,f} is the partition subdivision of R_C, so REDU={b,e,a,f}.

⑦U/{b,e,f}, U/{b,a,f} are not the partition subdivision of R_C, U/{e,a,f} is the partition subdivision of R_C, so REDU={e,a,f}.
⑧ Output REDU={e,a,f}.

8 Experimental Results

We choose Decision table 4 in this paper and some decision tables in UCI machine learning database, and implemented Algorithm 1 in this paper and Algorithm 2 in reference[1] by Java language on our PC(Intel(R) Core(TM)2 2.33GHz, 1.96GB RAM,WINXP). The experimental results are as follows:

Table 6. Experimental Results Table.

Decision table	If it is a consistent decision table	The number of instances	The number of condition attributes before reduction	The number of condition attributes in the minimal reduction	Algorithm 1in this paper		Algorithm 2 in reference[1]	
					The number of condition attributes after reduction	Execution time /s	The number of condition attributes after reduction	Execution Time /s
Table 5	No	10	5	3	3	0.01	3	0.02
Voting-records	Yes	435	16	9	9	0.12	9	0.15
Tic-tac-toe	Yes	958	9	8	8	0.32	8	0.38
zoo	No	101	17	10	11	0.06	10	0.07
mushroom	Yes	8124	22	4	4	3.23	4	3.80
chess end-game	Yes	3196	36	29	29	2.73	29	3.09

From Table 6. we can see that the execution time of Algorithm 1 in this paper is less than that of Algorithm 2 in reference[1].

9. Conclusions

Being illuminated by the set cluster R_C [1] and the decision power[3], this paper has found and proved the following laws by *Theorem 1* and *Theorem 2* : In decision table T=(U,C,D), $A \subseteq C$, $POS_A(D)=POS_C(D) \Leftrightarrow$ U/A is a partition subdivision of $R_C \Leftrightarrow \sigma_A = 1$ (σ_A is the consistent degree of A with respect to R_C).

Consequently, a heuristic knowledge reduction algorithm, *Algorithm 1,* is designed. Making use of *Theorem 1*, this algorithm judges if REDU is a subdivision of R_C instead of judging if $POS_{REDU}(D)=POS_C(D)$, so the calculation amount shrink evidently. From the proof of *Theorem 2* we can see that the smaller of σ_A, the less importance of A for decision attribute, so it is rational that this algorithm takes the consistent degree σ_A as the heuristic information to reduce the searching space. And the calculation of consistent degree is easier than the calculation of condition information entropy. The time complexity of this algorithm is lower too.

Finally, The results of experiment show that this algorithm is more efficient than Algorithm 2 in reference[1] actually.

References

1. LIU Qi-he, LI Fan, MIN Fan, YE Mao, and YANG Guo-wei,"An Efficient Knowledge Reduction Algorithm Based on New Conditional Information Entropy", Vol.20, No.8, pp.878-882,Control and Decision, 2005.
2. JIANG Si-yu and LU Yan-sheng,"Two New Reduction Definitions of Decision Table", Vol.27, No.3, pp.512-515, Mini- Micro Systems,2006.
3. XU Zhang-yan, SONG Wei, YANG Bing-ru, GAO Jing and HOU Wei,"Note on 'Two New Reduction Definition of Decision Table' ", Vol.28 ,No.9, pp.1686-1689,Journal of Chinese Computer Systems, 2007.
4. WANG Guo-yin: Rough Set Theory and Knowledge Acquisition, Xi'an Jiaotong University Publishing Company, Xi'an2001.
5. LIU Qing: Rough sets and Rough Reasoning, Science Publishing Company, Beijing 2001
6. Hu X.H. and Nick C. "Learning in relational databases: A rough set approach", Vol.11, No.2, pp.323-338,International Journal of Computational Intelligence, 1995
7. XU Zhang-yan, LIU Zuo-peng, YANG Bing-ru and SONG Wei,"A Quick Attribute Reduction Algorithm with Complexity of max $(O(|C||U|), O(|C|^2|U/C|))$", Vol.20, No.3, pp.391-399,Chinese Journal of Computers, 2006.
8. Pawlak Z, "Rough sets", Vol.11, No.5, pp.341-356, International Journal of Computer and Information Science, 1982.
9. Pawlak Z: Rough Sets: Theoretical Aspects of Reasoning about Data, Kluwer Academic Publishers, Dordrecht,1991
10. Pawlak Z, Slowinski R, "Rough set approach to multi-attribute decision analysis", Vol.72, No.1, pp.443-459, European Journal of Operational Research, 1994.

Object-based Image Retrieval with Attention Analysis and Spatial Re-ranking

Ke Gao[1], Shouxun Lin[2], Yongdong Zhang[2] and Sheng Tang[2]

[1]Key Laboratory of Intelligent Information Processing,
Institute of Computing Technology, Chinese Academy of Sciences
Graduate University of the Chinese Academy of Sciences
Beijing, 100080,China
kegao@ict.ac.cn

[2]Key Laboratory of Intelligent Information Processing,
Institute of Computing Technology, Chinese Academy of Sciences
Beijing, 100080
China
{sxlin, zhyd, ts}@ict.ac.cn

Abstract: In this paper, a new method is proposed for object-based image retrieval. The user supplies a query object by selecting a region from a query image, and the system returns a ranked list of images that contain the same object, retrieved from a large image database. The main outcomes of this research are as follows: (1) An novel object-based image retrieval framework that integrates effective pre-treatment and re-ranking is presented, (2) a new feature filtration method based on attention analysis is proposed for pre-treatment, (3) to further improve object retrieval precision, we add an efficient spatial configuration model to re-rank the primary retrieval result using Bag of Word method. Experimental results demonstrate the effectiveness of our method.

Keywords: Object-based image retrieval, attention analysis, spatial re-ranking

1 Introduction

OBIR (Object-based Image Retrieval) is an important branch of content-based image retrieval (J.Sivic and A.Zisserman, 2003; J.Phibin et al.2007). The goal of OBIR is to find images containing desired object by providing the system a selected region of a query image. It remains a challenging problem because an

---

Please use the following format when citing this chapter:

Gao, K., Lin, S., Zhang, Y. and Tang, S., 2008, in IFIP International Federation for Information Processing, Volume 288; *Intelligent Information Processing IV*; Zhongzhi Shi, E. Mercier-Laurent, D. Leake; (Boston: Springer), pp. 118–128.

object's visual appearance may be quite different due to viewpoint, illumination, affine transformation, and even partially occlusion.

The innermost core of OBIR is how to detect and measure the similarities of object regions. Recent work in this field can be divided into two categories: one is based on image segmentation, such as Blobworld and SIMPLcity (C. Carson *et al.*1999; Wang *et al.*2001); the other is so-called BoW (Bag of Words) method, which simulates simple text-retrieval system using the analogy of "visual words" (J.Sivic *et al.*2003). BoW doesn't rely on the precision of image segmentation, and can deal with a variety of affine transformations. In consequence, it has become increasingly attractive (Qing-Fang Zheng *et al.*2006; S. Lazebnik *et al.*2006).

In Bag of Words method, affine covariant local patches (Mikolajczyk and Schmid, 2002; Matas *et al*, 2002) are detected in images, and an affine invariant descriptor (Lowe, 2004) is computed for each patch. To effectively index these high-dimensional descriptors, they are clustered into a visual vocabulary, and each patch is mapped to its closest visual word. Then an image is represented as a bag of visual words and their frequency of occurrence. Usually, they are organized as an inverted file to facilitate efficient retrieval. The benefits of this approach are as follows: first, the use of local affine covariant patches and affine invariant descriptors can effectively present an object under various image transformations, such as different viewpoint, illumination, affine transformation, and even partially occlusion; second, feature matching has been pre-computed using vector quantization, so that any particular object can be retrieved at run-time.

Although BoW method is an effective analogy between "visual words" and text words, Object-based image retrieval using "visual words" and text words-based web pages retrieval are somewhat different. The "visual words" are calculated by unsupervised clustering, and can't be understood by the user. Accordingly, "visual words" are "noisier" than text keywords in two aspects: on one hand, patch detector often returns a large number of patches which have a low signal-to-noise ratio, because only a few of them are distinguishable, so informative patches need to be picked out through a sea of background patches; on the other hand, in BoW method, the spatial information about the image-location of the visual words is ignored, which is similar to retrieve documents only by orderless letters. This will result in false matching such as "abc=cba", and reduce the retrieval precision.

To utilize the spatial relation between patches, Sivic et al. use a search area containing the 15 nearest neighbors of each matched patch, and the neighboring patch which also matches within this area casts a vote for that image. Philbin adds affine matrix verification to nearby patches using LO-RANSAC. Zheng et al. propose a visual phrase-based approach using adjacent patch pair, which is hard to satisfy in images with sparse patches, and doesn't contain the information of distance and orientation. Furthermore, the above methods don't consider the spatial neighborhood' affine transformation under different viewpoints, and rely heavily on the clustering precision of visual words.

To solve the above problems, the benefits of this paper are as follows. (1)A novel object-based image retrieval framework that integrates effective pre-treatment and re-ranking is presented, (2) a new feature filtration method based on attention analysis is proposed for pre-treatment, (3) to further improve object retrieval precision, we add an efficient spatial configuration model to re-rank the primary retrieval result using Bag of Word method.

The remainder of the paper is organized as follows. Section 2 gives a overview of our system. Section 3 describes attention analysis based feature filtration in detail. Spatial re-ranking is discussed in Section 4, and Section 5 concludes this paper.

2 Overview of the object-based image retrieval system

As the system flow chart showed in figure 1, after local affine covariant patches are detected, attention-based filtration select informative patches from them. Then Bag of words model is used to obtain the candidate image set and greatly reduce the number of images that need to be considered. It is can be efficiently implemented as an inverted file data-structure. Finally, we use spatial configuration model to re-rank the candidate image set, and improve the primary retrieval precision. Following (K.Mikolajczyk et al, 2005), we use MS (Matas, 2002) algorithm as region detector and SIFT (Lowe, 2004) to describe the regions.

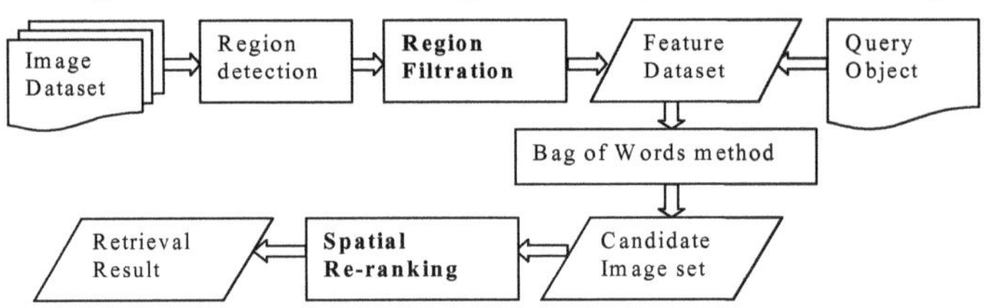

Figure 1. The flow chart of our OBIR system.

3 Attention analysis based region filtration

Although MS region detection algorithm can deal with various image affine transformation, it often generates a large number of patches which only a few of them are distinguishable, so informative patches need to be picked out through a sea of background patches. "Background patches" we mentioned here includes two kinds of patches: one kind comes from background rather than the salient region of the image; the other has little distinctive information thus can be found in both foreground object and background. Consequently, this section focuses on the above problem and proposes a novel method to filter these affine covariant regions based on attention model and local entropy.

Our contribution lies in proposing a novel method which is well-suited to filter MS patches based on attention model and local entropy. Using attention analysis and local entropy, all patches detected in an image are ranked with its saliency, and only the most distinctive patches will be reserved. In this way, the local patch information and global image distribution are both taken into account, and the background patches can be removed effectively.

3.1 Attention model and saliency region

Attention is at the nexus between cognition and perception. While interpreting a complex scene, a human being selects a subset of the available sensory information before further processing. This region is so-called "focus of attention" (Tsotsos *et al*, 1995). (Itti *et al*, 2001) proposed a saliency-based attention model for scene analysis. In his work, a "saliency map" is generated in a bottom-up manner as a combination of these feature maps. Recently, fuzzy growing (Ma *et al*, 2003) is proposed to find all of the saliency regions for original image. Considering the calculation complexity, the number of saliency regions per image is limited to 3. Figure 2 gives an example in practical application.

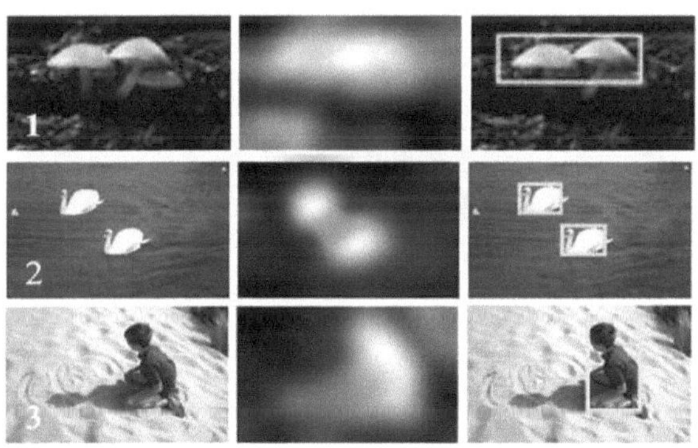

(a) (b) (c)

Figure 2. Samples of saliency regions detection. (a) original images, col. (b) attention model based saliency map, col. (c) saliency regions (as figured out by yellow rectangles), col.

Given a patch X lies in any saliency regions and its grey level distribution $D = \{ d_1 \ldots\ldots d_r \}$, local entropy is defined as:

$$H_X = -\sum_{i=1}^{r} p(d_i) * \log_2 p(d_i) \tag{1}$$

Where $p(d_i)$ is the probability of pixel taking the value d_i in patch X. Informative patches often have large entropy, so we remove those patches whose entropy is less than threshold $Entropy_{low}$.

As to the patches from trees or grass which have complex texture, because they have similar intensity distribution over large ranges of scale, we use self-similarity to remove them. For simplicity the sum of absolute difference of several grey-level histograms is defined as self-similarity.

$$SS_X = \int_{i \in D} \left| \frac{\partial}{\partial s} p_D(s, X) \right| di \tag{2}$$

To prevent deleting informative patches by mistake, we use dual threshold method. Only those patch whose self-similarity is smaller than $SelfSimilarity_{low}$ and local entropy is also smaller than $Entropy_{high}$ will be removed. The proper values of these thresholds are discussed in section 3.3.

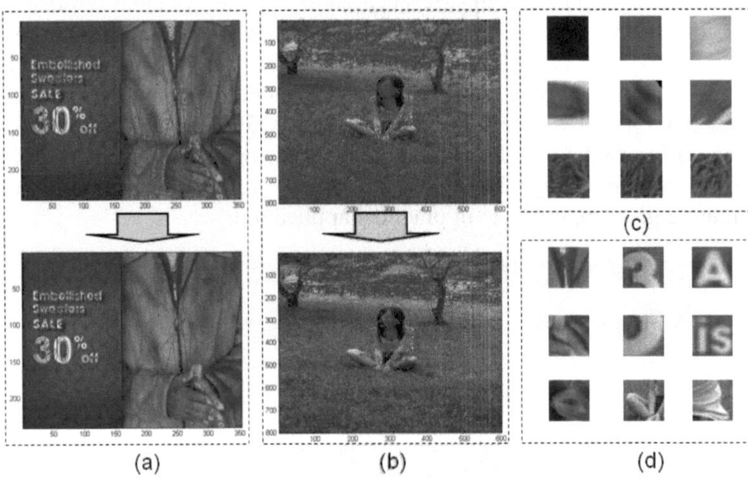

Figure 3. Samples of region filtration. (a) (b) Result comparison of region filtration.(c) Samples of removed background patches. (d) Samples of reserved patches.

3.2 Result on region filtrations

In this sub-section, the experimental result of patch filtration is discussed in detail. The image dataset used here are keyframes extracted from TRECVID 2005 news video retrieval database. Out of which 3000 images are selected. According to the objects they contain, these images are divided into 50 categories. The number of relevant images in each class ranges from about 20 to about 50 images, while the rest are thought to be disturbances. All the subsequent experiments are based on MS region and SIFT descriptors.

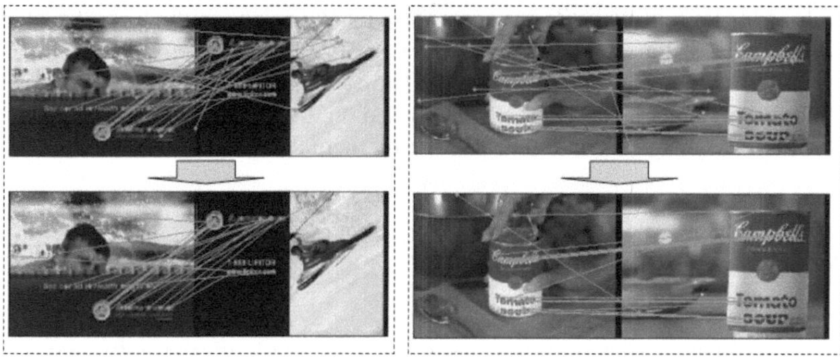

Figure 4. Examples for improved matching precision based on region filtration.

To measure the efficiency of patch filtration in section 3.2, we adopt exact point-to-point matching with SIFT in this sub-section. As shown in Figure 4, most of the false matching due to background patches are removed correctly.

There are 3 thresholds in our filtration process, among which $Entropy_{low}$ influences the performance mostly. So we test its influence in a sample image set including 200 images and about 28k patches are extracted, while we define $SelfSimilarity_{low}$=0.5 and $Entropy_{high}$=3.0. The influence on patches quantity and matching precision (the ratio of correct matching and all matching pairs found in each image) are shown separately in table 1 and Figure 5. We can see that when $Entropy_{low}$=2.0, the best balance can be achieved, while a lot of redundant patches can be removed correctly, and matching precision would be guaranteed at the same time. Accordingly, these filtration thresholds are adopted throughout our subsequent experiment.

Table 1. *Comparison of patches quantity*

$Entropy_{low}$	Delete amount	Delete ratio
1.0	589	2.1%
1.5	2407	7.3%
2.0	3786	13.5%
2.5	5076	18.1%

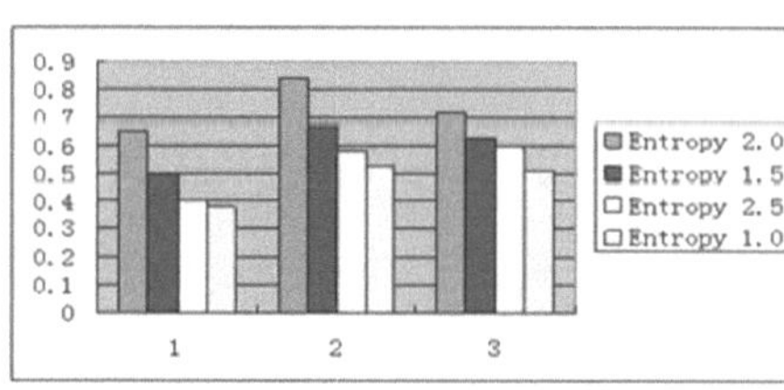

Figure 5. Comparison of matching precision

4 Spatial configuration model based re-ranking

Although region filtration can effectively remove a lot of background patches, the result of object retrieval still has some false matching due to the lack of spatial relation of these patches. In our system, we solve this problem with a novel method called spatial configuration model. The idea is implemented here by first retrieving query object using BoW method based on the selected regions, to obtain a small candidate image set, and then re-ranking them using the spatial model.

4.1 Spatial configuration model

The key issues of spatial re-ranking are spatial configuration definition and similarity measurement based on it. The following sub-sections describe our spatial configuration model in detail.

4.1.1 Spatial configuration definition

(J.Sivic, 2003; J.Phibin, 2007) defined the spatial configuration by the 15 nearest neighbours of each match using L2 distance (called L2-KNN method), and each patch which also matches with this area casts a vote for that matched patch. This definition doesn't consider the affine transformation of different images, and can't obtain the same spatial neighbouring area exactly. Here we define an affine covariant spatial configuration called Affine-KNN. According to the ellipse's parameter of central patch, those patches which lie in K (the experiential K in our system is 3) times the ellipse area are considered the spatial neighbours of this central patch. For example in figure 6(a), after affine transformation, L2-KNN mistakes the original neighbouring patch "b,c" for "d,e"(denoted with dashed circle), while our Affine-KNN method retains the original patch set exactly.

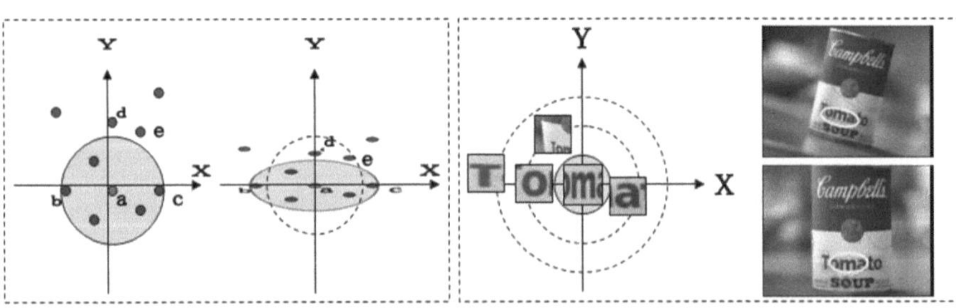

(a) (b)

Figure 6. Spatial configuration definition. (a) Comparison of L2-KNN and Affine-KNN. (b)Example of normalized Affine-KNN spatial configuration in real image .

4.1.2 Spatial configuration similarity measurement

Based on the definition, configurations of a pair of matched patch i, j can be recorded as two patch sets: $S1 = \{c_{11}, c_{12}, ..., c_{1m}\}, S2 = \{c_{21}, c_{22}, ..., c_{2n}\}$,where c_{ij} is the visual word each neighbouring patch belonging to, and m,n denote the number of patches in each spatial configuration set. Note here the set also contains the information of which spatial level the visual word belongs to (level is between 1,2…K). The size of spatial configuration set often varies due to different image scale. For instance, image with small resolution has less detail and generates fewer patches. Consequently, the distance between two spatial configuration sets is measured using the Earth Mover's Distance (EMD) (Rubner *et al*, 1998). Considering that EMD matches perceptual similarity well and can operate on variable-length representations of the distributions, it is suitable for our spatial configuration similarity measure. Based on the spatial configuration definition and similarity measure, we define a pair of patches with spatial configuration similarity more than T_{emd} as "spatial matched patches", and re-rank the candidate image set use these spatial score.

4.2 Result on Spatial re-ranking

To evaluate the effectiveness of our spatial re-ranking method in object retrieval, 20 categories are selected as query images in the image dataset mentioned above which includes about 3000 images, and the number of relevant images in each class ranges from about 20 to 50.

Some examples for object retrieval result are shown as Figure. 7, where query objects are demarcated using yellow rectangle in the left query images. The top 5 images of retrieval result are shown with descending object's similarities. We calculate the time used to retrieve the top 20 relevant images to each query object. Using a 3.2G Pentium 4 PC with 1.5G memory, the average retrieval time for each query ranges from 0.11 second to 1.83 second depending on the number of visual words in the query object.

Figure 7. Examples for object retrieval result.

We compare our spatial configuration model based approach (called SCM) with J.Sivic's method (called L2-KNN) and No-spatial result (BoW without spatial information). The effectiveness of each approach is judged by a score as Q.F.Zheng's method, which is defined as follows:

$$Score(I_1,\ldots,I_{20}) = \sum_{i=1}^{20} w_i X_i \tag{3}$$

$$w_i = \begin{cases} 2.0 & 1 \le i \le 5 \\ 1.5 & 6 \le i \le 10 \\ 1.0 & 11 \le i \le 15 \\ 0.5 & 16 \le i \le 20 \end{cases} \quad \text{and } X_i = \begin{cases} 1, & I_i \text{ contains query object} \\ 0, & I_i \text{ contains no query object} \end{cases} \tag{4}$$

Where Ii is the top i-th retrieved image to a query object, and the weight wi is defined as (4). The average retrieval performances of 20 classed of the three approaches are plotted in Figure 8. As shown below, our SCM-based method generally outperforms L2-KNN based approach, and both of them are much better than visual word-based approach without spatial information. We attribute this to that spatial configuration model contains abundant spatial information between patches, and EMD-based similarity measurement is more suitable than simple voting method. However, compare the best class "News" with the worst class "man", we can find that our method is more adopted for dense patch images such as "News" which including many distinctive and adjacent patch pairs, while in "man" there are few distinctive patches and they are often far from each other.

5 Conclusions and future work

We have presented an approach based on attention analysis and spatial re-ranking for object retrieval. In this system, a novel framework is proposed, and attention model is used to filter those background patches. Furthermore, The spatial relations of adjacent patches are described exactly and measured with EMD distance. Based on this, we use re-rank the BoW result with this information. Experimental result demonstrates that our method is efficient and outperforms the state-of-art object retrieval methods. We are currently investigating the extension of our proposed framework in the following aspects such as the amalgamation of more types of features and the use of relevant feedback.

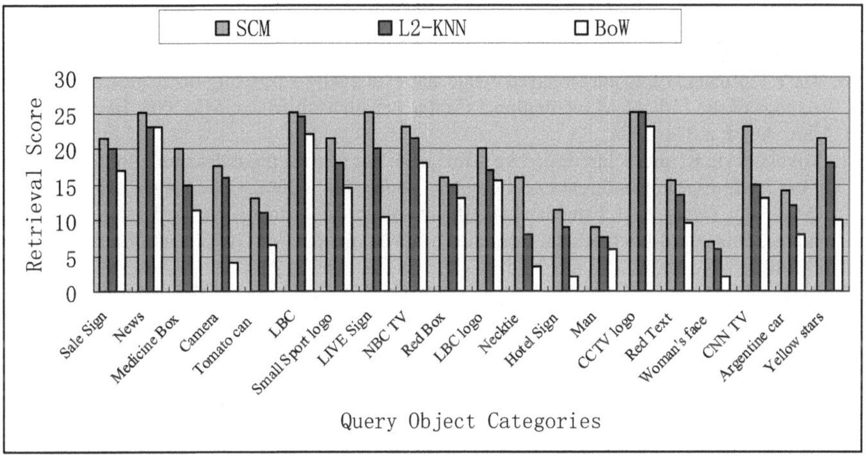

Figure 8. Average retrieval precision comparison.

6 Acknowledgements

This work was supported in part by the National High Technology and Research Development Program of China (863 Program, 2007AA01Z416) and the National Basic Research Program of China (973 Program, 2007CB311100), the National Nature Science Foundation of China (60773056), the Beijing New Star Project on Science & Technology (2007B071).

7 References

1. C. Carson, et al. Blobworld: A System for Region-based Image Indexing and Retrieval, In 3rd Int. Conf. on Visual Information Systems, 1999, Amsterdam, p. 509-516.
2. Itti L, Gold C, Koch C, Visual attention and target detection in cluttered natural scenes. Optical Engineering, 2001, Vol 40(9), p.1784-1793.
3. J. K. Tsotsos, S. M. Culhane, W.Y.K. Wai, et al, Modeling visual attention via selective tuning, Artificial Intelligence, 1995, p.507-545.
4. Jams Phibin, Ondrej Chum, Michael Isard, et al. Object retrieval with large vocabularies and fast spatial matching, IEEE Conference on Computer Vision and Pattern Recognition, CVPR2007.
5. J.Sivic, A.Zisserman. Video Google: A Text Retrieval Approach to Object Matching in Videos, International Conference on Computer Vision, ICCV2003, p.1470-1477.
6. J.Matas, O. Chum, M. Urban, and T. Pajdla. Robust wide baseline stereo from maximally stable extremal regions, British Machine Vision Conference, BMVC2002, p384-393.
7. K.Mikolajczyk, T. Tuytelaars, et al. A comparison of affine region detectors, International Journal on Computer Vision, IJCV2006, p. 43-72
8. K.Mikolajczyk, C. chmid. A performance evaluation of local descriptors. IEEE Transaction on Pattern Analysis and Machine lntelligence, PAMI2005, p.615-1630.
9. Lowe, D. Distinctive image features from scale-invariant keypoints, International Journal on Computer Vision, IJCV2004, Vol 60(2), p.91–110.
10. Ma Y F, Zhang H J, Contrast-based image attention analysis by using fuzzy growing. Proceedings of the 11th ACM International Conference on Multimedia, MM2003. Berkeley, CA, USA: ACM, p.374 – 381.
11. Mikolajczyk, K. and Schmid, C. "An affine invariant interest point detector", In Proceedings of the 7th European Conference on Computer Vision, ICCV2002, Copenhagen, Denmark.
12. Qing-Fang Zheng, et al. Effective and efficient object-based image retrieval using visual phrases, 14th ACM International Conference on Multimedia, MM2006, Santa Barbara, USA, p.77-80.
13. Rubner, Y., Tomasi, C., and Guibas, L., A Metric for Distributions with Applications to Image Databases. Proceedings of the IEEE International Conference on Computer Vision, ICCV1998.
14. S. Lazebnik, C. Schmid, and J. Ponce. Beyond bags of features: Spatial pyramid matching for recognizing natural scene categories, IEEE Conference on Computer Vision and Pattern Recognition, CVPR 2006.
15. Timor Kadir, Michael Brady. Saliency, Scale and Image Description, International Journal of Computer Vision, IJCV2001. Vol45 (2), p.83-105.
16. Wang, J. Z., Li, J., and Wiederhold, G., SIMPLIcity: Semantics-sensitive Integrated Matching for Picture Libraries, IEEE Transactions on Pattern Analysis and Machine Intelligence, PAMI2001, vol. 23.

Forecasting Stock Exchange Movements Using Artificial Neural Network Models and Hybrid Models

Erkam GÜREŞEN and Gülgün KAYAKUTLU

Istanbul Technical University, Department of Industrial Engineering,

Maçka, 34367 Istanbul, Turkey.

erkamguresen@gmail.com

kayakutlu@itu.edu.tr

Abstract: Forecasting stock exchange rates is an important financial problem that is receiving increasing attention. During the last few years, a number of neural network models and hybrid models have been proposed for obtaining accurate prediction results, in an attempt to outperform the traditional linear and nonlinear approaches. This paper evaluates the effectiveness of neural network models; recurrent neural network (RNN), dynamic artificial neural network (DAN2) and the hybrid neural networks which use generalized autoregressive conditional heteroscedasticity (GARCH) and exponential generalized autoregressive conditional heteroscedasticity (EGARCH) to extract new input variables. The comparison for each model is done in two view points: MSE and MAD using real exchange daily rate values of Istanbul Stock Exchange (ISE) index XU10).

1. Introduction

The financial time series models expressed by financial theories have been the basis for forecasting a series of data in the twentieth century. Yet, these theories are not directly applicable to predict the market values which have external impact. The development of multi layer concept allowed ANN (Artificial Neural Networks) to be chosen as a prediction tool besides other methods. Various models have been used by researchers to forecast market value series by using ANN (Artificial Neural Networks). Engle (1982) suggested the ARCH(p) (Autoregressive Conditional Heteroscedasticity) model, Bollerslev (1986) generalized the ARCH model and proposed the GARCH (Generalized ARCH) model. By considering the leverage effect limitation of the GARCH model, the EGARCH (Expo-

---

Please use the following format when citing this chapter:

Güreşen, E. and Kayakutlu, G., 2008, in IFIP International Federation for Information Processing, Volume 288; *Intelligent Information Processing IV*; Zhongzhi Shi, E. Mercier-Laurent, D. Leake; (Boston: Springer), pp. 129–137.

nential GARCH) model was proposed (Nelson 1991). Despite the popularity and implementation of the ANN models in many complex financial markets directly, shortcomings are observed. The noise that caused by changes in market conditions, it is hard to reflect the market variables directly into the models without any assumptions (Roh 2007). During the last few years research is focused on improving the ANN's prediction performance.

The objective of this study is to compare classical ANN models and new ANN methodologies with hybrid ANN models, such as GARCH-ANN and EGARCH-ANN models. The methods are compared by using MSE (Mean Square Error), MAD (Mean Absolute Deviation) and % MAD (Mean Absolute % Deviation).

The remaining sections of this paper are organized as follows: Section 2 provides a brief review of related studies. Section 3 introduces the models used in this study and Section 4 provides results of each model using daily exchange rates of Istanbul Stock Exchange (ISE) index XU100. Final section concludes the study with future researches.

2. Brief review of research on time series

ANN models have been used by researchers. A brief literature survey is given in Table 1. This survey clearly shows that ANN methods outperform the classical methods. Hybrid methods that use both classical methods with ANN have potential to avoid deficiencies in classical methods.

Many researchers pointed that hybrid methods are promising for future studies and with using hybrid methods advantages of each method can combine.

Table 1. Financial Time Series Researches (ANN and Hybrid Models)

Date	Researchers	Used Method	Data Years	Data Type	Goal	Prediction Period	Results
2007	Preminger and Franck	Robust Liner Autoregressive Robust Neural Nertwork	1971-2004	GBP/$ JPY/$	To optain better results than Standart linear autoregressive and Neural Network	1-3-6 months	Robust models are better than standart models but still are not better than RW (Random Walk)
2007	Hamzaçebi and Bayramoğlu	ARIMA ANN	2002-2006	ISE-XU100	To compare ARIMA and ANN	Daily	ANN has better results
2007	Pekkaya and Hamzaçebi	LR (Linear regression) ANN	1999-2006	YTL/USD	To compare the forecasts using macro economic variables	Monthly	ANN gives better results and predicts two important breaking point with 6.611 % error
2007	Roh	ANN,EWMA (Exponentially Weighted Moving Average) GARCH, EGARCH	930 trading days	KOSPI 200	To compare ANN with hybrid models	Daily	Classical ANN outperforms NN-EWMA NN-EGARCH For periods shorter than a month 100 % direction prediction and for periods shorter than 160 days min 50 % direction prediction, NN-GARCH For periods shurter than a month 100 % direction prediction and for periods shorter than 160 days min 50 % direction prediction
2007	Kumar and Ravi	ANN Fuzzy Logic Cased-Based Resoning Decision Trees Rough Sets			Review- Bankruptcy prediction (128 paper)		SVM outperforms logistic regression and BPNN Rough set based Ap. outferforms logistic regression and decision tree Logistic regression, LDA, QDA, FA clearly outperformed by ANN Hybrid methods combine the advantages and promising for future researches
2007	Celik and Karatepe	ANN	1989-2004	Monthly banking sector data series	Crises prediction		Financial ratios successfully predicted for 4 months
2005	Ghiassi, Saidane and Zimbra	ANN, ARIMA DAN2 (Dynamic Architecture for ANN)		Time series used in literature	To compare the methods		DAN2, is an alternative of ANN and gives better result and only needs to choose the inputs
2006	Menezes and Nikolaev	Genetic Programming (GP) Polynomial Genetic Programming (PGP)		Time series used in literature	To compare the methods		The polynomials in time series are found and promising for future researches
2007	Zhang and Wan	Fuzzy Interval NN (FINN)	1998-2001	JPY/USD GBP/USD	Exchange prediction	6 weeks	Promising for future researches
2007	Hassan, Nath and Kirley	Hidden Markov Model (HMM), ANN Genetik Algorithm (GA)	2003-2004	Stocks; Apple Computer Inc., IBM, Dell Inc.	Exchange prediction	5 weeks	Hybrid model is better than HMM and ARIMA
2005	Yümlü, Gürgen and Okay	Mixture of Experts (MoE) MLP RNN EGARCH	1990-2002	ISE XU100 daily values	Exchange prediction & To compare the methods	4 years	MoE outperforms the aother models EGARCH is outperformed by all other methods

3. ANN and Hybrid ANN Models

3.1. Multilayer Perceptron (MLP)

This model uses last four values of a time series as inputs and generated by using NeuroSolutions 5.06 software. MLP has two layers using tanh neurons. The number of neurons in each layer and learning rate are calculated by genetic algorithm using the same software.

3.2. Lagged Time Series (LTS)

This model is generated by using NeuroSolutions 5.06 software to use lagged values of the financial time series. LTS has 2 layers with tanh neurons and each layer have lagged connections. The number of neurons in each layer and learning rate are calculated by genetic algorithm using the same software.

3.3. Recurrent Neural Network (RNN)

This model is generated by using NeuroSolutions 5.06 software to have 2 layers with tanh neurons and each layer consisting of recurrent connections. The number of neurons in each layer and learning rate are calculated by genetic algorithm using the same software.

3.4. Dynamic Architecture for Artificial Neural Networks (DAN2)

This model is developed by Ghiassi and Saidane (Ghiassi and Saidane 2005) and compared with the classical ANN models using a known time series (Ghiassi et al. 2005). Figure 1 shows the structure of DAN2.

DAN2 uses all input data at a time to train the network. Training begins with a special F_0 node captures the linearity using classical linear regression. The training process stops when a desired level of accuracy is reached. Each time a nonlinear relation is hit, a new hidden layer is added. Each hidden layer has 4 nodes: one C node, one CAKE node (in Figure 1, F nodes) and two CURNOLE nodes (in Figure 1, G and H nodes). A CAKE (Current Accumulated Knowledge Element) node captures the previous layers using the CAKE node at the previous layer.

With a linear combination of CURNOLE (Current Residual Nonlinear Element) nodes, C node and previous CAKE node, existing CAKE node provides the results. Until the desired level of accuracy reached new hidden layers continue to be added to the model. After the special linear layer (F_0) DAN2 uses α_i's where α_i is the angle between the observation vector *i* and a defined reference vector. DAN2 uses the trigonometric transfer functions to capture the nonlinearity. Each *G* and *H* nodes at layer *k* uses the given formula:

$$G_k(X_i) = \text{Cosine}(\mu_i \times \alpha_i)\ ,\ H_k(X_i) = \text{Sine}(\mu_i \times \alpha_i) \qquad [1]$$

Using the given formula of $G_k(X_i)$ and $H_k(X_i)$ we can use the following formula for F nodes:

$$F_k(X_i) = a_k + b_k\, F_{k-1}(X_i) + c_k \text{Cosine}(\mu_i \times \alpha_i) + d_k \text{Sinse}(\mu_i \times \alpha_i) \qquad [2]$$

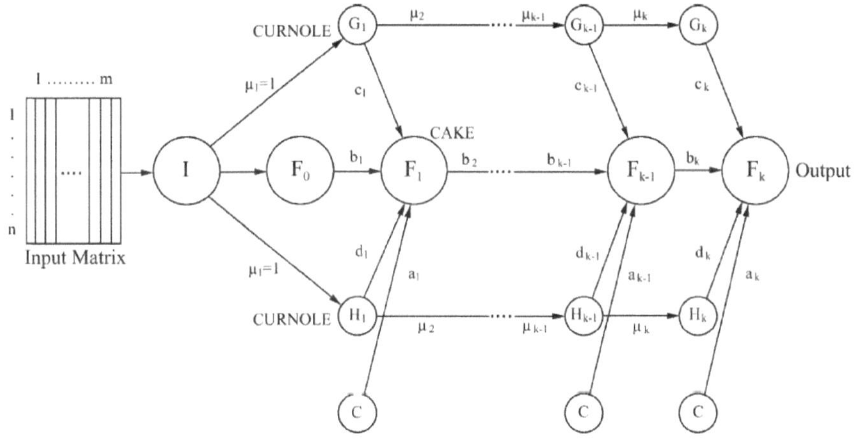

Fig. 1. The DAN2 Network Architecture (Ghiassi and Saidane 2005)

3.5. GARCH - ANN Models

Most of the financial series models are known to be easily modelled by GARCH(1,1), so this research uses the extracted variables from GARCH(1,1) as Roh suggests (Roh 2007). The GARCH(1,1) has the following formula:

$$\sigma_t^2 = \alpha_0 + \alpha_1 \varepsilon_{t-1}^2 + \beta_1 \sigma_{t-1}^2 \qquad [3]$$

Where σ_t is volatility at t, α_0 is the non-conditional volatility coefficient, ε_{t-1}^2 residual at $t-1$, σ_{t-1}^2 is the variance at $t-1$.

The newly extracted variables are as follows (Roh 2007):

- $\sigma_t^{2'} = \beta_1 \sigma_{t-1}^2$
- $\varepsilon_{t-1}^{2'} = \alpha_1 \varepsilon_{t-1}^2$

We use these new variables as additional inputs for every type of ANN given above.

3.6. EGARCH - ANN Models

EGARCH has the leverage effect with the following formula:

$$\ln \sigma_t^2 = \alpha + \beta \ln \sigma_{t-1}^2 + \gamma \left(\left| \frac{\varepsilon_{t-1}}{\sigma_{t-1}} - \sqrt{\frac{2}{\pi}} \right| \right) + \omega \left(\frac{\varepsilon_{t-1}}{\sigma_{t-1}} \right) \qquad [4]$$

Where α is the non-conditional variance coefficient, $\ln \sigma_t^2$ is the log value of variance at $t-1$, $(| \varepsilon_{t-1}/\sigma_{t-1} - \sqrt{(2/\pi)} |)$ is the asymmetric shock by leverage effect, and $(\varepsilon_{t-1}/\sigma_{t-1})$ is the leverage effect. The newly extracted variables are as follows (Roh 2007):

- $\ln \sigma_t^{2'} = \beta \ln \sigma_{t-1}^2$
- LE (leverage effect) $= \gamma(| \varepsilon_{t-1}/\sigma_{t-1} - \sqrt{(2/\pi)} |)$
- L(leverage) $= \omega(\varepsilon_{t-1}/\sigma_{t-1})$

4. Forecasting ISE XU100 Index

In this research daily stock exchange rates of ISE index XU100 from January 2003 to March 2008 are used. Graph of the data is given in figure 2. First 1132 days are used for training and cross validation and last 160 used for testing. For hybrid models also new variables extracted from GARCH and EGARCH are calculated using MS Excel. For MLP, LTS, RNN, GARCH-MLP, GARCH-LTS, GARCH-RNN, EGARCH-MLP, EGARCH-LTS and EGARCH-RNN NeuroSolutions 5.06 software is used. For calculating DAN2, GARCH-DAN2 and EGARCH-DAN2 MS Excel is used. Results are given in table 2. GARCH-DAN2 have the smallest training MSE and MAD, followed by EGARCH-DAN2 and DAN2. In all the other hybrid models, training MSE and MAD values are increased. However, GARCH-DAN2 and EGARCH-DAN2 have smaller training MSE and MAD, DAN2 has smaller testing MSE and MAD. DAN2 based neural networks outperformed the other neural networks. Hybrid RNN models decrease the training error but increase the testing errors.

Fig. 2. ISE XU100 closing values from January 2003 to March 2008

Table 2. Results of ANN and Hybrid Models

	Training			**Test**		
	MSE	**MAD**	**MAD %**	**MSE**	**MAD**	**MAD %**
MLP	332,121.4	431.074	2.02378	5,540,545.9	2,042.031	3.87061
LTS	4,040,290.2	1,270.136	8.091805	4,053,666.2	3,114.716	6.021672
RNN	2,215,589.2	1,073.526	6.182388	30,728,867.0	4,748.948	8.847816
DAN2	262,130.4	370.661	1.408297	1,176,015.7	840.700	1.679289
GARCH-MLP	468,823.2	514.225	2.627341	7,124,780.4	2,317.443	4.38835
EGARCH-MLP	450,787.2	512.206	2.705861	8,651,756.5	2,547.234	4.797743
GARCH-LTS	4,793,112.9	1,344.516	7.021188	82,679,183.4	8,259.680	15.56614
EGARCH-LTS	7,268,783.3	1,771.432	9.802969	86,388,074.0	8,383.227	15.77058
GARCH-RNN	1,588,036.6	839.538	4.413098	40,952,240.9	5,621.619	10.52457
EGARCH-RNN	2,331,406.0	806.284	4.545228	46,952,272.1	5,970.485	11.15228
GARCH-DAN2	261,378.6	370.218	1.4039	1,178,820.5	842.373	1.682031
EGARCH-DAN2	261,918.2	370.416	1.405955	1,177,072.3	841.188	1.680164

5. Conclusion

This study is in search for reducing the shortcomings of using ANN in predicting the market values. With this aim Hybrid models are developed and investigated. In order to present the differences in accuracy of prediction, all the models are applied on the same set of data retrieved from Istanbul Stock exchange.

This study shows that DAN2 is powerful neural network architecture. Hybrid models using GARCH and EGARCH can decrease the training error but do not guarantee a decrease in testing errors. The lowest error is achieved by DAN2 based hybrid model, which also shows that DAN2 has greater noise tolerance.

The achieved results indicate that DAN2 model is to be focused in the future studies to improve the noise tolerance. More attention is to be given to the hybrid models in defining the hybridization procedure clearly.

References

1. Bollerslev, T., "Generalized autoregressive conditional heteroscedasticity", Journal of Econometrics, vol 31, 1986, p. 307-327.
2. Celik A. E., Karatepe Y., "Evaluating and forecasting banking crises through neural network models: An application for Turkish banking sector", Expert systems with Applications, vol. 33, 2007, p. 809-815.
3. Engle R. F., "Autoregressive conditional heteroscedasticity with estimator of variance of United Kingdom inflation", Econometrica, 1982, 50(4), p. 987-1008.
4. Ghiassi M., Saidane H., "A dynamic architecture for artificial neural networks", Neurocomputing, vol. 63, 2005, p. 397-413.
5. Ghiassi M., Saidane H., Zimbra D.K., "A dynamic artificial neural network model for forecasting time series events", International Journal of Forecasting, vol. 21, 2005, p. 341-362.
6. Hassan M. R., Nath B., Kirley M., "A fusion model of HMM,ANN and GA for stock market forecasting", Expert Systems with Applications, vol. 33, 2007, p. 171-180.
7. Kumar P. R., Ravi V., "Bankruptcy prediction in banks and firms via statistical and intelligent techniques – A rewiev", European Journal of Operational Research, vol. 180, 2007, p. 1-28.
8. Menezes L. M., "Forecasting with genetically programmed polynomial neural networks", International Journal of Forecasting, vol. 22, 2006, p. 249-265.

Nelson D. B., "Conditional heterosdasticity in asset returns: a new approach", Econometrica, 1991, 59(2), p. 347-370.

9. Pekkaya M., Hamzaçebi C., "Yapay sinir ağları ile döviz kuru tahmini üzerine bir uygulama", YA/EM 27. National Congress, Izmir 2007, p. 973-978.
10. Preminger A., Raphael F., "Forecasting exchange rates: A robust regression approach", International Journal of Forecasting, vol. 23, 2007, p. 71-84.
11. Roh T. H., "Forecasting the volatility of stock price index", Expert Systems with Applications, vol. 33, 2007, p. 916-922.
12. Zhang Y., Wan X., "Statistical fuzzy interval neural networks for currency exchange rate time series prediction", Applied Soft Computing, vol. 7, 2007, p.1149-1156.

A Robot Emotion Generation Mechanism Based on PAD Emotion Space

Research on Robot Emotion

Gao Qingji*, Wang Kai* and Liu Haijuan**

* Robotics Institute,Civil, Aviation University of China
Tianjin, 300300, China
wangkaiblue@163.com

** Department of Automation, Northeast Dianli University
Jilin, 132012, China
cherygirl0829@yahoo.com.cn

ABSTRACT: A robot emotion generation mechanism is presented in this paper, in which emotion is described in PAD emotion space. In this mechanism, emotion is affected by the robot personality, the robot task and the emotion origin, so the robot emotion will change naturally when it senses the extern stimuli. We also experiment on Fuwa robot, and demonstrate that this mechanism can make the robot's emotion change be more easily accepted by people and is good for human-robot interaction.

KEYWORDS: artificial emotion, emotion space, OCC emotion model

1 Introduction

As the development of cognitive science, neuroscience and psychology, the research results show that emotion plays a crucial role in attention, planning, reasoning and decision-making. It was probably in 1981, that, for the first time, Sloman[7] proposed an idea that "the need to cope with a changing and partly unpredictable world makes it very likely that any intelligent system with multiple motives and limited powers will have emotions". In the society of mind, Minsky [3], noted that "The question is not whether intelligent machines can have any emotions, but whether machines can be intelligent without any emotions".

Robot endowed with emotion can enhance the performance of its behaviour. In recent years, researchers of robotics are being actively conducted to develop robotics that can help a user to do a desired job so as to accommodate the convenience of the user. Special interests are being taken to develop an intelligent robot that can make an intelligent determination through an interaction with a user

Please use the following format when citing this chapter:

Qingji, G., Kai, W. and Haijuan, L., 2008, in IFIP International Federation for Information Processing, Volume 288; *Intelligent Information Processing IV*; Zhongzhi Shi, E. Mercier-Laurent, D. Leake; (Boston: Springer), pp. 138–147.

and can perform a corresponding operation[4]. If robots make decision without emotions, they decide solely using mechanisms based on reason. Examples include planning algorithms and state machines etc.[4], and robot in those mechanisms cannot show its "feeling". As Picard argued[5], emotions influence the decision-making, learning and other cognitive functions of human. So, it is very significant if we equip robots with emotion, and the human-robot interaction (HRI) will be more natural.

Presently, researchers in artificial intelligence have some previous work in emotion robot; however, most of them are still in the phase of research, we cannot directly apply to the real system. The research of artificial emotion can be generalized to three aspects: emotion recognition, emotion expression and the emotion control architecture [6,8,9]; the emotion control architecture is the essential part of artificial emotion, and the emotion generation mechanism is the key of the emotion control architecture. Emotion generation mechanism mainly involves that how the robot's emotion changes when it responds to the environmental stimuli and how the variation of emotion can be easily accepted by human.

There ere several emotion generation mechanisms in this field. According to Picard[5], the affective computing model (it is assumed that the affect equals to the emotion, although there is some difference between them) can be divided into three types: discrete state model, emotion space model and the model based rules. However, the first two types are usually used in the practical system. The OCC model is a typical discrete state model (this model addressed that 22 emotion words related to real interaction), which computes the current emotion based on the event, object, and the agent state. The advantage of the model is that it considered the origin of emotions; The disadvantage of the model is that it can only describe the 22 kinds of emotion and it has the limitation of representing the strength or the intensity of emotion[12]. The computing model of emotion space commonly describes emotion in several abstract dimensions, so emotion can be easily represented in mathematics. The demerit of this model is that origin of emotion is not considered[12]. Wei Zhehua[11] presents a 3D emotion space generated by fear, indignation and relish, and any emotion can be represented in the combination of the 3D above. Broekens J. and D. DeGroot[1] employ the Pleasure-Arousal-Dominance (PAD) three dimensions to quantify emotion.

In order to make robot has an emotion generation method similar to that of human and enhance the flexible behaviour of robot in HRI, a robot emotion generation mechanism is proposed, and the merits of OCC model and PAD emotion space are adopted in this mechanism. The proposed mechanism is also applied in the practical system (Fuwa robot designed for the Beijing 2008 29th Olympic Games, as Fig 1.1) to show the effect of emotion. This paper is organized as follows: section 2 introduces the representation of emotion and personality; Section 3 shows the architecture of emotion generation mechanism; Section 4 shows the experiment with the proposed mechanism, and conclusions are given in Section 5.

Fig 1.1 *robot Jingjing*

2 Related Theory of Artificial Emotion

2.1 Representations of Emotion

It is very critical to define some kind of measures to describe each emotion state in emotion generation mechanism. This paper chooses PAD emotion space designed by Albert Mehrabian (1974) [1]. The PAD scale determines emotions using a three-dimensional emotion space with the axes representing pleasure, arousal, and dominance (with possible values between -1 and 1). Pleasure represents the overall joy of the agent, and arousal represents its desire to interact with the world, and dominance represents its feeling of control in the situation.

This model is selected for two reasons:

1) The PAD three dimensions are nearly orthogonal scales of emotion, and Mehrabian argues that any emotion can be expressed in terms of values on these three dimensions, and provides extensive evidence for this claim.

2) Any two similar types of emotion in PAD emotion space can be differentiated easily, while it is hard in other emotion space.

Mehrabian provides an extensive list of emotional labels for points in the PAD space (Fig 2.1), which gives an impression of the emotional meaning of combinations of pleasure, arousal and dominance.

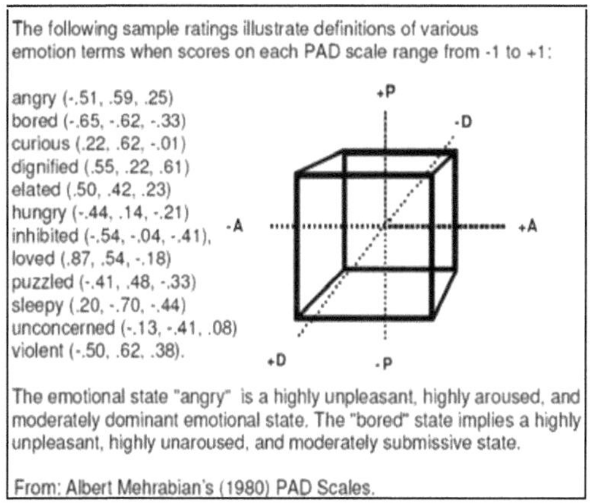

Fig 2.1 *the Mehrabian P-A-D emotion space*

In the PAD space, emotion state at time t can be represented as emotion vector:

$\mathbf{E}_t = (P_t, A_t, D_t)$.

2.2 Description of Personality

The human personality is affected by genetic factor and environmental factor. As a species our brains are almost identical which gives rise to our common sets of behaviours; However, because we are all genetically and environmentally unique, we are all different to varying degrees. It is these differences that give us our unique behavioural variations to common behaviour patterns. This paper assumes that the role of personality is to adjust the effect of the extern stimuli to robot emotion.

There are several methods to describe personality[10]. In fact, The OCEAN (Openness, Conscientiousness, Extraversion, Agreeableness, Neuroticism) 5D model and the EFA（Extroversion, Fear, Aggression）3D model are often used. Each dimension of the two models describes the special nature of personality.

We select the extraversion, neuroticism, and fear three dimensions to describe personality. Each dimension value varies between -1 and 1, and the extent of transfer correlated to the value of the dimension. The robot personality can be represented as follows:

$\mathbf{P} = (E, N, F)$

Let $\Delta\mathbf{E}_t$ is objective change of robot emotion at time t caused by extern event, and after weighted by robot's personality, objective emotion change $\Delta\mathbf{E}_t$ is converted into robot's emotion change $\Delta\mathbf{E}'_t$.Equations (2.1 ~2.3) describe the detail of personality effect.

$$\Delta\mathbf{E}'_t = P_c(\Delta\mathbf{E}_t) \quad (2.1)$$

$$\Delta\mathbf{E}_t = (\Delta P_t, \Delta A_t, \Delta D_t) \quad (2.2)$$

$$\Delta\mathbf{E}'_t = (\Delta P'_t, \Delta A'_t, \Delta D'_t) \quad (2.3)$$

Where P_c stands for the personality transformation, formula (2.4) implements this transformation.

$$P_c(\mathbf{\Delta E}_t)=\begin{bmatrix}1+1/N & 0 & 0\\ 0 & 1+1/N & 0\\ 0 & 0 & 1/F-1\end{bmatrix}\begin{pmatrix}E\\ N\\ F\end{pmatrix}\begin{bmatrix}1 & 0 & 0\\ 0 & 1 & 0\\ 0 & 0 & 1\end{bmatrix}\begin{pmatrix}\Delta P_t\\ \Delta A_t\\ \Delta D_t\end{pmatrix} \qquad (2.4)$$

If let

$$\mathbf{B}=\begin{bmatrix}1+1/N & 0 & 0\\ 0 & 1+1/N & 0\\ 0 & 0 & 1/F-1\end{bmatrix},\quad \mathbf{I}=\begin{bmatrix}1 & 0 & 0\\ 0 & 1 & 0\\ 0 & 0 & 1\end{bmatrix}$$

Formula (2.4) can be simplified as:

$$P_c(\mathbf{\Delta E}_t)=\mathbf{BP}^T\mathbf{I}\Delta E_t^T \qquad (2.5)$$

3 Emotion Generation Mechanism

Different person will give different psychological response, which all attributes to various goals. If extern stimuli are in favor of pursuing the goal, one may response with greeting, admiration or joyness etc. Otherwise, one may response with hatred or distaste.

The explanation for emotion in psychology is that emotions are evaluations for oneself or for the relation status between agents and environment by human body [2]. We integrate the status of robot body and the extern environment. The status of robot body composes of emotion state, personality and basic survival condition. The basic survival condition denotes the amount of robot's energy. Fig 3.1 shows the frame of emotion generation mechanism.

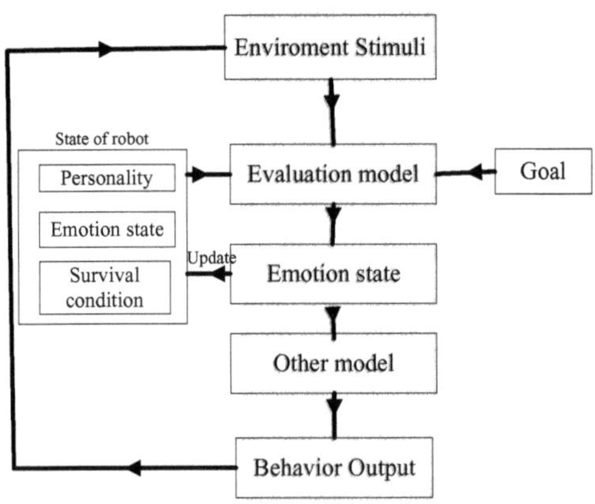

Fig 3.1 the frame of emotion generation system

In Fig 3.1, when robot perceives environmental stimuli, the environmental stimuli are sent to the evaluation model, in which the state of robot body and the goal are also considered at the same time. There is a priority problem between the need of current state of body and the current goal, that is to say, the agent should satisfy the survival condition first, and then finish the goal determined by human. After weighted by the evaluation model, the last emotion is updated by the current emotion. Finally, the output of robot changes the environment. Fig 3.2 illustrates the flow of the evaluation model.

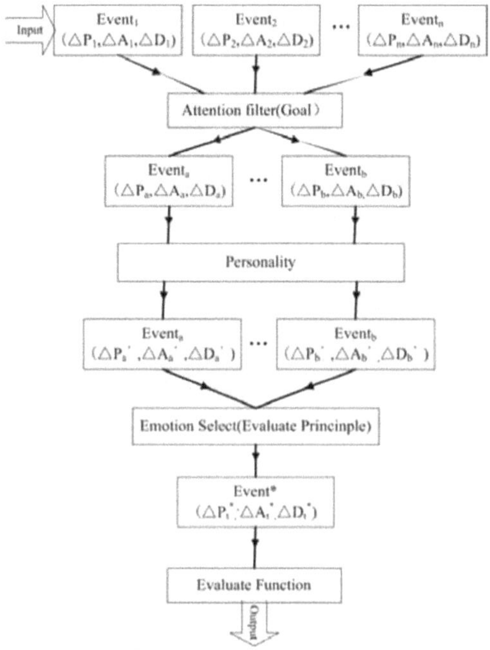

Fig 3.2 *the flow of evaluation model*

As in Fig 3.2, because of the inspiration from the OCC model, the extern stimuli are classified into several events according to the event features. At the beginning, the input events are $Event_1$, $Event_2$, …, $Event_n$, and the map from event to PAD emotion space is $(\Delta P_i, \Delta A_i, \Delta D_i)$, this vector is the objective change of emotion relative to event. The all events after filtered by the attention (decided by its goal), some events may be excluded, and the events reserved are $Event_1$, …, $Event_{n'}$, where $n' \le n$; the objective emotion change caused by these reserved events converted into the robot's subjective emotion change; and then we choose an optimal event based on the value principle as the input of evaluation function. The method here used is described as follows:

$$Event\ * = Event_{\ i} \quad (3.1)$$

$$\mathbf{E}_{t+1} = \mathrm{F}(\psi(\mathbf{E}_t) + \mathbf{\Delta E}_t) \quad (3.2)$$

$$\mathbf{\Delta E}_{\mathrm{t}} = (\Delta \mathrm{P}_{\mathrm{t}}^{*}, \Delta \mathrm{A}_{\mathrm{t}}^{*}, \Delta \mathrm{D}_{\mathrm{t}}^{*}) \quad (3.3)$$

Where $i = \arg\max_{k=1,\dots,n'} (\Delta P_k + \Delta A_k + \Delta D_k)$, $\Delta E_t = (\Delta P_t, \Delta A_t, \Delta D_t)$ is the delta of emotion at time t, ψ is the function that represents how Emotion decays; F is the function that constrains the intensity of emotion between -1and 1.

4 Experiment Result and Analysis

4.1 Introduction of Fuwa Robot

Fuwa robot is an amusement and service robot, which is developed by robotics institute of Civil Aviation University of China. Fuwa robot can be applied in the airport terminal, and the major task is comity and service. Not only has the autonomous navigation function of robot, but also has the following functions: welcoming guests with regards, dialoguing and handshaking with passenger, and performing the special show to the passenger etc.

4.2 Experimental Design

The available sensor information comprises the following three parts: (1) Face detection result through CCD camera image fuses with the result of the infrared sensor, and the finally fusing results judges whether the human exists. (2) The input of ultrasonic, which used to judge whether the obstacle exists in the process of navigation. (3) The input of person's voice signal through the microphone.

The change amount of robot emotion correlated to the various input. If the human do not interact with the robot in the long time, since the robot's drives of own task, the three dimensions of emotion will decrease. When the robot knows a person appearing in its vision, the robot emotion varies in each dimension along with the HRI degree, for instance, the emotion will change if the person says "You are so stupid", The detail of the change shows in Table 4.1.(the communication index denotes the degree of interaction).

Table 4.1.the map from the extern event to emotion change

Event	△P	△A	△D
Person Coming	0.05	0.05	0.05
Person going away	-0.1	0.2	-0.15
Person saying"You are stupid"	-0.15	0.25	-0.25
No person	-0.1	-0.2	-0.1
communication index 1	0.05	0.0	0.05
communication index 2	0.1	0.07	0.08
communication index 3	0.15	0.1	0.12

Considering the robot should handshake with person, the map relationship from PAD emotion space to the action of handshake must be constructed. As the arm of robot with five degree of freedom (DOF), we allows for the two DOF of shoulder and the one DOF of elbow. Let the three angles of the three DOF are α , β , γ individually, and t is the required time of completing the behaviour. The map function described as follows:

$$\alpha = \alpha_{\mathrm{Normal}}(0.5 + e_d) \; ; \; \beta = \beta_{\mathrm{Normal}}(0.5 + e_d)$$

$$\gamma = \gamma_{\mathrm{Normal}}(0.5 + e_d) \; ; \; t = t_{\mathrm{Normal}} \; /(0.5 + e_v)$$

$$e_d = \frac{2P + D}{6} + \frac{1}{2} \; ; \; e_v = \frac{A}{2} + \frac{1}{2}$$

Where α_{Normal}, β_{Normal}, γ_{Normal} are the movement angles of normal state, and t_{Normal} is the required time of finishing the behaviour in normal state. $e_d, e_v \in [0,1]$.

4.3 Experimental Process

In order to affirm the validity of the proposed mechanism, the experiment is performed on the Fuwa robot. The Robot's initial emotion is set at the origin of the emotion space. Robot emotion varies according to the extent of communication. The robot interacts with a participant through speech and handshake. To manifest robot's different emotion, the participant requests to shake hands with the robot and the robot emotion can be showed from the responses.

Fig 4.1 shows the experimental process, when t < 60, robot is in the idle state, and no person appears in its vision. When t = 60, the participant comes to the front of the robot; When 60 < t < 300, due to the communication content is simple, thus, the communication index is high. When t = 240, the participant requests to shake hands with robot for the first time. When 300 < t < 360, the communication index decreases because the communication content becomes complex. When t = 360, the participant says "You are so stupid". When t = 420, the participant requests to shake hands with robot once more. When t = 480, The participant goes away. When 480 < t < 600, No person communicates with the robot. When t = 60, we end the experiment.

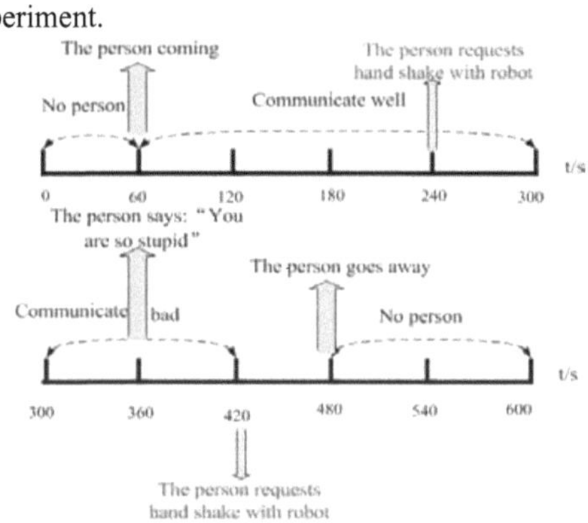

Fig 4.1 *the experimental process*

Two groups of personality parameter are set separately and are carried on the experiment twice according to the above experimental process.

4.4 Result and Analysis

Since the behaviour of handshake in the two experiments is similar, we only analyze the first experiment (Fig 4.2). The (a) of Fig 4.2 is the scene of the participant shaking hands with robot at the first time, and the (b) of Fig 4.2 is at the second time. Fig 4.3 and Fig 4.4 are emotion various curves with Personality = (0.09, 0.08, 0.06) and Personality = (0.2, -0.5, 0.06) individually.

(a) (b)

Fig 4.2 *the robot shaking hands with human*

As the two pictures of Fig 4.2 show, the angle of handshake in the Figure (a) is smaller than that in the Figure (b), that is because the interaction between robot and the participant is not fluent, therefore the robot displays unhappy emotion to shake hands with the participant.

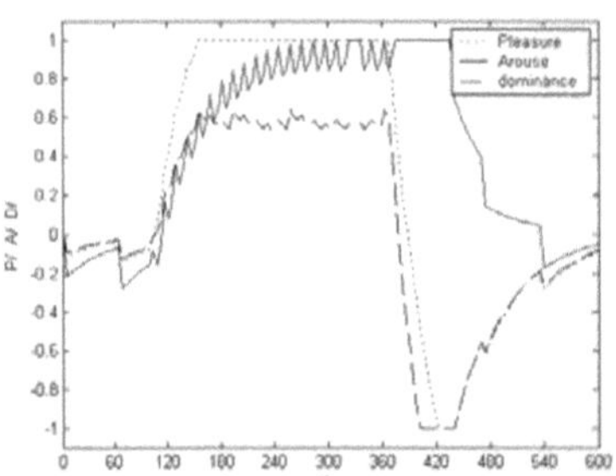

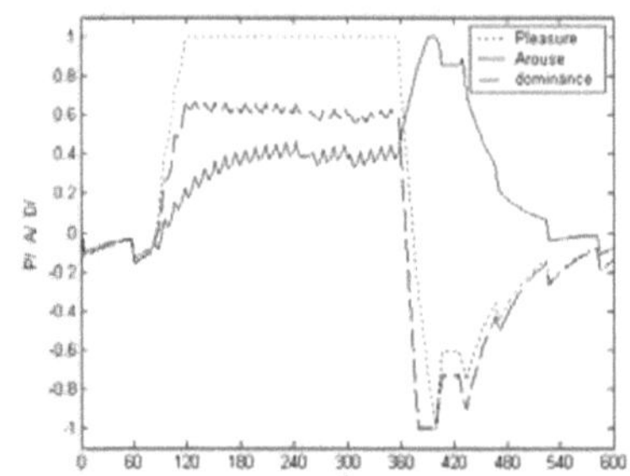

Fig 4.3 *the various curve of emotion 1* **Fig 4.4** *the various curve of emotion 2*

From the Fig 4.3 and Fig 4.4, we can see the tendencies of change are similar due to the same communication process. When $t < 60$, since there is no person interacting with the robot, the three dimensions of emotion began to decrease from the origin. When $60 < t < 300$, although the robot sensed both the coming of person and the existing of obstacle, the robot decided to communicate with the person because the drive of its own task, and then the dimensions of robot emotion start to vary corresponding to the communication index. As the increase of the communication index, the three dimensions of emotion increased too. When $300 < t < 420$, the robot emotion began to maintain invariable due to the decreasing of the communication index. When $t = 360$, after the participant said" You are so stupid", the pleasure curve began to drop, and the dominance curve dropped since the robot was unable to control the situation, but the arouse curve ascend because of the intense stimulation. When $480 < t < 600$, the three dimensions of emotion decayed to zero as the change of time because of the disappearing of the person. Even though the arouse curve had fluctuation, the entire curvilinear trend is reasonable, and may reflect the changing process of robot emotion. Because of the two groups of experiment with different personality, the emotion may be generated positive emotion easily. When $t = 120$, the pleasure curve in Fig 4.4 has reached the maximum, while in the Fig 4.3 the pleasure curve need more time to reach the maximum. When the arouse curve in the Fig 4.4 reaches the peak value, the arouse curve reduces quickly, while in the Fig 4.4 maintains a period of time. The reason is that the neuroticism parameter of personality in the second time is less than the first time. The results suggest that we can change the parameter of personality to generate various emotions.

5 Conclusions

In this paper, a robot emotion generation mechanism is proposed, and emotion is described in PAD emotion space. In this mechanism, emotion is affected by the robot personality, the robot task and the emotion origin. The experiments demonstrate that the robot emotion can be changed naturally when it senses the extern stimuli. This mechanism can be applied in the robot with emotion system, so as to make the robot behaviour more flexible. The robot decision making involved with emotion generation mechanism is the later work.

References

[1]Broekens, J. and D. DeGroot. "Scalable and Flexible Appraisal Models for Virtual gents," CGAIDE, 2004.[11-++1]

[2] JIANG Dao-Ping, BAN Xiao-J uan, YIN Yi –Xin. Research on Emotion Theory and the Decision odels Based on Emotion .COMPUTER SCIENCE. 2007. 34(2)154-157.[8+++2]

[3] Minsky M. The Society of Mind [M], New York, USA:Simon and Schuster, 1986.[2++3]

[4] Park, Cheonshu; Ryu, Jungwoo; Sohn, Joochan; Cho, Hyunkyu; An Emotion Expression System for the Emotional Robot, Consumer Electronics, 2007. ISCE 2007. IEEE International Symposium on Robot and Human Interactive Communication, 20-23 June 2007 Page(s):1 – 6[3+++++4]

[5] Picard R W. Affective Computing [M]. MIT Press, London, England, 1997.[4++5]

[6]Rani, P, Sarkar, N."Making Robots Emotion-Sensitive-Preliminary Experiments and Results," 14th IEEE International Workshop on Robot and Human Interactive Communication - ROMAN 2005[7---6]

[7] Sloman and Croucher, M. "Why Robot Will Have Emotions", In Proceedings IJCAI 1981, Vancouver.[1---7]

[8] SONG Yixu, J IA Peifa, A Control Architecture Based on Artificial Emotion for Anthropomorphic Robot, ROBOT.2004.29(4).491-495[5---8]

[9] WANG Guojiang, WANG Zhiliang,, Survey of Artificial Emotion.Application Research Of Computers .2006(11).7-11[6+++9]

[10] WANG Guo-Jiang,WANG Zhi-Liang,CHEN Feng-Jun .Emotion Model of Interactive Virtual Humans Based on MDP. COMPUTER SCIENCE 2006, 12(33):135-138.[12++10]

[11]Wei Zhehua. Research on Affective Computing of Emotional Robot Based Artificial sychology Theoy. [D].A Dissertation Submitted to Uninersity of Science and Technology Beijing For the Academic Degree of Master of Science, 2002[10++11]

[12]Youngmin Kim, Hyong-Euk Lee.Steward Robot: Emotional Agent for Subtle Human-Robot Interaction. The 15th IEEE International Symposium on Robot and Human Interactive Communication (RO-MAN06), Hatfield, UK, September 6-8, 2006[9++12]

Study of Personalized Network Tutoring System Based on Emotional-cognitive Interaction

Manfei Qi [1], Ding Ma [2] and Wansen Wang [1]

[1]Information Engineering College, Capital Normal University,

Beijing, 100037, China

qimanfei@163.com, wansenw@126.com

[2]Security and Protection Department, Chinese People's Public Security University,

Beijing, 102600，China

mading139@126.com

Abstract: Aiming at emotion deficiency in present Network tutoring system, a lot of negative effects is analyzed and corresponding countermeasures are proposed. The model of Personalized Network tutoring system based on Emotional-cognitive interaction is constructed in the paper. The key techniques of realizing the system such as constructing emotional model and adjusting teaching strategies are also introduced.

Keywords: Personalized Network tutoring system, affective model, cognitive model, teaching strategies

1. Introduction

Network tutoring system uses modern educational technologies to implement an ideal learning environment through integrating the information technology into curriculum, which can embody the learning styles of students' main-body function, reform the traditional teaching structure and the essence of education thoroughly [1].

Although the current Network tutoring system have many merits, many of them only treat the advanced information technology as the simple communication tools, and release some learning contents and exercise in the network [2]. This kind of movable textbook or electronic textbook is indifferent to the learners, which lacks of the interaction of emotion. Thus, some learning problems of the

---

Please use the following format when citing this chapter:

Qi, M., Ma, D. and Wang, W., 2008, in IFIP International Federation for Information Processing, Volume 288; *Intelligent Information Processing IV*; Zhongzhi Shi, E. Mercier-Laurent, D. Leake; (Boston: Springer), pp. 148–154.

learners in the learning process can't be solved and perplexity of the psychology can't get help.

How to measure cognitive emotion of learners in the E-learning system and realize harmonious emotion interaction and adjust teaching strategies becomes an important research topic in the distance education [3] .In this paper, facial expression recognition is used to construct affective model and calculation of cognitive ability is used to construct cognitive model. Teaching strategies and learning behaviors are adjusted according to learners' emotion state and cognitive ability. Thus, the system based on Emotional- cognitive interaction could help the learners to pleasure study essentially.

2. Personalized Network tutoring system model based on Emotional- cognitive interaction

The model of Personalized Network tutoring system model based on Emotional- cognitive interaction is shown in Figure 1.

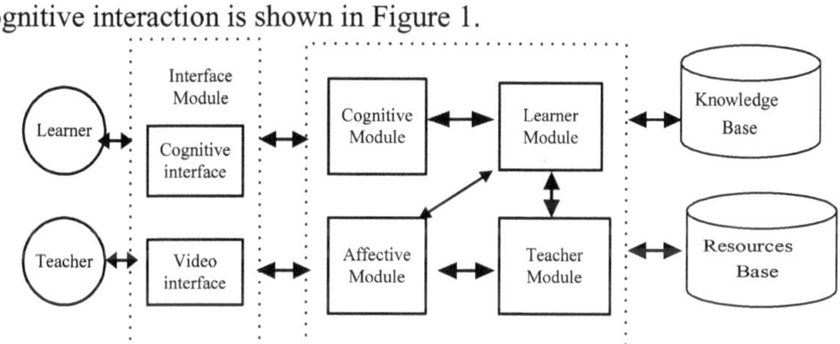

Fig.1 the model of Personalized Network tutoring system based on Emotional- cognitive interaction

The model is composed of six modules as follows:

Interface module: It is interacting interface between Personalized Network tutoring system and learners and teachers.

Learner module: It manages all important information about the learners in the learning process. Such as student basic information, personal characteristics, historical behavior, learning aptitudes, test records etc.

Teacher module: It generates teaching strategies, which are adjusted according to the evaluation parameters of cognitive ability and learning records of learner module and provide learners appropriate teaching contents and teaching strategies. Simultaneously, emotional encouragement and compensation is also given.

Affective module: It analyses learner's facial expressions to show they are interested in learning or tired, happy or distressed. According to learners' facial expressions, with the learning mood of psychology research, access to learners 'psychological status, it is the basis for the adjustment of teaching strategies.

Cognitive module: It is module response to the level of knowledge of the students. According to Bloom classification of the target will be divided cognitive ability into remember, understanding, application, analysis, synthesis and evaluation of six grades.

Knowledge base: It contains all characteristics of the knowledge to teach, storing information on the topics, tasks, excises, relationships between them, difficulty of each task, etc

3. Implementation of key technologies

3.1. Construction of affective model

There are many types of facial expressions, but emotional teaching, there is absolutely no need to study all the facial expressions, as long as they can seize those main emotion closely related to the learning process can be. The system analyzes the study expression from the following three aspects:

(1) Interest (that means the degree to elude), measured by the area of the face [4]. when the contour of the face detected becomes bigger compared with the normal state, it is suggested that learners are leaning forward during the learning process and are interested in the current subjects; in contrast, when the contour of the face detected becomes smaller, it is suggested that learners are leaning backward during the learning process and are not interested in the current subjects at all.

(2) Excitation (that is concentration), measured by eye spacing [4]. When the eye spacing becomes wider, it is suggested that learners are paying more attention to the current learning contents; in contrast, when the eye spacing becomes less narrow, it is suggested that learners are paying less attention to the current learning contents (tired emotionally).

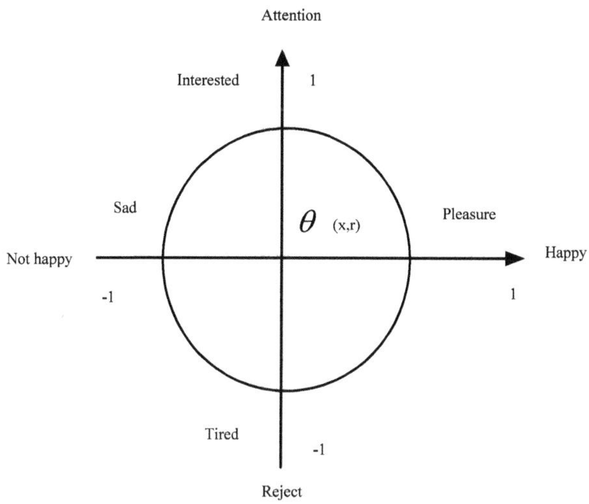

Fig.2 Two dimensional emotional spaces

(3) Happiness (roughly divided into pleasure and distress), measured by facial expressions. When facial expressions appear happy, it is suggested that learners are interested in learning stuff and can master them; when facial expressions appear distressed or confused, it is suggested that learners are not interested in learning stuff and can not master them at all.

According to the three groups of parameters above, we defined two-dimensional emotion space, which are “happy- not happy” dimension and “attention- reject” dimension [5], as shown in figure 2. It contains four basic emotion states such as pleasure, sad, interested, and tired. All normal emotions are represented by a point located in a circle with the radius of 1.Points outside the circle stands for abnormal emotions and the origin stands for calm state. Pleasure and sad are a pair of opposite emotion, which stands for 1 and -1 along the horizontal axis, respectively; interested and tired are a pair of opposite emotion, which stands for 1 and -1 along the horizontal axis, respectively. which

$$r=\sqrt{x^2+y^2}\ ;\quad \theta=\begin{cases}\arccos(\ x/\sqrt{x^2+y^2}),\ \text{if}\ \ y>0\\ \pi+\arccos(\ x/\sqrt{x^2+y^2}),\ \textit{if}\ \ y<0\end{cases}$$

3.2 Calculation of cognitive ability

Learners' cognitive ability scores of each knowledge point are stored in cognitive module. Values of all learners' six cognitive ability are defined as follows matrix.

$$A = |Rij|$$

Cognitive ability also depends on the time spent on learning knowledge point and the difficulty of knowledge point. Every knowledge point is assigned a standard time. Then, the coefficient of learning time can be got by comparing with the standard time. Assume L=S-time/U-time, where S-time stands for standard time and U-time stands for actual learning time. Then, the learning time coefficient T_v is defined as follows:

$$Tv = \begin{cases} 1.1 & \text{if } L \le 0.8 \\ 1 & \text{if } L \in (0.8, 1.2] \\ 0.95 & \text{if } L \in (1.2, 1.4] \\ 0.9 & \text{if } L \in (1.4, 1.6] \\ 0.85 & \text{if } L \in (1.6, 1.8] \\ 0.8 & \text{if } L \in (1.8, 2.0] \\ 0.75 & \text{if } L \in (2.0, 2.4] \\ 0.7 & \text{if } L \in (2.4, 3.0] \\ 0.65 & \text{if } L \in (3.0, 4.0] \\ 0.6 & \text{if } L \ge 4.0 \end{cases}$$

The coefficient between the difficulty of knowledge point and cognitive ability has the following form:

$$Dv = \begin{cases} 1.2 & \textit{difficult} \\ 1 & \textit{common} \\ 0.8 & \textit{easy} \end{cases}$$

Based on all the factors above, the function to measure cognitive ability is:

$$S = (\sum_{\substack{i=1 \\ j=1}}^{n,\sigma} (Rij * Vj * Tv * Dv) / n$$

In the formula above, Vj are weight values of the six cognitive abilities, which are provided by experienced teachers. In this paper they are 0.1 for memory ability, 0.1175 for understanding ability, 0.1625 for application ability, 0.18 for analysis ability, 0.2225 for overall ability, and 0.2175 for evaluation ability [6]. Fuzzy cognitive ability will be grouped into five levels: (Lower, low, average, high, higher), lower, s $\in [0,0.2)$;low ,s $\in [0.2,0.4)$; average ,s $\in [0.4,0.6)$; high ,s $\in [0.6,0.8)$; higher ,s $\in [0.8, 1)$.

3.3 Emotional-cognitive interaction

The relationship between emotion and cognition suggests that positive emotion promote learning and negative emotion prevents learning [7]. The change of learners' emotion is more complex in the learning process. If the learner has an idea to solve this problem, he will pleasure. If the learner is defeated repeatedly, he will suspect himself and changes into the sad state. If learners gaze at indifferent computer screens for a long time, they do not feel the interactive pleasure and understanding the problem, and they may have tired emotion. The system should apperceive this kind of emotional change and carry on emotion intervening, which make him turn to interested state and pay attention to study .Therefore, teaching strategies are adjusted dynamically according to the emotion and cognitive ability. Moreover, appropriate teaching strategies are generated by the inference engine to implement personalized learning. The system uses case-based reasoning (Figure 3).Figure 4 illustrates the process of reasoning in this system.

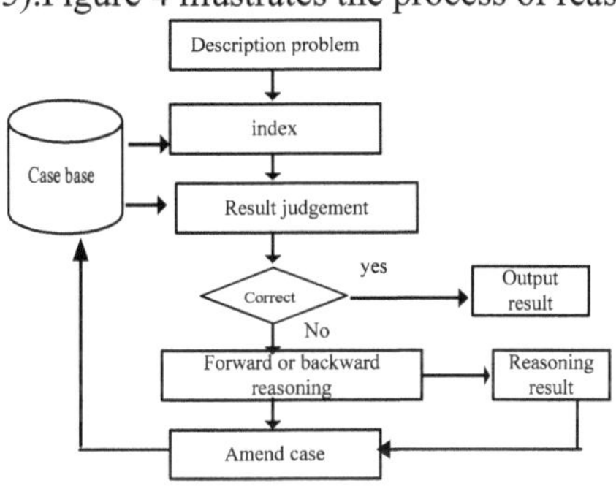

Fig.3 Case-based reasoning

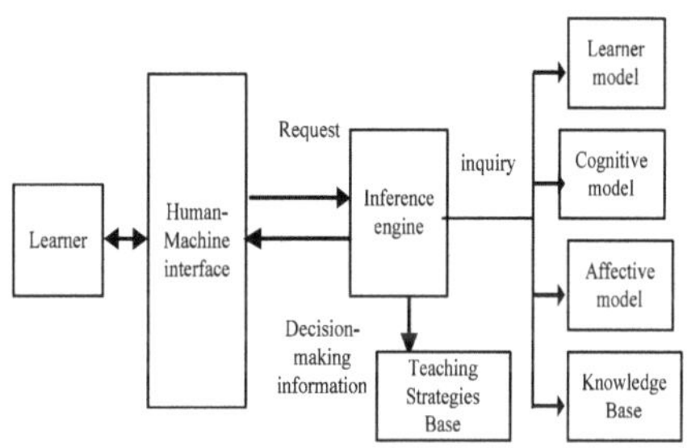

Fig.4 Process of reasoning

After learners enter the learning system, inference engine will inquire their learning history, testing records in the learner model, inquire knowledge point characteristics in the knowledge base, inquire their cognitive ability in cognitive model, and inquire the current emotion state in affective model. After that, the inference engine will compare the inquiry results and the rules in the teaching strategies base, if they are in good match, the operations described in the conclusions will be performed. Teaching strategies are adjusted through production rules:

IF (< premise1>, < premise2> … < premise n>)

THEN (< Conclusion 1 >, < Conclusion 2 > … < Conclusion n >)

For example:

IF (< emotion state= tired> and<cognitive ability=average> and)

THEN (<Entering video learning>)

IF (<emotion state= sad >and< cognitive ability=high>)

THEN (<Entering dynamic interaction learning>)

In the learning process, the teaching strategies are not invariable. When learners' emotion state or cognitive ability changes, the system will analyze the reasons and will generate several teaching strategies. Then, it will choose the strategy that is most suitable for current emotion and knowledge point to learner.

4. Conclusion

This study proposes that Emotional-cognitive interaction is applied in the traditional Network tutoring system. The system based on Emotional-cognitive interaction may solve emotion deficiency in the great degree. The feedback information of facial expression and cognitive ability that is used in adjusting teaching strategies can pro-vide the personalized environment for learners. Based on it, emotion encouragement and compensation are also provided through the analysis of facial recognition. The re-sults obtained in this study demonstrate that emotion recognition in facial is feasible. It have broad prospect in modern education.

Acknowledgements

Project supported by Key science project from Beijing Municipal Commission of Education, that is nature science funded key project of Beijing （KZ200810028016）

References

[1] Kekang. He, "E-learning essence-information technology into curriculum". E-education Research, 2002,vol. 105, no. 1, .3-4.
[2] Jijun. Wang, "Emotion deficiency and compensation in distance learning" Chinese network edu-cation, 2005.
[3] Xirong. Ma, "Research on harmonious man-machine interaction model", Computer science, 2005
[4] Yinggang. Xie, "The Research of Intelligent E-Learning System Based on Artificial Psychology". University of science and Technology Beijing, 2007.
[5] Xiuyan. Meng etal, "Teaching assistant System Based on Affective Modeling", Application Re-search of Computer, 2007, Vol. 24, No. 4, 74-76.
[6] Weiying. Zheng, "Intelligent network tutoring on based personalized", FuDan university, 2006.
[7] Wansen. Wang etal, " Study of Intelligent Network tutoring System based on Artificial Emotion" , MINI-MICROSYSTEM, 2006, vol. 27, no. 3, 569-572

A Novel Fingerprint Matching Method Combining Geometric and Texture Features

Mei Xie, Chengpu Yu and Jin Qi

University of Electronic Science and Technology of China.

Chengdu,P.R.China Post Code:610054

xiemei@ee.uestc.edu.cn

Abstract: In this paper, we proposed a new fingerprint matching algorithm based on local geometric feature of fingerprint minutia and texture feature for each minutia. To describe the geometric feature of fingerprint minutia, we build a bi-minutia based bar model and get the geometric relationship between the bar and ridges of two candidate minutia; to demonstrate the texture feature, we creatively adopt gradient angular histogram in the neighborhood region of minutia. Meanwhile, changeable sized boundary box of unique area adopted for minutia matching make this algorithm more robust to nonlinear fingerprint deformation. Finally, experimental results on the database FVC2004 demonstrate that our method is effective and reliable, whilst the matching accuracy can be improved to some extent after using gradient angular histogram as texture feature without adding extra amount of calculation.

1 Introduction

Automatic fingerprint recognition, which is established in modern information technology, is wildly used to civilian purposes such as access control, financial security, and so on. Fingerprint recognition technology is based on the reality that fingerprint of each person have its uniqueness and unchangeable properties.

Many researchers have made progress in the fingerprint matching algorithms. These algorithms can mainly be divided into several categories as follows: (1) minutia and ridge based method [15]; (2) minutia and texture based method [14]; (3) graph based method [12] [13]; (4) tri-minutia structure based method [7]. All the conspicuous features used in above methods are related and complemented. Taking into account of advantages of above methods, we propose the method based on bi-minutia based bar model, and add texture feature to fingerprint representation to improve the matching efficiency and accurateness.

The algorithm introduced in this paper adopts local geometric feature of mi-

Please use the following format when citing this chapter:

Xie, M., Yu, C. and Qi, J., 2008, in IFIP International Federation for Information Processing, Volume 288; *Intelligent Information Processing IV*; Zhongzhi Shi, E. Mercier-Laurent, D. Leake; (Boston: Springer), pp. 155–164.

nutia and texture feature around minutia. Bi-minutia based bar model used in this method can compromise the deficiency of solo-minutia based and tri-minutia based model, and it can effectively and reliably extract matched minutia pairs. Meanwhile, the gradient angular histogram as texture feature can generally reflect the profile of fingerprint ridge edges and the minutia type (bifurcation or ending).

This paper is organized as follows. Section 2 briefly describes preprocessing of fingerprint image. Section 3 demonstrates local structure and reference minutia selection. Section 4 illustrates fingerprint alignment and global matching. Section 5 shows the experimental results on the database FVC2004. In the end, we draw the conclusion in section 6.

2 Preprocessing of fingerprint image

In this paper, we adopt fingerprint features not only from thinned ridge image, such as minutia position and geometric feature, but also from original gray image, such as gradient angular histogram as texture feature. Since low quality fingerprint image often contains noises and contamination, it requires us to preprocess the image to enhance image. Main steps involved in the preprocessing include fingerprint segmentation, block orientation estimation, image enhancement, image binarization, thinning, and minutia extraction. LinHong [1] introduces the orientation estimation method based on gradient vectors of fingerprint ridges, which could compute directions more accurately in low quality image, see Figure 1(b). Zhu [2] proposes Gabor filtering enhancement method can overcome the deficiency that occurs when using method in LiHong[1], see Figure 1(c). X.P.Luo[3] describes binarization and post processing of fingerprint image with method based on knowledge and method based on combination of statistic and structure, see Figure 1(d).

Fig. 1 Fingerprint preprocessing.(a)An original fingerprint in DB1_Aof FVC2004,(b)its block orientation field,(c)enhanced image,(d) thinned image of fingerprint image

3 Local structure description and reference minutia selection

Minutia features (ending or bifurcation) are salient and stable features for fingerprint image of different discrimination. However, external interference will cause many pseudo minutias and create large error, and using multi-minutia based model can resist interference to some extent.

3.1 Feature description of solo-minutia based model and calculation of gradient angular histogram

Vector set of minutia $M^F = \{M_i^F = (x_i^F, y_i^F, \alpha_i^F, h_{i1}^F \Lambda\ h_{i8}^F);\ |M^F| \geq i \geq 1\}$ denote all comprehensive minutia in the fingerprint. Where $|M^F|$ is the number of minutia in a fingerprint image. M_i^F, the ith minutia, is denoted by a feature vector $x_i^F, y_i^F, \alpha_i^F, h_{i1}^F \Lambda\ h_{i8}^F$. Where

(a) x_i^F, y_i^F denotes its coordinates;

(b) α_i^F denotes the tangent direction of the ridge where the minutia locates;

(c) $h_{i1}^F \Lambda\ h_{i8}^F$ denotes gradient angular histogram in the circular neighborhood region whose radius is r. The algorithm of gradient vector computation [5] has been described in the section of fingerprint orientation field estimation. Then we transform the vector in Euclidean space to the polar coordinates, thus the magnitude and direction can be calculated as follows:

$$\nabla f = mag(\nabla \vec{f}) = [G_x^2 + G_y^2]^{1/2} \tag{6}$$

$$\alpha = \arctan(\frac{G_y}{G_x}) \tag{7}$$

$mag(\bullet)$ *and* ∇f in formula (6) represent magnitude calculation operator and magnitude value respectively. α in formula (7) represents direction of gradient vector, which is perpendicular to the direction of the corresponding image edge.

Gradient angular histogram is considered as texture feature for fingerprint recognition. Utilization of gradient angular histogram in this paper has much preponderance which are showed as follows: 1) it is more stable to the change of illumination, because it extracts the gradient angles of larger gradient magnitude here; 2) it is invariant to scale and displacement of the image; 3) it is invariant to rotation. Here, we define the tangent angle of the ridge where minutia locates as the reference direction.

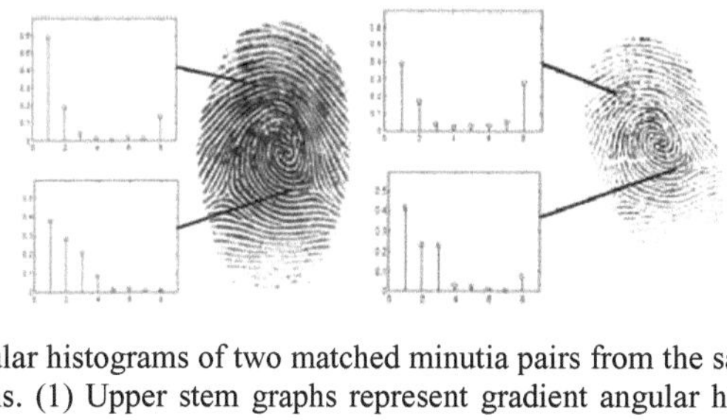

Fig. 2 Gradient angular histograms of two matched minutia pairs from the same fingerprint illustrated as stem graphs. (1) Upper stem graphs represent gradient angular histogram of endings, similarity between them is 0.929; (2) Lower stem graphs illustrate that of bifurcations, similarity between them is 0.975.

Gradient angular histograms of two matched minutia pairs have been demonstrated in Figure 2. In the stem graph, direction 1 and direction 8 are neighborhood. From the gradient angular histogram, we can observe that all the gradient angles concentrate in the region whose center is the direction of ridge where minutia locates. Gradient angular histogram adopted here can reflect the information of minutia type to some extent, and it also can reflect the texture information around the minutia.

3.2 Feature description of bi-minutia based model

Vector set of bi-minutia based model $E^F = \{E_i^F = (p_i^F, q_i^F, l_i^F, c_i^F, \theta_i^F, u_i^F, v_i^F), |E^F| \geq i \geq 1\}$ represents information of all bi-minutia bars, and these features are showed in Figure 3.

(a). $|E^F|$ is the size of bi-minutia bar set.

(b). p_i^F, q_i^F denote the serial numbers in the minutia set M^F. $M_{p_i}^F$ and $M_{q_i}^F$ are two ending minutia of bi-minutia bar E_i^F, and they contain all features listed in the minutia set.

(c). $l_i^F = \|(x_{p_i}^F, y_{p_i}^F) - (x_{q_i}^F, y_{q_i}^F)\|$ denotes the length of bi-minutia bar, and $(x_{p_i}^F, y_{p_i}^F), (x_{q_i}^F, y_{q_i}^F)$ represent coordinates of $M_{p_i}^F$ and $M_{q_i}^F$ respectively. In order to limit the number of bi-minutia bars in a fingerprint image, the length of bi-minutia bars are confined in range $L_l \leq l_i^F \leq L_h$

(d). c_i^F denote the number of fingerprint ridges that bar E_i^F passes through, because there will exist large error if we only calculate Euclidean distance; however, combining c_i^F to Euclidean distance can accurately describe corresponding distance.

(e). $\theta_i^F = \arctan\left(\dfrac{x_{p_i}^F - x_{q_i}^F}{y_{p_i}^F - y_{q_i}^F}\right)$ denotes the direction of bi-minutia bar.

(f). $u_i^F = \min\{|\alpha_{p_i}^F - \theta_{p_i}^F|, \pi - |\alpha_{p_i}^F - \theta_{p_i}^F|\}, v_i^F = \min\{|\alpha_{q_i}^F - \theta_{q_i}^F|, \pi - |\alpha_{q_i}^F - \theta_{q_i}^F|\}$ denote bi-minutia bar's directional deviations from $\alpha_{p_i}^F$ and $\alpha_{q_i}^F$, and this feature have rotation invariant ability..

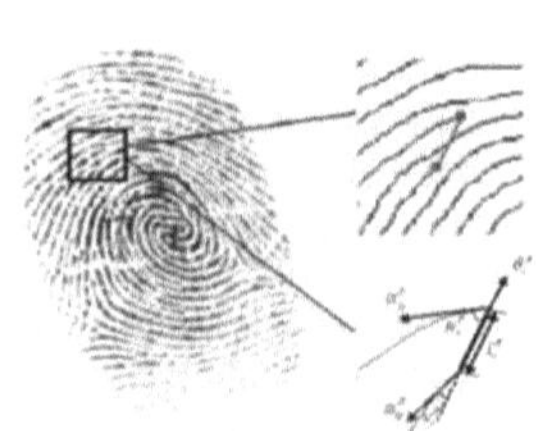

Fig. 3 Demonstration of minutia structure and features in a ridge image

Influenced by the low quality in a fingerprint, minutia extracted might not be so stable, hence we haven't added minutia type as a character in bi-minutia based model [11]. Here, the angular histogram around the minutia as the texture can express the type of minutia.

3.3 Selection of reference minutia pairs for fingerprint matching

As fingerprint image are extracted in the same device, subtle deformation of the fingerprint can be omitted. Solo-minutia based model [6] used in fingerprint matching will generate lots of pseudo matched minutia pairs; tri-minutia based model [7] used in fingerprint matching might have difficulty in looking for entirely matched triangle composed of three minutia, so that we adopt bi-minutia bar based model as the compromise of two above models.

Suppose bi-minutia bar sets E^F and E^G denote fingerprint representation of input and template fingerprints, and matching criteria includes:

(a). Constraint of bar-length: $|l_i^F - l_j^G| \le d_0$, where d_0 usually makes value about half the ridge period in the fingerprint;

(b). Constraint of ridge numbers the bar passes through: $|c_i^F - c_j^G| \le n_0$, where n_0 usually makes value about 1 or 2;

(c). Constraint of directional deviation of ridges and bi-minutia bar: $|u_i^F - u_j^G| \le u_0$ *and* $|v_i^F - v_j^G| \le v_0$, where u_0 and v_0 usually make values lower than $\pi/12$.

(d). Constraint of texture similarity: $s(M_{p_i}^F, M_{p_j}^G) \ge s_0, s(M_{q_i}^F, M_{q_j}^G) \ge s_0$, where s_0 should be larger than 0.9, which is obtained from numerous experiment. The similarity of two vector $s(\vec{h}_i, \vec{h}_j)$ can be estimated as correlation coefficient:

$$s(\vec{h}_i, \vec{h}_j) = \frac{<\vec{h}_i, \vec{h}_j>}{\|\vec{h}_i\|\|\vec{h}_j\|} = \frac{\sum_{k=1}^{L} h_i(k) h_j(k)}{\sqrt{\sum_{k=1}^{L} h_i^2(k)}\sqrt{\sum_{k=1}^{L} h_j^2(k)}} \tag{8}$$

Where $<\bullet>$ denotes inner production operator and $\|\bullet\|$ represents norm operator for a vector.

(e). Determination of two matched minutia pairs from two matched bars:

$$\begin{cases} p_i^F \leftrightarrow p_j^G, q_i^F \leftrightarrow q_j^G & \text{if } |u_i^F - u_j^G| \le u_0 \text{ and } |v_i^F - v_j^G| \le v_0 \\ p_i^F \leftrightarrow q_j^G, q_i^F \leftrightarrow p_j^G & \text{if } |u_i^F - v_j^G| \le u_0 \text{ and } |v_i^F - u_j^G| \le v_0 \end{cases} \tag{9}$$

Minutia pairs satisfying all above conditions may be selected as candidate reference minutia pairs. Through rigid constraints of features derived from local geometric and texture information, matched reference minutia pairs could dramatically decrease.

4 Fingerprint alignment and global matching

Jain[9] demonstrates minutia matching method utilizing polar coordinate system which is scale and rotation invariant. Suppose minutia M_i^F in input fingerprint and minutia M_j^G in template fingerprint are matched reference minutia, and alignment of input fingerprint and template fingerprint is carried out with locomotion and rotation of input fingerprint. Rotate angle of input fingerprint is $\theta^r = \alpha_j^G - \alpha_i^F$, and the coordinate vector of reference minutia is (x^r, y^r). Then, minutia coordinate (x_i, y_j) in Euclidean space can be transformed in to polar coordinate vector as follows:

$$\begin{pmatrix} r_i \\ e_i \\ \theta_i \end{pmatrix} = \begin{pmatrix} \sqrt{(x_i - x^r)^2 + (y_i - y^r)^2} \\ \arctan\left(\dfrac{y_i - y^r}{x_i - x^r}\right) \\ e_i + \theta^r \end{pmatrix} \tag{10}$$

Where (r_i, θ_i) is the final polar coordinate vector.

In order to search matched minutia pairs effectively and to guarantee robust to fingerprint deformation, we propose a changeable sized boundary box of unique area in this paper, because unique area of boundary box allows consistent error tolerance to each minutia. In Euclidean coordinate system, unique area of boundary box can easily be obtained; however, in polar coordinate system, parameters of a boundary box can be determined as follows:

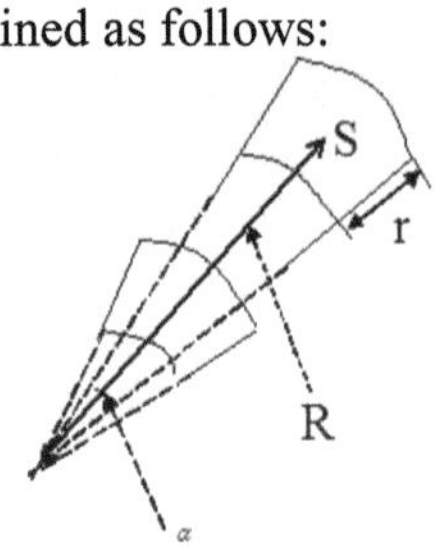

Fig. 4 Demonstration of changeable sized boundary box of unique area

In Figure 4, area of boundary box S is fixed in the experiment, and radius of boundary box r is also fixed in the experiment, then the polar angle of boundary box will decrease when polar radius of the corresponding minutia increases. The polar angle of boundary box can be calculated as follows:

$$\alpha \approx S/(r * R) \tag{11}$$

Where, all parameters in formula (11) are showed in Figure 5.

In order to determine whether two fingerprints are from the same source, we should calculate similarity of all possible minutia pairs in two fingerprints after alignment and compute global similarity of two fingerprints. Conditions that should be satisfied for two matched fingerprints are listed as follows:

a) $\left|\rho_i^F - \rho_j^G\right| \le r/2$ b) $\left|\alpha_i^F - \alpha_j^G\right| \le \alpha/2$

c) $\left|u_i^F - u_j^G\right| \le u_0$ d) $s(M_i^F, M_j^G) \ge s_0$

Where, (a) and (b) are used to test whether two minutia are in the same boundary box or not; (c) is used to test whether two tangent directions of corresponding ridges are consistent; (d) is used to test texture similarity of two minutia regions. Statistic all matched minutia pairs between input and template fingerprints which is marked as N_{match}, and global similarity of two fingerprint can be estimated as follows:

$$r_{match} = \frac{N_{match}}{\min\{N_{input}, N_{template}\}} \tag{12}$$

Where, r_{match} in formula (12) is regarded as minutia matching rate; N_{input} is considered as number of valid minutia in input fingerprint; $N_{template}$ is deemed as number of valid minutia in template fingerprint. Eventually, we could judge two fingerprints are matched if r_{match} is larger than a fixed threshold, and a optimal threshold should be determined in experiments in order to get global optimization to all performance indicators which will be discussed in section 5.

5 Experimental results

5.1 Advantages of gradient angular histogram as texture feature

In this experiment, we choose fingerprint images 1_3.gif and 1_6.gif representing average quality fingerprint and low quality fingerprint respectively from sub-database DB1_A in FVC 2004.

During the process of searching matched bi-minutia bars in this experiment, parameters involved are defined as follows: (1) Euclidean length of bi-minutia bar is confined in range between 5 and 15 times of ridge period, namely [10~80]; (2) Error constraint of bi-minutia bar's Euclidean length $d_0 = 4$; (3) Error constraint of ridges that bi-minutia bar passes through $n_0 = 1$; (4) Directional deviation constraint between ridge and bi-minutia bar of certain minutia $u_0 = v_0 = \pi / 12$; (5) Texture similarity constraint of gradient angular histogram $s_0 = 0.90$;

Table 1. Comparison of candidate reference minutia pairs

Fingerprint	Minutia numbers	Bi-minutia bars	Matched bars (without considering gradient angular histogram)	Matched bars (after utilizing gradient angular histogram)
1_3.gif	62	421	565	57
1_6.gif	37	221	565	57

From TABLE 1, we can observe that candidate reference bi-minutia bars decrease from 565 to 57 after considering constraint of texture similarity of gradient angular histogram, so that the amount of calculation of subsequent global matching will reduce about 9-10 times. Eventually, the ratio of retained candidate reference bi-minutia bars to all involved bars is $\frac{57}{421 \times 221} = 0.06\%$.

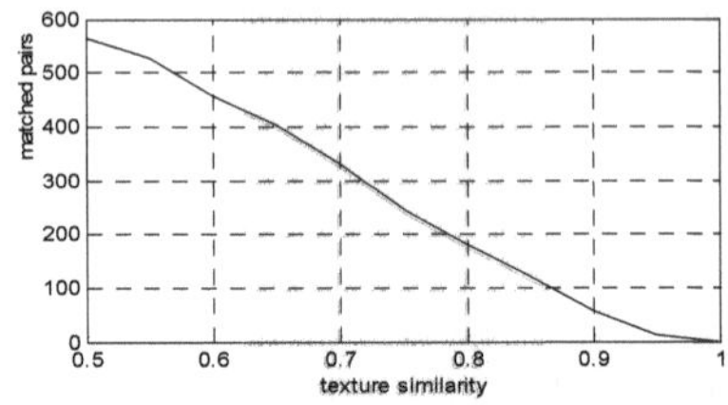

Fig. 5. Curve in the graph represents the number of reference minutia pairs with similarity of gradient angular histogram of images 1_3.gif and 1_6.gif in DB1_A of FVC2004.

From Figure 5, we can observe that matched candidate bi-minutia bars will decrease dramatically when texture similarity as constraint becomes higher. However, the threshold of texture similarity shouldn't be too high from numerous experimental observations. If the threshold of texture similarity is too high, it will omit many genuine and vital bi-minutia bars; inversely, matched bi-minutia bars will increase significantly.

After selecting optimal candidate reference bi-minutia bar, parameters used to statistic global matched minutia are defined as follows: (1) Radius error of boundary box $r = 10$; (2) Polar angular error of boundary box $\alpha = S/(r \times R) = 10/R$; (3) Tangent directional error of two corresponding ridges $u_0 = \pi/12$; (4) Threshold of texture similarity constraint $s_0 = 0.9$.

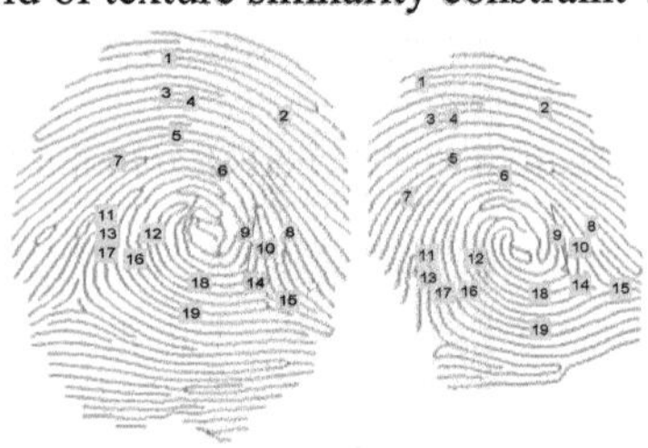

Fig. 6 Matched minutia pairs in two images of the same fingerprint; the red lines in the picture denotes optimal reference bi-minutia bar; the blue numbers in the picture represent corresponding orders of matched minutia pairs. The left is the ridge image of 1_3.gif in DB1_A of FVC2004, while the right is 1_6.gif.

From Figure 6, we can observe that the algorithm proposed in this paper can accurately find reference bi-minutia bar and obtain matched minutia pairs of the whole fingerprint. In this case, it has detected 19 pairs of matched minutia, and smaller minutia set has 37 valid minutia points, thus final minutia matching rate attain 50%.

5.2 Performance of our method on FVC2004

Nowadays, performance indicators of fingerprint matching that are wildly accepted include FNMR, FMR, EER, FNMR100, FNMR1000 and ZeroFMR. All above indicators can be reflected from the ROC curve, whose horizontal axis denotes FMR and vertical axis denotes FMNR.

Every subset in FVC2004 contains 100 fingerprints, and each fingerprint has 8 samples, thus it has 800 fingerprint images in a subset. Experimental data in estimating FNMR has ((8*7) /2) * 100 = 2,800 pairs; and total Experimental data in estimating FMR has ((100*99) /2) = 4,950 pairs when only utilizing the first sample for each fingerprint.

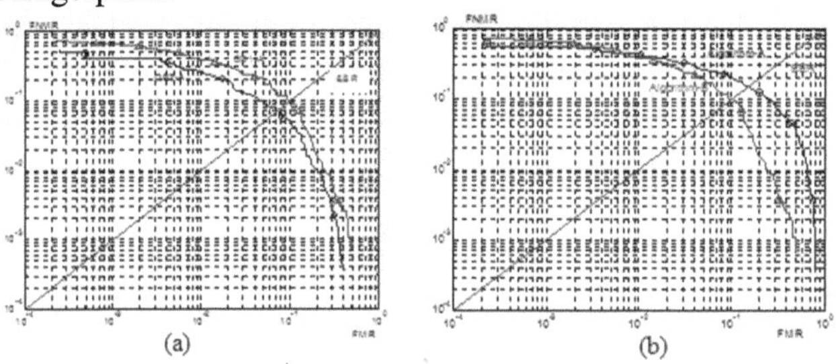

Fig. 7 ROC curves of the experiment results for database FVC2004. (a) Red curve illustrates the experiment results of DB1_A of FVC2004, whilst blue demonstrates DB2_A. (b) Blue curve represents the experiment result of bi-minutia bar model without texture similarity for DB1_A in FVC2004, whilst red represents the experiment result of our method for DB1_A.

From Figure 7(b), we can observe that ROC curve of our method in this paper illustrates better performance than that of method only considering bi-minutia bar model. Moreover, EER is about 10% observed from EER line, which is much lower than method only utilizing bi-minutia bar model whose EER is **15%.**

Table 2. Results of Our New Method over the Two Databases among FVC2004

Database (FVC2004)	EER (%)	FMR100 (%)	FMR1000 (%)	ZeroFMR (%)
DB1_A	9.56	17.2	23.0	37.2
DB2_A	7.46	20.0	25.4	42.0

Observing from TABLE 2, experimental results of the algorithm in this paper are actually close with that of many excellent algorithms [10],[11], which demonstrates robustness and reliance of our method in this paper. Of course, the experimental results will become much better if we have a good performance of fingerprint preprocessing, such as segmentation, enhancement and binarization. Especially, many genuine minutia points will be omitted and pseudo minutia points will be forged if parameters of Gabor filter are not optimal.

6 Conclusions

In this paper, we introduce a novel algorithm of fingerprint matching based on combination of minutia geometric and texture features. We adopt gradient angular histogram as texture feature in this paper, which effectively represents fingerprint information where minutia locate, because it can generally reflect profile of ridge edges and minutia types to some extent. In addition, we adopt bi-minutia bar model [10] as the geometric feature in this paper.

The new texture feature of gradient angular histogram in this paper can guarantee the accuracy of minutia matching of fingerprint; nonetheless, the gradient angular histogram will create deviation for the reason of low quality fingerprint. In the process of global fingerprint matching, using ratio of matched minutia pairs to total minutia can largely measure the similarity of two fingerprints. However, the matching accurateness might be improved if we could measure similarities from diverse aspects of corresponding weights [8].

7 References

[1] Lin Hong, Fingeprint Image Enhancement: Algorithm and Performance Evaluation, IEEE Trans. Pattern Analysis and Machine Intelligence, Vol. 20, No. 8, August 1998.
[2] Zhu En, Automatic fingerprint recognition technology, Publishing House of National University of Technology of Security, May 2006:95-107.
[3] Xiping Luo, Knowledge Based Fingerprint Image Enhancement, 15th ICPR, Vol.4, P783-786.
[4] Jie Tian, Technology of Biometric Feature Recognition and its Application, Publishing House of Electronic Industry, September 2005: 85-97.
[5] Rafael C. Gonzalez, Digital Image Processing (Second Edition), Publishing House of Electronics Industry, July 2005:567-585.
[6] Xiping Luo, A minutia matching algorithm in fingerprint verification, 15th ICPR, Vol.4, pp.833~836, Barcelona, 2000.
[7] Xudong Jiang, Fingerprint minutiae matching based on the local and global structures, IEEE,2000:1042~1045.
[8] MiaoLi Wen, Integration of multiple fingerprint matching algorithms, Proceedings of the Fifth International Conference on Machine Learning and Cybernetics, Dalian, 13-16 August 2006.
[9] A.K.Jain,LinHong,On-line identity authentication system using fingerprints, Proceedings of IEEE, 1997,85:1365~1388.
[10] Yuliang He,Jie Tian, Fingerprint Matching Based on Global Comprehensive Simility, IEEE Trans. Pattern Analysis and Machine Intelligence, Vol. 28, No. 6, August 2006.
[11] Zhu En, Automatic fingerprint recognition technology, Publishing House of National University of Technology of Security, May 2006:138-154.
[12] D.Isenor, S.Zaky . Fingerprint identification using graph matching. Pattern Recognition, 1986,19:113~122
[13] XiaJian Chen,Jie Tian. A matching algorithm based on local topologic structure. Proceedings of ICIAR2004, LNCS3211,2004:360~367.
[14] Jain A.K.,Hong L..Filterbank-based Fingerprint matching. IEEE Transactions on Image Processing, 2000, 19(5):846~859.
[15] Aparecido Nilceu Marana. Ridge-Based Fingerprint Matching Using Hough Transform. Proceedings of the XVIII Brazilian SIBGRAPI'05:1530~1834.

Distinctive Image Region Features from Color Invariant Moments

L. Guo[1,2,3], Z. Shi[2], J. Zhao[1] and R. Zhang[1]

1.Faculty of Information Science & Engineering,

Ningbo University

No.818, Fenghua Road, Ningbo City,

Zhejiang, China

guolijun@nbu.edu.cn

zhao_jieyu@nbu.edu.cn

zhangrong@nbu.edu.cn

2.Institute of Computer Technology, CAS

Beijing, China

shizp@ics.ict.ac.cn

3.Graduate University of Chinese Academy of Sciences

Beijing, China

Abstract: This paper proposes color invariant moment features based on color clustering. Similarity measure method based on the color invariant moment descriptors is given. This method is applied in a practical application system. The experimental result shows that, the proposed feature has both a wider and steadier invariant and a stronger ability in color based image region similarity discriminating than the traditional color features.

Please use the following format when citing this chapter:

Guo, L., Shi, Z., Zhao, J. and Zhang, R., 2008, in IFIP International Federation for Information Processing, Volume 288; *Intelligent Information Processing IV*; Zhongzhi Shi, E. Mercier-Laurent, D. Leake; (Boston: Springer), pp. 165–173.

1. Introduction

Some problems of image processing can be dealt with finally by computing similarity of two image regions, for example, CBIR or object class recognition[1][2]. A number of features, such as color, texture, shape, corner, et al, can be used for computing similarity of two image regions [3]. As such, some descriptors invariants based on simple features can also work well like shape context, differential invariants, SIFT and moment invariants [4]. But in some practical applications, for example, for judging if two regions from two images are of the same object, especially when the detected object is non-rigid (e.g., human body), it is not applicable of these features and descriptors. The fact is that it may be difficult even impossible to get satisfying results only by them. Factually, the perplexing problem arises in comparison and discrimination of human target from different monitor videos [5] [6], in which the images often are of low resolution and from different types of video equipment, and there exist changes in viewpoint, size, background, illustration and body deformation. In this case, the clothing color is a more reliable feature than other image content (assumed that the detected human does not change his/her dress). However, the previous experiments have proved that the traditional color features are inefficient in the actual applications. This paper proposes the introduction of color invariant moment features based on color clustering information. The experimental result shows that, the proposed feature has not only a wider and steadier invariance but also a stronger ability in color based image region similarity discriminating than the traditional color features.

The reminder of this paper is organized as follows. First, color invariant feature and relative issues are discussed in Section 2; in Section 3, the presented color invariant moment feature and the methods of similarity measurement are described in detail; and in Section 4, the experimental results on discriminating similarity of two image regions based on clothing color are given; followed by the conclusion and future work in Section 5.

2. Color invariant feature

Color features have been applied wildly by virtue of relative low dependence on location, size and direction; and good robustness as well as being easy to extract. Generally, color features include color histogram, color moments, color correlogram, et al. Though color histogram are based on various color spaces, HSV color space and CIE Lab color space are more often used in practice because their space structures are in accordance with people's subjective judgment much better [7][8]. Gevers[9] adopts a transform C4=(R-G) /(R+G), C5=(R-B)/(R+B), C6=(B-G)/(B+G), to realize the transformation from RGB space into C4C5C6 space, in which color component Ci does not vary with the angle and intensity of the incident light and other , and as a result, a invariant histogram is obtained. Furthermore, color histogram based similarity can be computed with L1 distance and L2 distance based on corresponding vector spaces and histogram intersection which is more often used in practice. However, results, using color histogram based similarity measurement, are unsatisfactory because of the problem of color quantization which probably gives rise to very small similarity values among almost the same images. Color moments, based on the assumption that the distribution of color in an image can be interpreted as a probability distribution, are more simple and effective measure presented by Stricker and Orengo[10]. Probability distributions are characterized by a number of unique moments. Consequently, the distribution of color in an image can be represented as three central moments that are means, variance and skewness. Compared with color histogram, this method avoids feature quantization. But it is often used before other features to help narrow range as a filter due to the limited discrimination ability of color moments. Totally, traditional color features, generally used with other features, can describe global color distributions of selected regions in an image but fail to describe accurate color distributions. Conclusively, traditional color features are unable to distinguish if two regions are from the same object.

The traditional moment invariants are computed for an image region based both on the pixels on the shape boundary and the interior. Hu [11] derived functions based on the scale normalized central moments, and proposed seven RST (Rotation, Scaling and Translation) invariants of the second and third-order moments. Mindru et al. [12] proposed several types of generalized color moment invariants based on the Hu group methods. These invariants are developed according to the combinations of geometric and photometric transformations. Obviously these generalized color moments aren't fit in the application proposed above because it is difficult to obtain geometric features and the objects are non-rigid.

Geusebroek [13] obtained 6 kinds of color invariants in their physics experiment. These color invariants can be used to extract correct color distribution features of image regions. But these features are obtained in different physical environment which not only include factors such as illumination and viewpoint, but also include material quality (reflection coefficient), roughness degree that we cannot consider in common applications.

In order to avoid the deficiencies of color features, considering changes in viewpoint and illumination, we present a novel color feature based on color invariant moments. The basis of the feature lay in color cluster. The experimental results have shown this method works better than other color invariant features in similarity distinguishing of two image regions under the condition of fixed background and single camera.

3. Color invariant moments

Different from common image retrieval, this paper presents a similarity calculation method based on color invariant moment.The method is described in detail as follows.

3.1 Color clustering and color invariant moments

The proposed color invariant moments are founded on color clustering. So the preliminary work is color clustering calculation on object image regions. K-mean clustering method is applied. For convenience, object image mentioned below refers to object image region and retrieved image refers to retrieved image region.

In the process of clustering, means and variances corresponding to color channels of each clustering color are calculated, which are respectively represented as means[k][ch] and vars[k][ch] (k is the clustering color index, ch is the color channel index), and pixel number of each clustering color, represented as pck(k is the clustering color index), is calculated too. In general case, the clustering color number is specified artificially according to object image.

After color clustering, color variant moments for object image are computed according to the following formulas:

Formula 1:

$$Xmoment[k] = \sum_{i=0}^{I.hteight} \sum_{j=0}^{I.width} i, \quad k \in [1 \;..\; N] \quad Color(p_{ij}) = k$$

Formula 2:

$$Ymoment[k] = \sum_{i=0}^{I.hteight} \sum_{j=0}^{I.width} j, \quad k \in [1 \;..\; N] \quad Color(p_{ij}) = k$$

Where Pij represents the image pixel at the ith row and the jth column in an object image and color (Pij) =k further shows that the color of the current pixel belongs to the k-th color cluster. Xmoment[k], Ymoment[k] and pck construct moment of the k-th color cluster. In other words, color invariant moments include 3 channels.

3.2 Color projection

Obtaining color invariant moments of retrieved image is divided into two steps, color projection and feature computation. Color projection is a projection from pixels in retrieved image region onto cluster colors in object image. In this process, the pixels in retrieved image region are compared with the values of means and variances of each color in object image obtained by color clustering so as to distinguish the cluster class the retrieved image region belongs to. Formally this is described as :

Formula 3:

$$\sum_{k=1}^{N1}\sum_{ch=1}^{N2}\left|p_{ij}[ch]-means[k][ch]\right| > 2 * \sqrt{\text{var}s[k][ch]}$$

Formula 4:

$$\sum_{k=1}^{N1}\frac{\sum_{ch=1}^{N2}(P_{ij}[ch]*means[k][ch])}{\sqrt{\sum_{ch=1}^{N2}(p_{ij}[ch]*p_{ij}[ch])}*\sqrt{\sum_{ch=1}^{N2}(means[k][ch]*means[k][ch])}} > const$$

Where k is the index of cluster color, ch is the current color channel index, N1 and N2 respectively represent the number of clustered colors and the number of color channels, Pij[ch] is the pixel value at the i-th row and the j-th column in reretrieved image, means[k][ch] and vars[k][ch] respectively represent mean and variance of the ch color channel of the k-th color, which are obtained from object image clustering mentioned above. If a pixel in retrieved image simultaneously satisfies Formula 3 and Formula 4, it can be determined that the color of the pixel is the same to the k-th clustered color in object image and the pixel value is assigned as the corresponding cluster color index and otherwise, it is assigned as 0. After projection of retrieved image (single component/channel image is acquired), color cluster information of retrieved image is acquired and therefore color invariant moment features are computed by Formula 1 and Formula 2.

3.3 Color similarity computing

After obtaining color variant moments of the object image and the retrieved image, in order to compute color similarity of the two images we adopt the following formulas, where Ixmo [k] and Iymo [k] (Sxmo [k] and Symo [k]) represent the moment of the kth clustering color of object image (of retrieved image); Ipck (Spck) represents the number of pixels belonging to the kth clustering color in object image (in retrieved image). Finally, color similarity is calculated by Formula 8, where W1, W2, W3 are weight parameters, which are determined from experience.

Formula5:

$$S_{pc} = \frac{\sum_{k=1}^{N1}\left(Ipc_k * Spc_k\right)}{\sqrt{\sum_{k=1}^{N1}\left(Ipc_k * Ipc_k\right)} * \sqrt{\sum_{k=1}^{N1}\left(Spc_k * Spc_k\right)}}$$

Formula 6:

$$S_x = \frac{\sum_{k=1}^{N1}\left(Ixmo[k] * Sxmo[k]\right)}{\sqrt{\sum_{k=1}^{N1}\left(Ixmo[k] * Ixmo[k]\right)} * \sqrt{\sum_{k=1}^{N1}\left(Sxmo[k] * Sxmo[k]\right)}}$$

Formula 7:

$$S_y = \frac{\sum_{k=1}^{N1}\left(Iymo[k] * Symo[k]\right)}{\sqrt{\sum_{k=1}^{N1}\left(Iymo[k] * Iymo[k]\right)} * \sqrt{\sum_{k=1}^{N1}\left(Symo[k] * Symo[k]\right)}}$$

Formula 8:

$$S = W_1 * S_{pc} + W_2 * S_x + W_3 * S_y \quad \left(W_1 + W_2 + W_3 = 1\right)$$

Color invariant moments and color similarity computed by the above formulas have the following strong features: (1) Extraction of color invariant moments does not involve color space quantization; (2) Based on color clustering, this method is able to eliminate the difference of color systems caused by different devices; (3) Location information and number information of pixels are taken into account in the calculation of color invariant moment and color similarity so as to successfully eliminate the effect of viewpoint and illumination. In the next section we will give experimental results which can prove them.

4. Results

We have applied the proposed color invariant moment features to the practical human detection system based on clothing. Considering that the detected object is a region in an image, we design two experiments, shown in Figure 1 and Figure 2 respectively.

In Figure 1, there is one object image and four retrieved images. All retrieved images, which are different in background, viewpoint and illumination and are from different image devices, and the object image include the same human object. HSV space based color histogram features, C4C5C6 space based color histogram features and color invariant moments are applied separately. The experimental results show that the novel features work better than HSV color histogram features and C4C5C6 color histogram features.

In this experiment, by transforming RGB space of the original image into the corresponding HSV space and C4C5C6 space we obtain HSV color histogram features and C4C5C6 color histogram features. Following that, by OpenCV based histogram computation and comparison similarity measure values are obtained. Relevant parameters in color invariant moment features are set as follows: the number of cluster color N1=2; W1=0.6; W2=W3=0.2; in formula 4, const=0.95. The next experiment applies the same parameters.

Figure 2 illuminates another experiment. The experimental results show that bigger is the value of Formula 8, the similarity of two image regions is higher. Meanwhile, the experiment results support the conclusion drawn from previous experiment.

Fig.1 . (a) is the object image with specified object region in red. (b), (c), (d) and (e) are retrieved images (obtained from video by moving object detection), in which detected results based on HSV color histogram features, C4C5C6 color histogram features and color invariant moments are shown respectively in yellow, blue and red. In (b), the similarity measure values are 0.172, 0.260 and 0.972 corresponding to the three feature methods; in (c), 0.797, 0.882 and 0.987; in (d) 0.425, 0.760 and 0.998; in (e), 0.423、 0.566、 0.981.

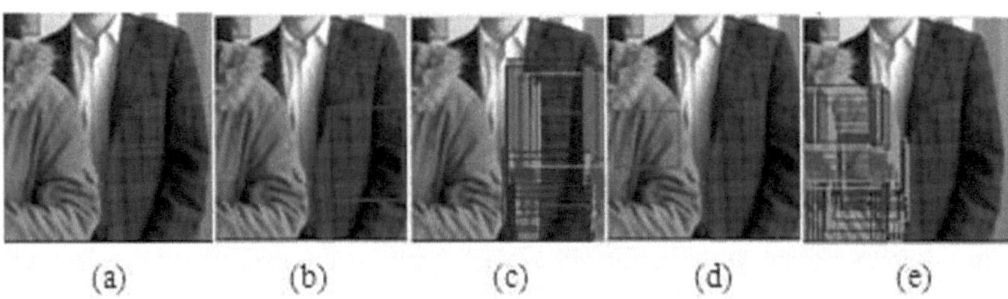

Fig.2 . (a) is the original image. (b) and(d) show object color region in red. (c) and(e) are retrieval results corresponding to the object regions in (b) and (d). Regions with higher similarity in retrieved images are outlined in red, followed by green (threshold >0.98) and blue (threshold >0.97)

5. Conclusion

In this paper, we present color invariant descriptors. Analysis on experimental data show that the descriptors have some shortcomings: (1) Mistaken detection probably happens as other descriptors but it can be reduced by adding texture descriptor. This is our prime work in future. (2) The color invariant descriptors proposed in this paper are not suitable for images which include a great number of colors in detected regions. Because more colors, color cluster error is bigger and the discrimination ability of the color invariant moment descriptors based on color cluster gets worse.

Our future work includes two aspects. On one hand, we will revise and optimize the color invariant moment descriptors to improve the discriminating ability and expend the application range. On the other hand, aiming at improving detection efficiency, we will perfect the object human detection framework by improving color cluster method and adding moving human detection, texture feature into the system.

6. Reference

[1] Gevers, T., Smeulders, A.W.M., PicToSeek: Combining Color and Shape Invariant Features for Image Retrieval,IP(9), No. 1, January 2000, pp. 102-119.
[2] Gy. Dorko and C. Schmid. Object class recognition using discriminative local features. IEEE Transactions on Pattern Analysis and Machine Intelligence, 2004. submitted.
[3] FAN Zi-zhu ,A Survey of Content-based Image Retrieval ,Journal of East China Jiaotong University .
[4] K. Mikolajczyk, C. Schmid, A performance evaluation of local descriptors, in: Proceedings of IEEE Conference on Computer Vision and Pattern Recognition, Madison, USA, June 2003.
[5] J. Sivic, F. Schaffalitzky, A. Zisserman, Efficient object retrieval from videos, in: Proceedings of the 12th European Signal Processing Conference, Vienna, Austria, 2004.
[6] Mark. S. Drew, Jie Wei, Ze-Nian Li, On Illumination Invariance in Color Object Recognition, Technical report 1997, School of Computing Science, Simon Fraser University, Vancouver, Canada.
[7] DOU Jian-jun , WEN Jun , LIU Chong-qing. Histogram-based color image retrieval. Infrared and Laser Engineering, 1999(1)
[8] Yao Qiong, Lai Jianhuang, Feng Guocan. Color-based Image Retrieval :An Overview of Current Research, Journal of Image and Graphics. 2003(z1)
[9] Gevers, T., Smeulders, A.W.M., PicToSeek: Combining Color and Shape Invariant Features for Image Retrieval,IP(9), No. 1, January 2000, pp. 102-119.
[10] M. Stricker, M. Orengo, Similarity of color images, in: Proc. SPIE Storage and Retrieval for Image and Video Databases, San Jose, 1995, pp. 381-392.
[11] M. Hu, Visual pattern recognition by moment invariants, IEEE Transactions on Information Theory IT-8 (1962) 179 - 187.
[12] F. Mindru, T. Moons, L.V. Gool, Color-based moment invariants for the viewpoint and illumination independent recognition of planar color patterns, in: Proceedings of International Conference on Advances in Pattern Recognition, 1998.
[13] J. M. Geusebroek, R. van den Boomgaard, A. W. M. Smeulders, and H. Geerts. Color invariance. IEEE Trans. Pattern Anal. Machine Intell., 23(12):1338-1350, 2001.

Inter-video Similarity for Video Parsing

Arne Jacobs, Andree Lüdtke and Otthein Herzog

Abstract In this paper we present a method for automatic detection of visual patterns in a given news video format by investigating similarities in a set of videos of that format. The approach aims at reducing the manual effort needed to create models of news broadcast formats for automatic video indexing and retrieval. Our algorithm has only very few parameters and can be run fully unsupervised. It shows good performance on a news format of the TRECVID'03 data which had already been modeled with hand-selected visual patterns and served as ground truth for evaluation.

Key words: Data Mining, Image Processing, Information Retrieval

1 Introduction and Related Work

News video broadcasts often expose a strong audiovisual and temporal structure, i.e., they are conventionalized in many ways. In most cases this structure is made pretty obvious to the viewers, for they shall be able to follow the structure of the broadcast. Paired with an audiovisual design which is characteristic to a news format this helps the viewers, on the one hand, to understand what is currently going on and, on the other hand, to recognize a certain news format. These common properties of news videos can be exploited in automatic video analysis algorithms, particularly those that focus on so-called "video parsing" [Swanberg et al(1993)Swanberg, Shu, and Jain]. In this paper we present a method to automatically detect visual patterns in a given news video format by investigating similarities between several videos of that format. It represents the logical continuation of the algorithm presented in [Jacobs(2006)] and helps in fur-

Arne Jacobs · Andree Lüdtke · Otthein Herzog
Universität Bremen, Am Fallturm 1, D-28359 Bremen, e-mail: {jarne|aluedtke|herzog}@tzi.de

Please use the following format when citing this chapter:

Jacobs, A., Lüdtke, A. and Herzog, O., 2008, in IFIP International Federation for Information Processing, Volume 288; *Intelligent Information Processing IV*; Zhongzhi Shi, E. Mercier-Laurent, D. Leake; (Boston: Springer), pp. 174–181.

ther reducing the manual effort needed to create models of news broadcast formats for automatic video indexing and retrieval.

In the next section we will describe our algorithm in detail. This is followed by experimental results which will be evaluated in Sect. 4. We conclude in Sect. 5.

2 Proposed Approach

Our goal is to find sequences in a given news broadcast format that are used to structure videos of that format and that can be used as "tokens" in a grammar for that broadcast. To achieve this goal we try to find visually near-identical subsequences that occur in most of the videos of the given format. The algorithm is based on the assumption that each news video follows a certain audiovisual design which is characteristic for its format and relatively fixed over time.

We denote a video V as a series of frames $V(t)$ at time t. We denote a subsequence of V with length l, starting at t_0 , and thus spanning the interval $[t_0, t_0 + l)$, with $V(t_0, l)$. To measure the similarity between two given subsequences we first define a similarity measure S for two single frames, where high values denote high similarity and low values denote little similarity:

$$S(V(t), V'(t')) \in [0, 1] \tag{1}$$

As we are interested in finding near-identical sequences we define a binary similarity $\dot{S}$ by applying a threshold $s_{\min}$ to our real-valued similarity measure:

$$\dot{S}(V(t), V'(t')) = S(V(t), V'(t')) \geq s_{\min} \tag{2}$$

By application of this threshold we account for slight differences between nearly identical frames caused by, e.g., different recording conditions of different videos of the same broadcast format, noise, encoding artifacts, ticker text independent of the actual news content, etc. Based on Eq. (2) we define a binary similarity measure between two video sub-sequences of the same length by the logical conjunction of the binary similarities of all temporally corresponding frames of the two sequences:

$$\dot{S}(V(t_0, l), V'(t'_0, l)) = \bigcap_{i=0}^{l-1} \dot{S}(V(t_0 + i), V'(t'_0 + i)) \tag{3}$$

To find such similar sequences we apply the following scheme: We choose a reference video V_r from the set of n videos $\{V_1, \ldots, V_n\}$ for a given news broadcast format. This is compared to every other video in the set. Given another video V' from the set we compare each frame $V_r(t)$ of the reference video with each frame $V'(t')$ of the second video. If a correspondence is found, i.e. if $\dot{S}(V_r(t), V'(t'))$ is true, we determine the longest interval $[t - a, a + b)$ for which

$$\dot{S}(V_r(t - a, a + b), V'(t' - a, a + b))$$

holds true. For each frame $V_r(t)$ we thus get a number of sub-sequences $V_r(t - a_i, a_i + b_i)$ for which a near-identical sequence $V'(t' - a_i, a_i + b_i)$ was found in V'. From these sequences we take the one with the highest similarity $S(V_r(t-a, a+b), V'(t'-a, a+b))$, which is defined as the average of the corresponding frame-wise similarities of the two sequences:

$$S(V(t_0,l),V'(t'_0,l)) = \sum_{i=0}^{l-1} \frac{S(V(t_0+i),V'(t'_0+i))}{l} \tag{4}$$

We also apply a constraint on the minimum length $l_{\min} \leq a+b$ of a sequence to account for the fact that for a human to recognize a characteristic sequence it has to exceed a certain length. To reduce the computational cost, we can use this minimum length constraint and only compute the similarity to every $l_{\min}$th frame of the reference video. This results from the observation that a sequence of minimum length $l_{\min}$ necessarily contains one of these frames and is thus still found by our algorithm.

We can now determine the set of frames of the reference video that belong to sequences for which we have found near-identical sequences in one or more of the $n-1$ other videos. By using a threshold $n_{\min} \in [1, n-1]$ on the minimum number of other videos with near-identical sequences and creating the set union of all corresponding sequences in the references video we have our result: A set of sequences from the reference video that have corresponding near-identical sequences in a specified minimum number of other videos.

2.1 Frame-wise Similarity Measure

For our algorithm to work we rely on a real-valued frame-wise similarity measure S as referenced in Eq. (1). For our purpose we use a color and texture based similarity measure as described in [Jacobs et al(2007a)Jacobs, Hermes, and Wilhelm]. It has been designed for indexing of very large (i.e., containing several millions of images) still image databases. It is sufficiently robust against noise and encoding artifacts. In contrast to [Chum et al(2007)Chum, Philbin, Isard, and Zisserman], who focus particularly on time efficient detection of nearidentical video sequences, we do not apply any sort of hashing or reverse file indexing and use a rather simple approach. However, as we only have a limited set of videos to be analyzed and as our algorithm aims at modeling news broadcast formats rather than being deployed in the actual retrieval stage, we find this approach sufficient.

2.2 Parameters of the Algorithm

The proposed algorithm has very few parameters that influence the results:

- The threshold $s_{\min}$ for frame-wise similarity (see Eq. (2))
- The minimum sequence length $l_{\min}$
- The minimum number of other videos with corresponding near-identical sequences $n_{\min}$

We believe that these parameters are intuitive and easy to select. In the following section we will demonstrate this by applying our approach to part of the TRECVID'03 set and showing some experimental results.

3 Experimental Results

The TRECVID'03 data set contains news videos from different news formats. We chose a subset of one particular news broadcast format – CNN Headline News – covering approximately three weeks with half an hour of video footage per day. We chose "CNN Headline News" because we already have additional ground truth data available for this particular format, which we will use in the evaluation section.

Our test set consists of 16 videos of "CNN Headline News" recorded on separate, mostly successive days. Each video has a length of approximately half an hour. We use the first video as reference.

As parameters of our algorithm we set $s_{\min} = 0.9$, which we found an adequate threshold for the underlying still image similarity measure to identify near-identical images. As minimum sequence length we chose $l_{\min} = 15$, which corresponds to approximately half a second. We assume that shorter sequences are not really useful for structuring a news broadcast, as they have to be recognized by the human viewers. We believe that these two parameters do not need to be tweaked and can remain fixed regardless of the news format the algorithm is applied to. We vary the third parameter $n_{\min}$ from 8, which is half of our videos, to 12 (three fourths) to test its influence on the results. In total there were 16 sequences identified by the algorithm, which are shown with manually chosen key frames in Fig. 1.

Table 1 shows a short description of the sequences and the detection results in the different runs with varying parameter $n_{\min}$.

Sequence nr. 5 – marked with * in Table 1 – contains a commercial at the end in addition to the title sequence in the first run. This was due to the fact that the same commercial appears in the reference video and also in 8 other videos of the set, always directly following the title sequence. In all other runs, sequence nr. 5 only contains the title sequence.

Fig. 1 Result sequences 1-16 (from top to bottom and from left to right), in order of their appearance in the reference video

Table 1 Detection results with varying $n_{\min}$, in order of their appearance in the reference video

Nr.	Description	$n_{\min}$=8	9	10	11	12
1	Weather map	X	X	X	X	
2	Coming Up screen	X	X	X	X	X
3	Your Health intro sequence	X	X	X		
4	Your Health end sequence	X	X	X	X	X
5	Headline News title sequence 1*	X	X	X	X	X
6	AT&T commercial	X	X	X	X	
7	Top Stories intro sequence	X	X	X	X	X
8	Dollars & Sense intro sequence	X	X	X	X	X
9	Financial News screen 1	X	X			
10	Financial News screen 2	X	X	X		
11	Financial News screen 3	X	X	X	X	
12	Headline News title sequence 2	X	X	X	X	X
13	Sports News intro sequence	X	X	X	X	X
14	Sports News end sequence	X	X	X	X	X
15	Play of the Day intro sequence	X	X	X	X	X
16	Headline News title sequence 3	X	X	X	X	X

4 Evaluation

For our evaluation we use the results of a project of the Delos Network of Excellence which focused on news video modelling and parsing [Jacobs et al(2007b)Jacobs, Ioannidis, Christodoulakis, Moumoutzis, Georgoulakis, and Papachristoudis]. In the course of the project the "CNN Headline News" format was manually analyzed and a context-free grammar based on hand-selected visual tokens structuring the news broadcast was created by extensive examination of "CNN Headline News" example videos. The tokens finally found useful for the structural grammar were:

- "Black Frames" – a sequence of black frames
- "Channel Logo" – an animation showing the "CNN Headline News" logo
- "Coming Up" – a screen showing what is coming up next
- "Dollars and Sense Intro" – an introduction sequence to the financial news
- "Extended Forecast Map" – a weather map
- "Face" – a sequence showing a presenter in a studio setting (anchor shot)
- "Island Map" – a weather map
- "Play of the Day Intro" – an introduction sequence to the "Play of the Day" sports section
- "Pressure Map" – a weather map
- "Sports Intro" – an introduction sequence to the sports section
- "Studio" – a sequence showing an arbitrary view of the studio
- "Temperature Map" – a weather map
- "Top Stories Intro" – an introduction sequence to the "Top Stories" section
- "Your Health Screen" – an introduction/end sequence of the "Your Health" section

We can now map our automatically detected sequences to the hand-selected ones shown above. Table 1 lists the respective precision and recall values for the different runs in the second and third column. In practice, however, we find that our previous work already covers the detection of anchor shots – "Face" in the above grammar [Jacobs(2006)] – and we never expected the approach presented here to detect those sequences. By examining the grammar we can also see that all visual tokens corresponding to different weather maps always occur directly after one another. Thus it makes sense to combine them into one single token. Also, the "Black Frames" token has no real structural purpose in the grammar as it only occurs together with other structural tokens. In fact, our algorithm included the black frames into the detected sequences. The fourth column in Table 2 shows the "improved" recall values taking these observations into consideration.

Table 2 Performance of the algorithm based on manually selected ground truth sequences. R_1=Recall; P_1=Precision; R_2="Improved" recall

n_{min}	R1	P1	R2
8	57%	69%	89%
9	57%	75%	89%
10	57%	80%	89%
11	57%	85%	89%
12	50%	100%	78%

5 Conclusions

An approach for automatic detection of visual structural sequences in news broadcasts was presented. It shows good performance on a standard data set which has already been modelled with hand-selected visual patterns. Structural tokens that vary greatly between several instances of a given format, e.g., anchor shots varying due to changes in presenter and/or clothing and general studio shots, are not detected by our algorithm, but this was expected.

References

[Chum et al(2007)Chum, Philbin, Isard, and Zisserman] Chum O, Philbin J, Isard M, Zisserman A (2007) Scalable near identical image and shot detection. In: Proceedings of the 6th ACM international conference on Image and video retrieval, pp 549–556

[Jacobs(2006)] Jacobs A (2006) Using self-similarity matrices for structure mining on news video. In: Proceedings of the 4th Hellenic Conference on AI SETN 2006, Heraklion, Crete, Greece, pp 87–94

[Jacobs et al(2007a)Jacobs, Hermes, and Wilhelm] Jacobs A, Hermes T, Wilhelm A (2007a) Automatic image annotation by association rules. In: Electronic Imaging & the Visual Arts EVA 2007, Berlin, Germany, pp 108–112

[Jacobs et al(2007b)Jacobs, Ioannidis, Christodoulakis, Moumoutzis, Georgoulakis, and Papachristoudis] Jacobs A, Ioannidis G, Christodoulakis S, Moumoutzis N, Georgoulakis S, Papachristoudis Y (2007b) Automatic, context-of-capture-based categorization, structure detection and segmentation of news telecasts. In: Proceedings of the First International DELOS Conference - Revised Selected Papers, Pisa, Italy, pp 278–287

[Swanberg et al(1993)Swanberg, Shu, and Jain] Swanberg D, Shu C, Jain R (1993) Knowledge guided parsing in video databases. In: Proceedings of the IS-T/SPIE Conference on Storage and Retrieval for Image and Video Databases, San Jose, CA, USA, vol 1908, pp 13–24

Image Segmentation of Historical Handwriting from Palm Leaf Manuscripts

Olarik Surinta and Rapeeporn Chamchong

Department of Management Information Systems and Computer Science
Faculty of Informatics, Mahasarakham University
Mahasarakham, Thailand
e-mail: olarik.s@msu.ac.th, rapeeporn.c@msu.ac.th
Telephone: +6643754322 ext 2497
Fax: +6643754359

Abstract: Palm leaf manuscripts were one of the earliest forms of written media and were used in Southeast Asia to store early written knowledge about subjects such as medicine, Buddhist doctrine and astrology. Therefore, historical handwritten palm leaf manuscripts are important for people who like to learn about historical documents, because we can learn more experience from them. This paper presents an image segmentation of historical handwriting from palm leaf manuscripts. The process is composed of three steps: 1) background elimination to separate text and background by Otsu's algorithm 2) line segmentation and 3) character segmentation by histogram of image. The end result is the character's image. The results from this research may be applied to optical character recognition (OCR) in the future.

Keywords: Palm Leaf Manuscript, Image Processing, Image Segmentation, Background Elimination, Otsu's Algorithm

1. Introduction

Palm leaf manuscripts have been a popular written media for over a thousand years in Southeast Asia. [1-3] Palm leaves were used for recording the history, knowledge and local wisdoms such as medical treatments, Buddhist doctrine, astrology and the story of dynasties. There are various texts written on palm leaf manuscripts. [4] An example page of palm leaf manuscript is shown in Fig. 1. . With the passage of time, most of these palm leaves are nearing the end of their natural lifetime or are facing destruction from elements such as dampness, fungus, ants and cockroaches. For this reason, Mahasarakham University is establishing Palm Leaf Manuscript Preservation Project for the discovery, preservation and protection of palm leaf manuscripts from Northeast Thailand. [5]

Please use the following format when citing this chapter:

Surinta, O. and Chamchong, R., 2008, in IFIP International Federation for Information Processing, Volume 288; *Intelligent Information Processing IV*; Zhongzhi Shi, E. Mercier-Laurent, D. Leake; (Boston: Springer), pp. 182–189.

2. Proposed framework

To extract data from historical handwritten palm leaf manuscripts, the BILAN (palm leaf manuscripts) system is proposed. The user can understand the system by utilizing an easy to use graphical user interface. [5] The system will display image results step by step. Fig. 1 represents the modules within the proposed system.

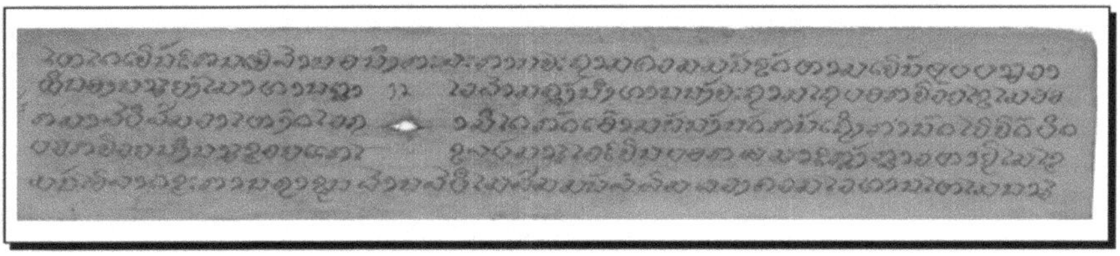

Fig. 1. An example page from palm leaf manuscript.

In our work, we use palm leaf manuscripts consisting of 227 pages to do research work. We implement the system to extract data from palm leaf manuscripts. The system processes consist of background elimination, line segmentation, and character segmentation.

2.1 Convert Image from RGB Color to Grey Image

A RGB color is another format for color images. It represents an image with three matrices of sizes matching the image format. Each matrix corresponds to one of the colors red, green and blue. [1] When we convert it into a grey scale (or intensity) image it depends on the sensitivity response curve of detector to light as a function of wavelength. [6, 7] The equation is:

$$Y = 0.3R + 0.59G + 0.11B \tag{1}$$

A result from this equation is shown in Fig. 3.

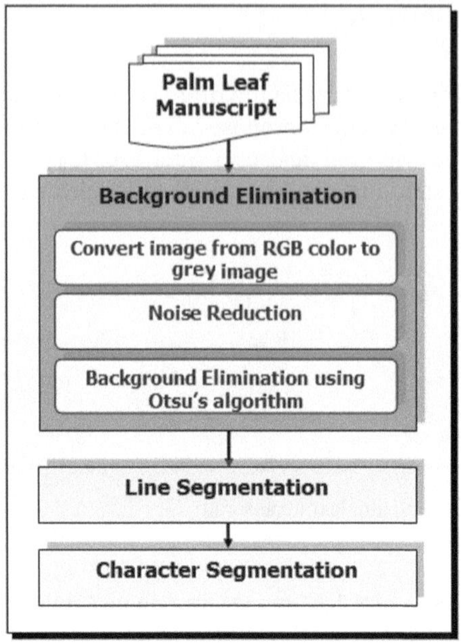

Fig. 2. Framework of the proposed system.

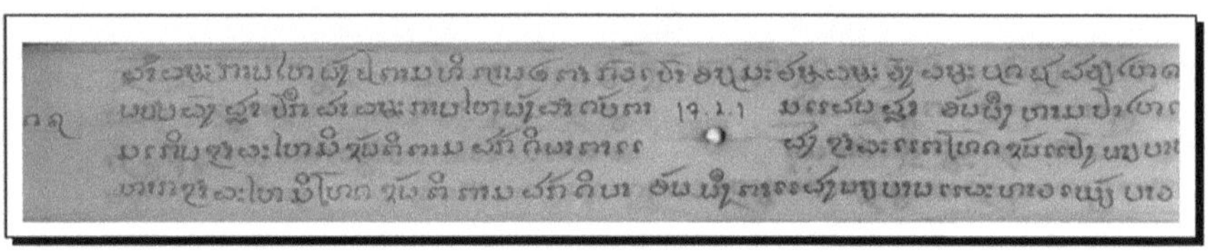

Fig. 3. Figure 1. An example showing a grey image.

2.2 Noise Reduction

Noise reduction is the process of removing noise (from the scanning process) from a signal. A popular technique for removing noise from a grey image is Gaussian filtering. This techniques for calculate the transformation to apply to each pixel in the image. The equation is: [5]

$$f_f(i,j) = \frac{1}{S_k} \sum_{m=1}^{k} \sum_{n=1}^{k} B_{mn} * f_{gr}(m,n) \tag{2}$$

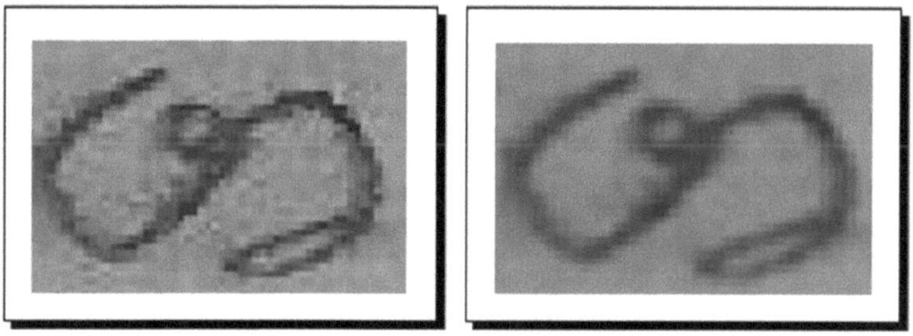

(a) Noise grey image (b) Grey image after reduction

Fig. 4. An example showing a grey image before and after noise reduction.

2.3 Background Elimination using Otsu's Algorithm

The background elimination method proposed by Otsu [5, 8, 9] has the advantage of not needing any prior knowledge of the image, based only on its grey level histogram. The main idea is to find in the histogram an optimal threshold that divides the image objects by constructing two classes from any arbitrary grey level, using the discriminated analysis shown in Fig. 5.

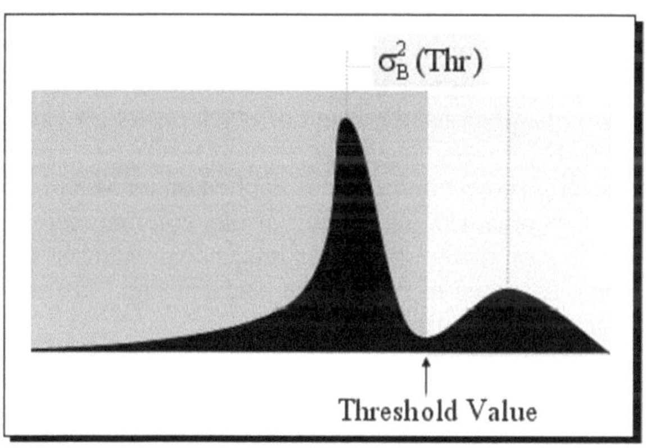

Fig. 5. Otsu's threshold value method.

To find the optimal threshold (*Thr*) we can use the following criteria equation which respects *Thr*.

$$\eta = \frac{\sigma_B^2}{\sigma_{Thr}^2} \tag{3}$$

Where σ_{Thr}^2, that is the total variance, is independent from the grey level, only being necessary to minimize the function σ_B^2, that is the within-class variance. The optimal threshold *Thr** will be defined in the following equation.

$$Thr^* = ArgMin\ \eta \tag{4}$$

A result from this equation is shown in Fig. 6.

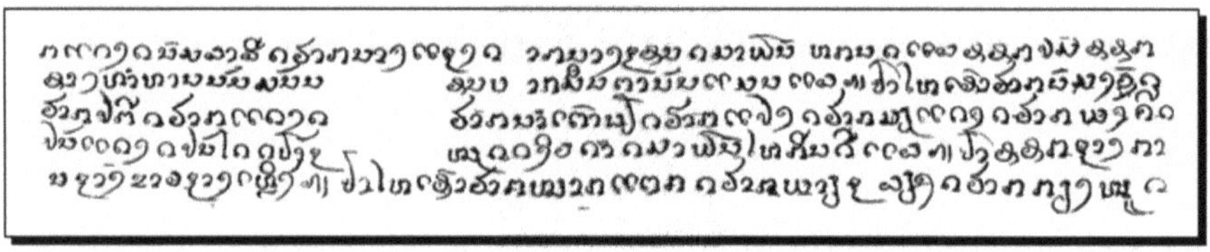

Fig. 6. An example showing a binary image after background elimination.

2.4 Line Segmentation

For the next step, projection profile analysis is a popular technique for line segmentation. We use horizontal projection profile analysis because the texts in most document images are aligned along horizontal lines. The technique computes horizontal projection histograms, the count of black pixels for each column of the raster image. [5, 10, 11]

When the horizontal projection profile is applied on an $M \times N$ image, a column vector of size $M \times 1$ is obtained. Elements of this column vector are the sum of pixel values in each row of the document image. An example of the projection profiles of an image is shown in Fig. 7. The peaks in Fig. 7(a), which correspond to the horizontal projection profile of the image.

(a) Line segmentation histogram

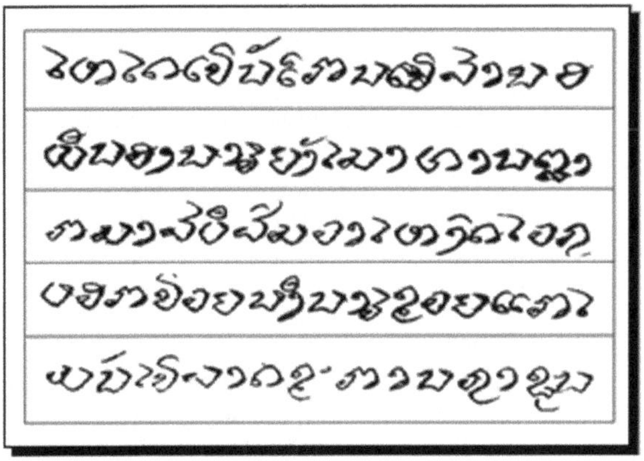

(b) Image after line segmentation

Fig. 7. An example showing an image after horizontal projection profile.

2.5 Character Segmentation

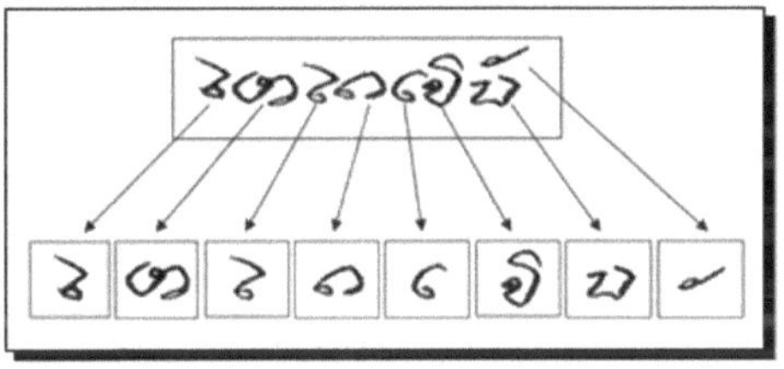

Fig. 8. An example showing an image after vertical projection profile.

As a final step, the extracted lines are segmented into characters. [11-13] To find the boundaries between the characters, we apply a threshold value on the length of the space in between the characters. After finding the positions of the spaces between characters we also eliminate the parts of the line segment. An example character segment is shown in Fig 8.

3. Experimental Results

The method was tested using a set of 227 palm leaf manuscripts. An example palm leaf manuscript is shown in Tables 1 and 2 give an indication of the accuracy.

Table 1. Background Elimination Results

Background Elimination	Accuracy	
	Number of documents	Percentage of background elimination segmented
Complete	138	61
Incomplete	89	39
Total	227	100

Table 2. Line Segmentation Results

Number of Segmented Lines	Percentage of lines correctly segmented
4	78%
5	87%
Average	82.5%

4. Conclusion

In this paper we presented image enhancement techniques for historical palm leaf manuscript document images. Our algorithm first converts the color image into a grey image, then converts the grey image into a binary image using Otsu's algorithm, and finally produces the segmented lines and characters using projection profile analysis.

5. References

[1] Shi Z, Setlur S, Govindaraju V. Digital Enhancement of Palm Leaf Manuscript Images using Normalization Techniques. 5th International Conference On Knowledge Based Computer Systems; 2004 December 19-22, 2004 Hyderabad, India; 2004.

[2] Shi Z, Govindaraju V. Historical Document Image Segmentation Using Background Light Intensity Normalization. 12th SPIE Document Recognition and Retrieval; 2005 January 16-20, 2005; California, USA; 2005.

[3] Shi Z, Govindaraju V. Historical Document Image Enhancement Using Background Light Intensity Normalization. 17th International Conference on Pattern Recognition; 2004 23-26 August 2004; Cambridge, United Kingdom; 2004.

[4] S.A. Shahab, Wasfi G. Al-Khatib, Sabri A. Mahmoud. Computer Aided Indexing of Historical Manuscripts The Inte6rnational Conference on Computer Graphics, Imaging and Visualisation (CGIV06); 2006 April 7, 2006; Sydney, Australia; 2006.

[5] Chamchong R, Surinta O. Text Line Segmentation from Palm Leaf Manuscripts. The 3rd National Conference on Computing and Information Technology (NCCIT2007). Bangkok, Thailand 2007.

[6] Surinta O, Jareanpon C. Comparison of image analysis for Thai handwritten character recognition. 4th International Conference on Intelligent Information Processing (IIP2006); 2006 September 20-23, 2006; Adelaide, Australia: Springer; 2006.
[7] Surinta O, Nitsuwat S. Handwritten Thai Charactr Recognition Using Fourier Descriptors and Robust C-Protytype. Information Technology Journal. 2006 January - June 2006;2(3):96.
[8] Otsu N. A threshold selection method from gray-level histograms. IEEE Transactions on Systems, Man and Cybernetics. 1979 January 1979;9(1).
[9] Otsu's method. 2008 February 20, 2008 [cited 2008 February 20]; Available from: http://en.wikipedia.org/wiki/Otsu's_method
[10] Tacnet LL-SAZB. Text Line Segmentation of Historical Documents: a Survey. International Journal on Document Analysis and Recognition, Analysis of Historical Documents. 2006.
[11] C. Weliwitage, A. L. Harvey, A. B. Jennings. Handwritten Document Offline Text Line Segmentation. In: Cairns Q, Australia 4870, editor. The Digital Imaging Computing: Techniques and Applications (DICTA2005); 2005; Queensland, Australia; 2005.
[12] Ataer E, Duygulu P. Retrieval of Ottoman Documents. 8th ACM SIGMM International Workshop on Multimedia Information Retrieval; 2006 October 26-27, 2006; California, USA: MIR 2006. 8th ACM SIGMM International Workshop on Multimedia Information Retrieval; 2006.
[13] A. Cheung, M. Bennamoun, N. W. Bergmann. An Arabic optical character recognition system using recognition-based segmentation Pattern Recognition Society. 2001 February;3(2).

Virtual Organizations: Trends and Models

Mohammad Reza Nami[1] and Abbaas Malekpour[2]

[1]Faculty of Electrical, IT, and Computer Engineering,

Islamic Azad University- Qazvin Branch, Iran

nami@iau-saveh.ac.ir

[2]Department of CS & EE, University of Rostock, Germany

abbas.malekpour@uni-rostock.de

Abstract: The Use of ICT in business has changed views about traditional business. With VO, organizations with out physical, geographical, or structural constraint can collaborate with together in order to fulfill customer requests in a networked environment. This idea improves resource utilization, reduces development process and costs, and saves time. *Virtual Organization (VO)* is always a form of partnership and managing partners and handling partnerships are crucial. Virtual organizations are defined as a temporary collection of enterprises that cooperate and share resources, knowledge, and competencies to better respond to business opportunities. This paper presents an overview of virtual organizations and main issues in collaboration such as security and management. It also presents a number of different model approaches according to their purpose and applications.

Key words: Collaborative Networks, Virtual Organization, Virtual organization Breeding Environment (VBE), Virtual Enterprise (VE).

1. Introduction

The terms of like virtual team, virtual company, or virtual corporation have been introduced in the early 1990s, including the work of Davidow and Malone [1], and Introna , More , and Cushman [2]. Then a large body of literature has been produced mainly in two communities, the ICT and the management. However, the concepts of VE/VO are still evolving. Advances in computer networks also affected marketing and business systems so that traditional business systems have been metamorphosed.

Please use the following format when citing this chapter:

Nami, M.R. and Malekpour, A., 2008, in IFIP International Federation for Information Processing, Volume 288; *Intelligent Information Processing IV*; Zhongzhi Shi, E. Mercier-Laurent, D. Leake; (Boston: Springer), pp. 190–199.

Virtual Organization has been introduced as a new organizational schema including a temporary set of geographically organizations collaborating sharing skills and resources to fulfill customer requests in a networked environment [3]. Network or Breeding Environment [4] is the source of virtual organizations. It is used for a long-term supporting network in order to enable efficient collaboration in virtual organizations and handle virtual organization activities. The preparation actions for a network are the development of procedures, ICT, and common processes to support customer deliveries. This preparation sets up a virtual organization to fulfill a customer task.

Main reasons for collaborating in a VO include saving time and decreasing development process, spreading costs and risks with partners, improving resource utilization, and access to new markets through partnership. Modeling is a suitable means for designing, communicating, and implementing virtual organizations. There are different types of VO modeling approaches that are explained in this paper. A practical VO modeling moves from high level architectural design to more detailed levels according to the project requirements.

1.2 Structure of the Paper

This paper is organized as follows. Section 2 presents related works. An overview of VO concepts are presented in Section 3. In section 4, VO modeling approaches are described. Section 5 discusses important challenges such as VO management. Finally, conclusions are presented.

2. Related Work

Although VO is still studied, but many researchers are working on different issues and various projects are defined in this field. The most researches have been categorized in the following:

- **Planning and launching:** R. Camacho et al [5] have presented a reference model that integrates all information related with VO planning. On the other hand, it integrates the elements involved in the VO creation in three dimensions: VO lifecycle, modeling views including resources, organizational, functional, and information views.
- **VO management:** As a VO model represents interactions of VO members, resources, organizations, knowledge exchanged among VO members, and functions views form the basis of VO modeling and VO managing is based on the VO models. In fact, a VO management should allocate and coordinate resources, manage VO member cooperation, evaluate partners, and define some rules to achieve the goal.

Effective management needs to VO respond to fast changes in the environment. I. Karvonen et al have presented some VO management approaches in [6].

- **VO characteristics:** With respect to VO nature, Eckstein has described basic characteristics of a VO in [3]. They are explained in this paper.
- **VO modeling:** Since the analysis of past VO modeling indicates that researchers are not fully aware of a suitable modeling process and methodology, the VO modeling approaches is one of important issues. Authors in [7] [8] present some enterprise models.
- **VO products:** Different projects and case studies have been performed in virtual organization field. L. M. Camarinha-Matos, H. Afsarmanesh, and M. Ollus [3] have outlined some of these products.

3. VO Core concepts

There are three concepts used in this context: Virtual Organization (VO), Virtual Enterprise (VE), and Virtual organization Breeding Environment (VBE). This section presents definition, properties, and some concepts.

3.1 VE, VO, and VBE Definitions

A virtual enterprise is defined as a networked, reconfigurable, and temporary collection of enterprises that cooperate and share resources, knowledge, and competencies for better responding to business opportunities. A VO is defined as a temporary coalition of reconfigurable, independent, networked, geographically dispersed organizations including high level trust and competencies that collaborate and share their resources and competencies in order to respond to the customer request.

As mentioned, partners in a VO should collaborate in order to achieve business opportunities. Trust among them and operation according to a common agreement are essential things for collaborating. Networks or breeding environments are an appropriate context for effective creation of dynamic VOs. Authors in [9] have called this context as Virtual organization Breeding Environment (VBE) and defined it as "an association of organizations and their related supporting institutes, adhering to a base long term cooperation agreement, and adoption of common operating principles and infrastructures, with the main goal of increasing both their chances and their preparedness towards collaboration in potential VOs".

VBE can be local and global. Local VBE initiates dynamic VOs from organizations located in one geographical region while global VBE incorporates involved organizations from geographically distributed regions to effectively create VOs.

3.2 VO Properties

Virtual organization characteristics help researchers to gain competitive advantages outlined in the following:

- Combining competencies and resources from different VO partners *(Integrative Atomization)*
- Project-oriented organization with fast recombination of partners *(Temporalization)*
- No legal or other formal structures *(Dematerialization and Non-Institutionalization)*
- Geographically dispersed working *(Delocalization)*
- Improving competitiveness and better fulfilling customer demands and capturing market *(Individualization)*

These properties can be categorized in three groups: product and service (Dematerialization and Individualization), VO conditions and environment (Temporalization, delocalization, and asynchronous), and effective VO operational characteristics (Integrative atomization and non-institutionalization) too.

3.3 VBE Functionality

Efficient creation of dynamic VOs requires a proper environment that the members of new VOs are selected in it according to their capabilities and trust among them. The main goal of VBE is to improve the preparedness of its member organizations for efficiently creating VOs.

3.3.1 VBE Members

VBE Members can be different organizations such as business entities, ministries, legal service providers, and environmental organizations. These organizations should be registered at the VBE, accept the general VBE rules and policies, and have access to common information and tools for operation in a VO.

A VBE member can have different *roles* in different VOs established. The different member roles are listed in the following:

• **VBE Member:** The basic role for organizations that is registered in VBE for participation.

• **VBE Administrator:** Responsible for providing better cooperation among VBE and VBE management. It can find some organizations with high competencies from outside the VBE as a member.

• **VBE Broker:** Responsible for identifying and obtaining new business opportunities.

• **VO Planner:** Identifying, evaluating, and selecting the best partners for creating a new VO in terms of the competency and capabilities are performed by VO planner. In some cases, the roles of broker and planner are performed by the same actor.

• **VO Coordinator:** Responsible for coordinating a new VO during its life cycle.

Of course, some researchers believe that other roles can be defined in a VBE with considering needs. VBE advisor and VBE service provider are some examples in this context.

3.3.2 VBE Life cycle [2]

VBE life cycle consists of three stages: *creation, operation,* and *dissolution.* Each stage can be divided into sub stages. The VO life cycle is similar to VBE life cycle. It is also formed from three stages: *creation, operation and evolution,* and *termination.* The stages are described in the following:

1. **Creation:** VBE initiation and start up are two steps at this stage. Initiation is related to define objectives of the VBE, load base information of the domain, and establish plans and rules. Next step is to create common database, find new VBE members to join the VBE, and set up the VBE.

2. **VBE Operation and evolution:** This stage is the main part of VBE life cycle. Evolution occurs for the reason of some small changes in memberships or daily changes in working principles. Operations supported at this stage include management of rules and common knowledge, registration of new members including characterization of competencies, management of competencies and resources, and evolution of ontology for the considered domain. It also holds a history of past performance and collaborating members, uses this information for partner selection, creation, and registration of a new VO into the VBE and prepare assistance tools for the VBE members.

3. **VBE Dissolution:** After fulfillment of the business opportunity by VO created into a VBE, the VBE should reorganize and keep knowledge collected during the VBE operation. This knowledge can be transferred to the VBE members or other organizations. As the large number of members and open systems are involved and integrated in E-business and VBE creation, the virtual world will need the automation in reconfiguring and healing them. If one of them is modified in VBE or added to VBE, the entire VBE will need to act correctly and effectively

[9]. Autonomic Computing [10] can manage e-business and VO field with the minimal human intervention. VO challenges can be considered as important challenges in the design and implementation of a VBE.

4. Virtual Organization Modeling Approaches

Modeling and models are derived either by human thinking or formally using drawing and other representations including computer models. The models must be the simpler and easier to understand. Complexity of the model and the flexibility to change the models are major problems in enterprise and VO modeling [7]. This section presents a number of different VO model approaches.

4.1 Management Models

Management models depict the elements, architecture, and core concepts of the VOs. They usually set high-level architecture of the VOs and provide a structure for thinking about and defining organizations. There are two types of management models: framework models that are used as structures to design organization, and concept models that depict the principle of structure and operations. Concept models will provide a library of architectural reference models [8] for different types of virtual organizations.

4.2 Management-oriented Process Models

Business and management processes are defined as operative work in organizations. Such processes define the order and relationships between activities to reach a business objective such as fulfilling a customer order. This type of models must depict the collaboration and coordination spanning different locations or organizations. They often do not need to be very detailed. They are suited for building reference process libraries for VO processes.

4.3 Enterprise Engineering/ System Requirement (EE/SR) Models [8]

Different model notations such as UML (Unified Modeling Language, www.uml.org) and modeling tools such as Rational Rose were developed to support the translation of the business domain and its requirements into suitable system designs and configurations. System engineering drives EE/SR models. Management does not drive this type of modeling. A developer can derive from this model the requirement for the system design. EE/SR models provide tools and applications for supporting virtual organizations.

4.4 Enacted Models

Capturing the business activities, necessary data, and driving IT applications and tools are supported by enacted models. Enacted model approaches seem to accelerate the process from definition to system deployment and to support fast reconfiguration.

5. Virtual Organization Management

As a VO is composed of different members located at dispersed sites, different issues can affect the VO. Therefore, the VO management [11] must be examined in different aspects. They can be categorized in human issues, technology and context issues. Communication between the partners, trust among them, VO planning, and security are important challenges from technical point of view.

5.1 Virtual Organization Planning

VO planning activities include receiving and analyzing business opportunities, selecting proper partners, determining high level Work Breakdown Structure (WBS), and setting up VO. R. Camacho et al [5] present a reference model for VO planning and launching. This model integrates the elements involved in VO creation in VO creation, modeling, and knowledge management dimensions. After VO planning activities mentioned in above, VO modeling is created in four views: Resource, organization, functional, and Knowledge. Resource view represents all resources used in the VO operation. Organization view represents responsibilities and authorities of the elements involved in the VO. Functional view represents the behavior of the elements involved in VO life cycle. Knowledge view represents the structure of knowledge among the elements involved in the VO and relationships between these elements (VO partners). This knowledge includes VO structure, VO members profiles, procedures of VO member responsibilities, and reports developed into VO life cycle [9].

5.2 Security Management

Due to Altering in the organizational structure of institutions and changes in information system configuration security management is a continuous process. The objective of security management in VO is to reach and maintain the optimal security level of the entire system and the components of the system [11]. To assure security of VOs, the following issues are addressed:

- Communication security with confidentiality and integrity of information being preserved
- Authentication of the members participating in the operation
- Authorization and access control to resources managed
- Security elements and policies that are categorized into legal, organizational, and technical security policies

There are different threats to VO security such as threats caused by an activity that breaks the protection in order to illegally use resources or threats resulting malfunction of the system.

5.3 Trust Management

Trust among VO members (partners) is one of important issues in collaboration and VO creation, and affects the result of VO operations. It means that one organization as a VO member expects other to behave reliably in performing their tasks for achieving desirable goal of the VO [12].

VO modeling is based on Trust. Modeling is an appropriate tools to enhance planning and implementation. The basis of trust management are Trust Parameters (TPs) such as customer response time as an operational TP and damages by natural disasters as a Economic TP. Jochen Haller [13] has defined trust, reputation, and recommendation, as master concepts in creating a successful VO whose partners trust to each other to perform their roles and actions. He has categorized TPs in operational TP, economic TP, organizational TP, and legal TP. He also presents some trust requirements such as identifying and selecting TPs, aggregating them, considering trust values for reputation, and managing trust in collaboration. Trust accelerates collaboration among VBE members, enhances information sharing and knowledge creation, and reduces the management cost and transaction costs between the members.

5.4 Competency Management

Competency of an organization is defined as the validated capability of an organization to perform business processes, in collaboration with associated partners, having available the necessary resources (e.g. human, physical, technological), and applying known practices, with the aim to offer creation services/ products to customers. The competencies allow to perform processes and require resources as input that have product or services as output. The processes are supported by associated partners. The advance functionalities of competency management [14] include as follows:

- Automatically collecting competency data from organizations
- Competency gap analysis: This is based on matching domain competency ontology and a set of competencies existing in the VBE database
- Discovery of new competency in VBE: This is based on matching competencies needed for future business strategy and a set of competencies existing in the VBE database

Competency ontology is a part of the VBE ontology.

6. Conclusion and Future Work

Virtual Organization has been introduced as a new organizational schema including a temporary set of geographically organizations collaborating sharing skills and resources to fulfill customer requests in a networked environment. This idea improves resource utilization, reduces development process and costs, and saves time. This paper addresses some issues and open challenges in virtual organization such as VO management, and security management. It also presents a number of different model approaches according to their purpose and applications. With merging autonomic computing and virtual organization, an autonomous model can be designed and implemented as future research.

ACKNOWLEDGEMENTS

Mohammad Reza Nami is a PhD researcher in autonomic computing domain. He got a scholarship from the MSRT (Ministry of Science, Research, and Technology) of Iran. He has more than 15 journal and conference papers. He has run many projects in formal methods, software engineering, virtual organizations, and self-managing systems. He has worked at Delft University of Technology with Prof. Stamatis and Dr. Bertels. Some of his research has been supervised by Prof. Afsarmanesh at Amsterdam University.

REFERENCES

1. Davidow W. and Malone T., *The Virtual Corporation,* Harper Business, 1992.
2. Introna L. D., More H., Cushman M., The VO technical or social innovation? Available at http:// is.se.ac.uk/wp/pdf/wp72.pdf
3. Camarinha-Matos L. M., Afsarmanesh H., and Ollus M., *Virtual Organizations: systems and practices*, In Springer Science, 2005.
4. Camarinha-Matos L. M. and Afsarmanesh H., *Creation of virtual organizations in a breeding environment,* In the Proceedings of INCOM 2006, 12th IFAC Symposium on Information Control Problems Manufacturing, Saint-Etienee, France, May 2006.
5. Camacho R. et al, *An integrative approach for VO planning and launching*, PRO-VE'05, 2005.
6. Karvonen J., Salkari I., and Ollus M., *Characterizing virtual organization and their management.* In PROVE' 05, September 2005.
7. Toole M., et al, Reference models for virtual enterprises, Collaborative Business Ecosystems and virtual enterprises, L. Camarinha-Matos, Kluwer publisher, pp. 3-10, 2002.
8. Chen D., et al, Developing an Unified Enterprise Modeling Language (UEML)- Requirements and Roadmaps, Collaborative Business Ecosystems and virtual enterprises, L. Camarinha-Matos, Kluwer publisher, pp. 247-254, 2002.
9. Afsarmanesh H. and Camarinha-Matos L. M., *A framework for management of virtual organization breeding environment, PRO-VE'05*, 2005.
10. Nami, M.R., Sliarifi, M., 2006, in IFIP Intemational Federation for Information Processing, Volume 228, Intelligent Information Processing III, eds. Z. Shi, ShimoharaK., Feng D., (Boston: Springer), pp. 101-110.
11. Magiera J. and Pawlak A., *Security frameworks for Virtual Organizations*, In Virtual Organizations, Springer, 2005, pp.133-148.
12. Dimitrakos T. et al, *Towards a Trust and Contract Management Framework for Dynamic Virtual Organizations*, Proceeding of the e-Challenges 2004, Vienna, Austria, October 2004.
13. Haller J., *A stochastic approach for trust management*. In 22nd International Conference on Data Engineering Workshops (ICDEW'06), Atlanta, GA, USA, April 2006.
14. Ermilova E. and Afsarmanesh H., *Competency and profiling management in VBEs*, in the Proceedings of PRO-VE '06, Springer, Helsinki, Finland, September 2006, pp. 131-143.

A Survey of UML Based Regression Testing

Muhammad Fahad and Aamer Nadeem

Mohammad Ali Jinnah University Islamabad, Pakistan.

mhd.fahad@gmail.com, a.n@acm.org

Abstract: Regression testing is the process of ensuring software quality by analyzing whether changed parts behave as intended, and unchanged parts are not affected by the modifications. Since it is a costly process, a lot of techniques are proposed in the research literature that suggest testers how to build regression test suite from existing test suite with minimum cost. In this paper, we discuss the advantages and drawbacks of using UML diagrams for regression testing and analyze that UML model helps in identifying changes for regression test selection effectively. We survey the existing UML based regression testing techniques and provide an analysis matrix to give a quick insight into prominent features of the literature work. We discuss the open research issues like managing and reducing the size of regression test suite, prioritization of the test cases that would be helpful during strict schedule and resources that remain to be addressed for UML based regression testing.

1 Introduction

The purpose of regression testing is to selectively retest the software after certain modifications to ensure that they have not caused unintended effects on unchanged parts and changed parts of the software behave as intended [1]. Therefore, regression testing process focuses on identification of changes so that those unchanged parts that are already tested should not be tested again to reduce cost, and only changed parts corresponding to those changes should be tested. The objectives of regression testing include not only selective retesting of the software to check its conformance to the new specification, but also enhancing the confidence of the clients that the software product can be changed according to their requirements and the environment [2]. Through the effective regression testing, the programmer also comes to know about the implications and side effects of the changes that have been made. Reusing previous test cases not only reduces the cost of newer test case generation but also reduces other costs of creating test case execution set-up, building oracle and crafting data that can be used [2].

Please use the following format when citing this chapter:

Fahad, M. and Nadeem, A., 2008, in IFIP International Federation for Information Processing, Volume 288; *Intelligent Information Processing IV*; Zhongzhi Shi, E. Mercier-Laurent, D. Leake; (Boston: Springer), pp. 200–210.

Software has to go through a repetitive process of refinement during its development lifecycle. Software engineers have to pay much attention to produce high quality bug free software and it may require many testing techniques at various levels. Regression testing can be applied at any level of testing i.e. unit testing, integration testing, and system level testing. It is different from development testing as in regression testing an existing test suite is available for reuse [3]. It is the most costly process in software lifecycle and according to a study, about 80% of testing budget and one-third of the total cost of software is spent on regression testing and maintenance of the product [4]. Many techniques exist in the literature for maintenance and regression testing of software. Most of the work has been done on code based regression testing in which test suite is built about the delta change between the original code and the changed code, and a survey on code based regression test selection techniques is provided by Rothermel and Harrold [5]. Very few techniques use specification or UML design for change impact analysis to revalidate the software. The main effort is to reduce the cost of testing by selecting cost minimized subset of test cases for regression suite maintenance because rerunning all test cases would be time-consuming and would result in huge cost [2]. Besides cost, a trade-off between the selection and execution of test cases and the fault detection ability of the test cases that are executed is paid great attention during regression test selection. Cost-effectiveness of testing techniques depends upon many factors. Rothermel et al. identify the effect of grouping of test inputs into test cases on the cost-effectiveness of regression testing techniques [6]. Some researchers provide test case prioritization techniques that help when to test an artifact with limited budget and strict schedule [7]. Test case prioritization is also important for UML based regression testing techniques but none of the existing UML regression techniques incorporate this feature.

In this paper, we survey the UML based regression testing techniques. Although there is not much work in the literature that uses UML design for regression testing but this has certain advantages over code based regression testing. We highlight these advantages and significance of using *UML Design* versus *Code* for Regression Testing. While working with UML based regression testing techniques, we observed that UML with OCL constraints can be modeled for Regression Testing of Component Based Systems for systematic regression testing.
Rest of the paper is organized as follows: Section 2 discusses the advantages and significance of using UML design rather than code for regressing testing. Section 3 discusses categories of regression test selection techniques based on certain criteria. Section 4 comprises of survey on UML based regression testing techniques with their salient features. Section 5 discusses our analysis on existing techniques, and provides an analysis matrix. Section 6 concludes the paper.

2 UML Design versus Code based Regression Testing

UML design based regression testing techniques have many advantages over code based regression testing techniques, as outlined below:

- *Traceability:* Identification of change is easily traceable from design rather than the code [8]. Finding delta change in modified and original code is much difficult, and is protracted without code change history that is often ignored by developer during the implementation.
- *Scalability:* Code based regression testing is done only on a small scale, i.e., at unit level [9]. When applied to test large components, scalability becomes the main hindrance to manage all the information and to create corresponding traceability matrices. UML design based regression testing techniques are practical at all levels of testing and of large software applications as well.
- *Understandability:* Tester has to understand the code programmed by others which is a tedious and time-consuming task [9]. UML design is easier to understand and gives quick insights about the requirements and specification.
- *Language dependence:* Code based regression testing process is language dependent. Software that is built on different languages needs many code based regression-testing techniques [9], which increases complexity of the whole process. Regression testing by means of UML designs is free from this limitation as they are based on the standard UML notations [8].
- *Cost:* Code based regression testing detects faults at later stages of software lifecycle and thus consumes huge amount of cost in correcting them. But regression testing at design time gives early detection of faults and reduces the overall cost to apply correction procedures earlier during design phase [10].
- *Code Dependence:* Code based regression testing techniques are only applied when source code is available and hence they are not practical for component based software engineering. Component based systems are built-up by reusing existing components whose implementation is not available [11]. The only thing that component users have is interface specification and modified data information. Thus UML design based regression testing is effectively used for maintenance and correction purposes without the dependency of code.
- *Complexity:* UML designs provide an easy retrieval of relevant static and dynamic information from its various static and dynamic diagrams [8]. This task would be much difficult while extracting information about dynamic bindings between methods from code.
- *Executable UML:* UML based regression testing techniques are also effectively used for validation of executable forms of UML such as Executable UML and the UML virtual machine.

UML based regression testing techniques have some drawbacks [8] too:

- *Invisible Changes:* There are certain changes that may not be visible in design and need special ways to document them, e.g. a change in a method's body.
- *Consistent and up-to-date Design:* UML design based regression testing techniques assume that the diagrams used are consistent with each other. Change can only be detected if this assumption holds; violating this assumption makes the technique awkward and generates poor performance. Furthermore, they require design to be complete and up-to-date.

- *Low Precision:* UML design based regression testing techniques do not precisely build test suite as compared to techniques that utilize detailed code analysis. Precision of a technique means that testing strategy only selects required test cases from existing tests to build regression test suite, i.e., obsolete test cases are detected and ignored.

3 Regression Test Selection Techniques

To achieve successful regression testing, Hsia et al. identify four phases to ensure that the system behaves as intended after changes have been made [12]. First, the process starts by identification of changes made in certain parts, because we have to analyze that software has not been adversely affected by the modifications. Second, we have to build regression test suite by identifying three types of testcases from original testcases, i.e., i) test cases which are no more valid due to the changes made, as invalid test cases are no more useful, ii) test cases which are still valid but not useful as they are already tested and iii) testcases which should be retested to ensure correct software behavior with newer changes. Third, a cost effective testing strategy is made. Finally, selection of cost-minimized subset of test suite to retest the system after changes has been made.

Graves et al. [4] categorize the Regression test selection techniques as:

- *Minimization Techniques:* These techniques focus on selectively retest the software with minimum testcases covering modified or affected portions.
- *Dataflow Techniques:* These techniques select those test cases, which execute data interactions that have adverse effect by changes made.
- *Safe Techniques:* These techniques are designed to reveal the same faults as a retest-all strategy reveals. Thus those test cases that exercise the suspected portion having faults are more focused because they can reveal other most likely faults and exercise the critical functionality.
- *Ad-Hoc /Random Techniques:* These techniques build regression test suite by choosing randomly test cases from original test suite. Randomly rerunning test cases do not address the coverage of affected portions and may not find the most severe faults.
- *Retest-All Techniques:* These techniques rerun the entire original test suite to ensure that modifications have not regress the software functionality, but this requires enough time or resources to rerun the entire test suite.

4 Survey on UML Based Regression Testing Techniques

A variety of regression testing techniques have been described in the research literature. This section throws the light on their summarized features.

- **Specification-based Regression Test Selection with Risk Analysis.** Chen et al. [9] use activity diagram that describes the requirements, behaviors and workflows of underlying system to test. For regression testing, they select two types of tests, i.e., Targeted Tests and Safety Tests. Targeted Tests focus on those features that are still valid in newer version. Safety tests are built to test the modification parts. Chen et al. have uses the Amland's [13] proposed risk model, and emphasis on the cost minimization by detecting the most critical defects first. For regression testing, they apply CFG-based algorithm to activity diagram for detection of affected entities. Then, they form *Targeted Test* which executes the affected edges for regression analysis. For safety tests, they calculate the *Risk Exposure* for each test case. Safety Tests are chosen from the tests that have the highest value of risk exposure. The cost estimation and risk exposure calculations would be more attractive when time and cost is short.
- **Automating Impact Analysis and Regression Test Selection Based on UML Designs.** Briand et al. [8] use consistent sequence diagram, class diagram and use case diagram for identification of changes made to generate regression test suite. For regression testing, they detect changes by comparing previous and new version of Sequence diagrams and Class diagrams. Changes in sequence diagrams are obtained by viewing messages with different conditions, due to change in triggered messages and deleted sequence of boundary messages. Detected changes refer to changes in actions i.e. changed operations and changed classes. Then, they compare two versions of Class diagram to detect the set of changed attributes, operations, relationships and classes. They emphasize on OCL expression analysis of both versions in order to detect changes in operation's contract or in messages. On basis of identification of changes obsolete, retestable and reusable testcases are chosen for regression analysis. They evaluated their work on three industrial case studies and showed effectiveness of their work. Their case studies showed that the number of reusable test cases represented a large proportion (up to 100%). Moreover, they gave evidence about automation of their work by providing Regression Test Selection tool (RTSTool).
- **Maintaining Evolving Component-Based Software with UML.** This UML-based technique was proposed by Wu et al. [14] for component-based software systems that are particularly built on reusable components. Component-based systems need three types of maintenance i.e. Corrective, perfective and adaptive maintenance. In this paper, author gave a regression testing strategy for corrective maintenance as it involves modification on individual classes in a component, leaving none effect on the structure of component as a whole. They use collaboration diagram and statechart diagram to identify changes. For each change in collaboration diagram, test cases are selected which traverse such modified or changed parts. Furthermore, they analyze impacts of change on control sequences and on data dependencies separately to build regression test suite. For identification of change on control sequences, they suggest to retest the modified artifacts in collaboration diagram and all possible affected scenar-

ios that are represented in the statechart diagram. For identification of change on data dependencies, they suggest to retest all the dependent interfaces as well.

- **Efficient Object-Oriented Integration and Regression Testing.** Traon et al. [15] propose a strategy for integration and regression testing from an object oriented model. They produced a model of structural system, Test Dependency Graph (TDG) mapped from the class diagram that evolves with the refinement process of the OO design. Vertices of this graph represent the component and directed edges represent dependencies between classes or methods. Once the TDG is constructed, integration and regression testing strategies are applied on decomposition of the TDG. To build regression test suite, dependencies of both versions of TDG are compared for identification of changes. When the edges are found to be modified that represent dependencies between vertices (components), test cases are build up to cover all the dependant vertices and edges. They formulate two coverage criteria's for testing a component C in a system. Weakest criteria suggest that only those components are tested which are directly dependent from C. But the Strongest coverage criteria suggest testing each component that is included into a path containing C.
- **Model-based Testing and Maintenance.** Deng et al. [16] propose a Semantic Software Development Model (SSDM) for object oriented software and model-based regression test selection for software testing and maintenance. This model is more complete as it incorporates all the phases of the software development process: requirements, design, implementation, testing and maintenance. Information captured by the testing objects and maintenance objects are utilized in order to select regression test suite from original test cases. First, they define the tight-coupled relationships between UML diagrams for efficient and flexible testing and maintenance. For test selection they suggest that when a particular operation is modified, find all the operations that are dependant on this operation, and all the dynamic UML diagrams that include the corresponding behaviors for that operation. Then find all the use cases that are described by the found dynamic UML diagrams. For regression testing, test all the use cases whose corresponding operations need to call modified operation.
- **Regression Testing UML Designs.** Pilskalns et al. [10] propose a safe and efficient regression testing technique based on test cases for UML designs, where test cases always map to sequence diagram scenarios. They use the knowledge of existing approaches to build their regression testing approach, i.e., as a general framework[17], to identify changes[8], to classify test cases[18]. But unlike others, his work was the initial work that was done on identifying change impact for UML test cases rather than code test cases and map changes between UML model and UML test cases. For the purpose of testing, first they made an integrated model named Object Method Directed Acyclic Graph (OMDAG) from Class Diagrams, Sequence Diagrams and OCL. When the OMDAG integrated model is created, test cases are generated which are sets of inputs by using a non-binary analysis technique to partition values that can be

assigned to variables in conditional nodes. When the test case is executed it traverses a path in the OMDAG. And when a path changes, it affects one or more test cases associated with the path. They classify changes into three sets i.e. NEWSET, MODSET, and DELSET, according to whether they create, modify or delete elements in the design. They use delta function to find the test cases affected by a design change, which compares vertices and edges affected by the change made to the paths associated with a test case. Only Pilskalns et al. claimed by experimentation that their strategy selects the test cases with run-time less than as compared to retest-all technique.

- **Integrating White- and Black-Box Techniques for Class-Level Regression Testing.** Beydeda et al. [1] first propose a Class-Level testing of object-oriented prototypes by integrating two existing white box [17] and black box [19] techniques. Rothermel's idea [17] of white box testing is based on traversing both versions of a class, represented by class control flow graphs (CCFGs) to detect and analyze changes. Hong's idea [19] is based on identifying def-use pair of each attribute from class flow graph (CFG) and test suite is built by covering these def-use pairs. For regression testing, Beydeda et al. used a CFG and CCFGs to construct an integrated model called class specification implementation graph (CSIG) [20]. They built regression test suite by the algorithm which takes two versions of CSIG and previous refined test suite. For analyzing safe regression, previous refined test suite is obtained by manually deleting obsolete test cases from original test suite. First test cases are generated by white box testing criteria in which both graphs are traversed to analyze changes in the statements against the nodes. Once changes are identified, test cases covering those changes are generated. Then the algorithm generates test cases from black box criteria by testing inter-method data flow for def-use pairs.
- **An Approach for Selective State Machine based Regression Testing.** Farooq et al. propose an approach for selective state machine based regression testing [21]. For change identification, they use Behavioral state machine (UML 2.1) and class diagram, and classify the changes as class-driven changes and state-driven changes. For building the regression suite, they adopt Briand's test suite classification mechanism, i.e., Obsolete, Reusable, and Retestable. First, they generate class-driven changes by comparing original class diagram, and modified class diagram. The identified class-driven changes are propagated to state machine comparator that identifies state-driven changes that are passed as input to the regression test selector that separates the Obsolete, Reusable and Retestable test cases. The validity of the approach is tested on a small case study.
- **UML Based Regression Testing for OO Software.** Mansour and Takkoush [22] propose a UML based regression testing for object-oriented software by using the interaction overview diagram, class diagram and sequence diagram. Their strategy works by assuming that the test suite contains tests for unit level testing as well as system level testing, and works in phases by selecting tests for each level. First, they identify changes from class diagram. Then, they iden-

tify unit and system level tests from interaction overview diagram that are directly affected by the changes detected in the first phase either by traversing or dependency analysis. If a change is identified in sequence diagram, their algorithm suggests selecting the test cases that execute changed methods. They provided the empirical results of their experiment on nine subject applications and showed that their strategy identified all the tests similar to the retest-all strategy. Their experiment also showed the good precision results by ignoring non-modification test case.

Table 1. Comparison of UML based Regression testing Techniques.

Parameter/Reference	[9]	[8]	[16]	[10]	[20]	[14]	[15]	[21]	[22]
UML Notation*	AD	CD, SD, OCL	All	CD, SD, OCL	CSM	COD, SCD	CD	CD, BSM	IOD,CD, SD
Risk Based	Yes	No	No	No	No	No	No	No	No
Transformation needed	No	No	Yes	Yes	Yes	No	Yes	No	No
Test case classification*	Safety, targeted	ORR	No	ORR	No	No	No	ORR	No
Cost Analysis	Yes	No	No	No	No	No	No	No	No
Change impact*	CT	CT	CT	UMLT	CT	CT	CT	UMLT	IMLT
Safety	High	High	No	High	Low	Low	Low	High	High
Tool Support	No	Yes,	No	No	No	No	No	No	No
Case Study Evidence	Yes	Yes	No	No	No	No	Yes	Yes	Yes
Feasibility	Yes	Yes	No	Yes	Yes	Yes	Yes	Yes	Yes
Generality	Yes	Yes	No	No	No	No	No	Yes	Yes
Precision	High	High	No	High	No	Low	Low	High	High
Inter. Model name	No	No	SSDM	OMDAG	CSIG	No	TDG	No	No

*Notations used in comparison matrix

CD: Class Diagram, **IOD**: Interaction Overview Diagram, **SD**: Sequence Diagram, **AD**: Activity Diagram, **SCD**: State Chart Diagram, **COD**: Collaboration Diagram, **BSM**: Behavioral State Machine, **OCL**: Object Constraint Language, **CT**: Code testcases, **UMLT**: UML testcases, **ORR**: Obsolete, Reusable and Retestable classification

5 Analysis

This section narrates the identified analysis parameters to compare the efficiency and effectiveness of existing regression techniques. On basis of these parameters, analysis matrix is created to give quick insights on each of the approaches explained above as shown in Table 1. The parameters are:

- **UML Artifact:** Which UML diagram is used for change identification for building regression test suite.
- **Risk-Based:** Whether a technique builds risk matrices to quantitatively measure the safety of a test suite. By safety we mean whether a technique has the ability to reveal a fault in the modified program and build test cases that exercise the suspected portion having faults. While analyzing UML based regression-testing techniques, we found only one technique by Chen et al. that uses the risk model and calculates the safety of a test suite.
- **Transformation Needed:** Whether the technique is capable of identifying changes from the diagrams directly or builds the intermediate model that is efficient and conveys easy interpretation while identification of change impact analysis. [8,9,14,21,22] have not built any intermediate model, while Pilskaln's OMDAG is easy to understand because nodes of the model are similar to the classes in Class Diagram, and edges represent sequences between classes. But others form very complex intermediate model.
- **Test Case Categorization:** Whether a technique divides the original test suite to build regression test selection. [9] builds safety and targeted tests, and [8,10,21] identify Obsolete, Reusable and Retestable regression test cases.
- **Cost-Analysis:** Whether a technique calculates costs of each test case, and involves cost efficient strategy to select build regression test suite. Only Chen et al. involve the cost aspects in their strategy.
- **Change impact on Code Testcases/UML Testcases:** Some techniques identify changes that impact code test cases rather than UML test cases. [10,21,22] focused on identifying changes that affect UML test cases and their classification upon mapping changes between a UML design and UML test cases.
- **Safety:** Whether a strategy selects the test cases that reveal the same faults and helps in exposing errors caused by changes as a retest-all strategy reveals. Only works from Pilskalns et al. and Mansour et al. is very safe in this regard.
- **Feasibility:** Whether the testing criterion is feasible in a sense of identifying the impact of changes in the artifact, and is cost effective to be used for particular scenarios during software lifecycle.
- **Generality:** Whether the technique can be extended and applied to a wide and practical range of situations.
- **Precision:** Whether the strategy detects obsolete test cases and ignores them effectively, and change impact analysis only selects those test cases that are really beneficial to ensure the revalidation of software.

- **Tool Support:** Whether proposed technique is tool supported. Only Briand et al. provided the tool named "*RTSTool*" along the technique.
- **Case Study Evidence:** Whether the authors have made some experiment or case study to give evidence of their testing strategy. [8,9,15,21] build a case study evidence while analyzing their testing techniques to promote understanding.

6 Conclusion and Future directions

Regression testing, as a means of quality control measure, is one of the most costly testing techniques to ensure that modifications have not affected the working correct behavior of system and newly created modifications behave as intended. This paper surveys the regression testing techniques based on UML designs. We analyze that UML based regression testing opens a number of advantages and is practical for small and large applications. Classification of regession test suite into Obsolete, Retestable and Reusable test cases is highly significant and most of the literature techniques employed the same classification. UML models with OCL expressions can be effectively used for regression testing of component based systems. Safe techniques that identify the same test cases as the retest-all strategy identifies, are good for small scale test suites and small applications. However, safety for large applications and test suites is difficult to achieve as prioritization is needed for the selection of cost minimized subset for retesting. Identification of changes that affect on UML test cases and Code test cases are different and needs special attention. Little research has been done on identifying changes that impact UML test cases and classify test suite based on mapping changes between UML design and UML test cases, unlike others consider the behavior of the code. One of the future directions on this topic is to perform more work on classifying test cases based on UML designs. Another direction could be to analyze different aspects of cost, test suite minimization, testing of UML executable models, systematic revalidation of UML models and test case prioritization for UML, as these are important during regression testing in a controlled environment.

References

[1] S. Beydeda, and V. Gruhn, Integrating white- and black-box techniques for class-level testing object-oriented prototypes. In Software Engineering and Applications Conference, Las Vegas, Nevada, pp. 23–28, 2000.
[2] H. K. N. Leung, and L. J. White, A Cost Model to Compare Regression Test Strategies. Proc. Conference on Software Maintenance, Italy, pp. 201-208, October 15-17, 1991.

[3] Y. Chen, R. L. Probert, D.P. Sims, Specification based Regression test selection with risk analysis, IBM Center for Advanced Studies Conference. Proceeding of the Conference of the center for advance studies on collaborative research, 2002.

[4] T. L. Graves, M.J. Harrold, J. Kim, A. Porter, and G. Rothermel, An Empirical Study of Regression Test Selection Techniques, ACM Transactions on Software Engineering and Methodology, Vol. 10 (2001), No. 2, pp 184-208.

[5] G. Rothermel, and M.J. Harrold, Analyzing Regression Test Selection Techniques. IEEE Transactions on Software Engineering, Vol. 22 (1996), No.8, pp. 529-551.

[6] G. Rothermel, S. Elbaum, A. Malishevsky, P. Kallakuri, B. Davia, The Impact of Test Suite Granularity on the Cost Effectiveness of Regression Testing. Proceedings of the 24th International Conference on Software Engineering Orlando, Florida, pp.130-140, 2002.

[7] G. Rothermel, R.H. Untch, Chu. Chengyun, M.J. Harrold, Prioritizing test cases for regression testing. Transactions on Software Engineering, Vol. 27 (2001), No.10, pp. 929 – 948.

[8] L.C. Briand, Y. Labiche, G. Soccar, Automating Impact Analysis & Regression Test Selection Based on UML Designs, Proc. of Intl. Conference on Software Maintenance, IEEE,2002.

[9] Y. Chen, R.L. Probert, D.P. Sims, Specification based Regression test selection with risk analysis, Proc. of the center for advance studies on collaborative research, 2002.

[10] O. Pilskalns, G. Uyan, A. Andrews, Regressin Testing UML Designs, 22nd IEEE international Conference on software maintenance (ICSM'2006).

[11] S.A.M. Sajeev, and B. Wibowo, UML modeling for regression testing of component based systems. Published by Elsevier Science, B.V., 2003.

[12] P. Hsia, X. Li, D.C. Kung, C. Hsu, L. Li, Toyoshima, A technique for the selective revalidation of OO software, software maintenance: research and practice, Vol. 9(1997), pp. 217-233

[13] S. Amland, Risk Based Testing and Metrics: Risk analysis fundamentals and metrics for software testing including a financial application case study, The Journal of Systems and Software, Vol. 53(2000), pp. 287-295.

[14] Y. Wu, J. Offut, Maintaining Evolving Component-based Software with UML, Proc. of 7th European Conference on Software Maintenance and Reengineering (CSMR'03), 2003, IEEE.

[15] Y.L. Traon, T. Jeron, J. Jezequel, and P. Morel, Efficient Object-Oriented Integration and Regression Testing, IEEE Transactions on Reliability, Vol. 49 (2000), No. 1.

[16] D. Deng, P. C.Y. Sheu, Model-based Testing and Maintenance, Proceedings of International Symposium on Multimedia Software Engineering (ISMSE'04), IEEE, 2004.

[17] G. Rothermel, M.J. Harrold, and J. Dedhia, Regression test selection for C++ software. Software Testing, Verification & Reliability, Vol. 10(2000), No. 2, pp. 77–109.

[18] H.K.N. Leung, and L. White, Insights into Regression Testing. Proc. IEEE Intl. Conference on Software Maintenance (ICSM), Los Almitos, pp. 60-69, October 16-19, 1989.

[19] H.S. Hong, Y.R. Kwon, and S.D. Cha, Testing of object oriented programs based on finite state machines. In Proc. of the 2nd Asia-Pacific Software Engineering Conference, Brisbane, Australia, pp. 234–241, 1995.

[20] S. Beydeda, and V. Gruhn, Integrating White- and Black-Box techniques for Class Level Regression Testing. IEEE computer society, 2001.

[21] Q. Farooq, M.Z.Z. Iqbal, Z.I. Malik, A. Nadeem, An approach for selective state machine based regression testing, Proceeding of AMOST '07, July 2007, UK, pp. 44-52, ACM.

[22] N. Mansour, and H. Takkoush, UML based regression testing for OO software, Proc. of 11th IASTED conference software engineering and applications. Nov, Cambridge, USA.

Virtual Organizations: An Overview

Mohammad Reza Nami

Faculty of Electrical, Computer, and IT Engineering,

Islamic Azad University of Qazvin, IRAN

Nami1352@gmail.com

Abstract: The need to remain competitive in the open market forces companies to concentrate on their core competencies while searching for alliances when additional skills or resources are needed to fulfill business opportunities. The changing business situation of companies and customer needs have motivated researchers to introduce *Virtual Organization (VO)* idea. A Virtual Organization is always a form of partnership and managing partners and handling partnerships are crucial. Virtual organizations are defined as a temporary collection of enterprises that cooperate and share resources, knowledge, and competencies to better respond to business opportunities. This paper presents base concepts of virtual organizations including properties, management concepts, operational concepts, and main issues in collaboration such as security and authentication.

Keywords: Collaborative Networks, Virtual Organization, Virtual organization Breeding Environment (VBE), Virtual Enterprise (VE).

1. Introduction

Advances in Communication and Internet technology especially Internet services, and trends such as agility, globalization, and increasing demands for products and services with high productivity have motivated different organizations to cooperate and come together to explore business opportunities and fulfill customer tasks. In short, evolution of the Internet and rapid changes in customer demands for extended services and products have motivated organizations toward a new cooperation schema including geographically and legally organizations that collaborate to achieve the goal. This cooperation is supported by computer networks. A Collaborative Network (CN) [1] is an alliance constituted by a variety of entities that are largely autonomous, geographically, distributed, and heterogeneous in terms of their operating environment, culture, social, and goals, but that collabo-

Please use the following format when citing this chapter:

Nami, M.R., 2008, in IFIP International Federation for Information Processing, Volume 288; *Intelligent Information Processing IV*; Zhongzhi Shi, E. Mercier-Laurent, D. Leake; (Boston: Springer), pp. 211–219.

rate to better achieve common or compatible goals, and whose interactions are supported by computer network. Collaborate Networks are categorized into ad-hoc collaborations and Collaborative Networked Organizations (CNOs). Virtual teams, virtual workspaces, and virtual workers are defined in such extended enterprises. Virtual organizations are a part of goal-oriented CNOs.

1.1 Reasons and Motivations

The idea of VO/VE has not been invited by a single researcher rather it is a concept that has matured through a long evolution process. Co-operation between organizations or enterprises is not a new phenomenon too. The terms like virtual company, virtual enterprise, or virtual corporation have been introduced in the early 1990s, including the work of Malone and Davidow [2]. Then, a large body of literature has been produced mainly in two communities, the ICT, and the management. However, concepts and definitions of VO/VE paradigm are still evolving. During last 10-15 years, a large number of research projects have been run in Europe through the European commission funded programs, Japan, USA, Australia, and Mexico [3]. Therefore, research and discussion on virtual organization idea can improve distributed processing.

Virtual Organization has been introduced as a new organizational schema including a temporary set of geographically organizations collaborating sharing skills and resources to fulfill customer requests in a networked environment. Networking can be seen as a proper way to build up co-operation with other organizations. Cost-effective, saving time, high quality, flexibility, agility, and management of risks are some benefits of using network as breeding environment for virtual organizations [4].

1.2 Structure of the Paper

This paper is organized as follows. Section 2 presents an overview of virtual organizations and virtual enterprises concepts including different virtual organization including definitions, properties and quality factors. Section 3 discusses the most common issues in a collaborative work environment especially VO management. Finally, conclusion and future work are presented.

2. Base concepts

This section explains different definitions and properties of virtual organizations.

2.1 VO Definitions

L. M. Camarinha-Matos, H. Afsarmanesh, and M. Ollus [3] define VO as a "set of co-operating (legally) independent organizations, which to the outside world provide a set of services and act as if they were one organization. It is also reconfigurable. The co-operation is supported by computer networks". T. Dimitrakos et al [5] have also defined VO as "a temporary or permanent coalition of geographically dispersed individual, group, organizational units or entire organizations that pool resources, capabilities, and information to achieve common objectives.

Partners or virtual organization members in a VO should collaborate in order to achieve business opportunities. Important attributes for good partnerships are basic principles of human interaction and business perspectives. Basic principles of human interaction include:

- Fairness: Just to all parties, equitable
- Trust: Reliance on the integrity.
- Integrity: Adherence to a strict moral or ethical code
- Competency: Qualities of features that distinguish a person or group
- Open communication: Exchanging data freely between two partners

Business perspectives include:

- Balance of rewards versus risks or resources required
- Self-interest of both partners

Networks or breeding environments are an appropriate context for effective creation of dynamic VOs.

2.2 VBE Definitions

The authors in [6] called this context as Virtual organization Breeding Environment (VBE) and defined it as "an association of organizations and their related supporting institutes, adhering to a base long term cooperation agreement, and adoption of common operating principles and infrastructures, with the main goal of increasing both their chances and their preparedness towards collaboration in potential VOs".

For each business opportunity found by one of VBE members, acting as a broker, a subset of the VBE enterprises may be chosen to form a VO for that specific business opportunity. VBE also evaluates and coordinates created VO during its life cycle. Each VBE has a life cycle. The aim of a VBE is to improve preparedness of the partners.

Some benefits of VBE include [4,6]:

- Agility in dynamic VO creation
- Facilitating VO reconfiguration
- Providing a bag of assets, resources, tools, policies, and knowledge for better collaborating among members. It also holds the past performance measurements of members for selecting in new virtual organizations
- Managing competencies and reduction of risk in selecting members
- Defining criteria for evaluation of members trust with recording their performance history and introducing methods for building trust among the members

Each VBE serves a specific domain and attempts to select the best members to achieve its specific aims in the domain.

2.3 VO Benefits

Some benefits of virtual organizations include saving time such as time to market and reducing development process, spreading costs and risks with partners, improving quality factors such as performance and flexibility, exchange and share knowledge, and marketing in high scale, matching virtual organizations with dynamic changes in marketing, access to new technology and new customers, access to new markets through partnership, and improving access to financial resources. In most cases a mixture of these will be the driver for operating and doing business in networks.

2.4 VO Properties

Some basic characteristics of the virtual organization are often referred to [3, 7] and described in the following.

Delocalization is potentially space dependence. Therefore, enterprises become independent off space and capacity. It eliminates the need for a particular space. **Temporalization** refers to inter organizational relations and to the internal process organization, in the sense of the modular and fractal organization. **Asynchronous**

causes members to asynchronously communicate and interact with each other via the ICT in the context of innovations with the release of time. **Non-Institutionalization** of inter-organizational relationships in virtual environments can be waived because operations are performed in an environment without physical attributes. **Dematerialization** means that all object areas are immaterial. Existing mutual confidence for members, absence of physical attributes and administrator can affect system performance and flexibility. Increasing consumer demands is motivated **Individualization** property. Mass customization is one approach for manufacturers to fulfill customer demands and capture new markets. **Integrative Atomization** refers to integrate all atomized core competencies of the participants for satisfying customer.

These properties can be categorized in three groups: product and service, VO conditions and environment, and effective VO operation characteristics. Virtual organization properties also affect quality factors. It is outlined in table 1.

Table1. Relationships between Virtual Organization Properties and Quality Factors (QFs)

Virtual Organization Properties	Quality Factors
Delocalization	Portability
Temporalization	Functionality
Asynchronous	Functionality, Efficiency
Non-Institutionalization	Portability, Maintainability
Individualization	Maintainability, Functionality
Integrative Atomization	Reliability, Efficiency
Dematerialization	Efficiency, Portability, Flexibility.

3. Virtual Organization Challenges

This section presents some challenges and trends in virtual organization.

3.1 Challenges of Virtual Organization Creation

Since a VO is fixing as a master component of dynamic collaborative networks, there are different issues and challenges in VO creation, management, design, and implementation. Virtual organization life cycle includes three stages: creation, operation along with evolution, and termination. Identifying business opportunities, examining the partner competencies, selecting partners from within or outside the VBE (network), forming the best partnership in terms of the competencies, creating the necessary databases, registering new members, and VO setting up are the key tasks in VO creation. Main challenges of VO creation are outlined in the following:

- Negotiation of virtual organization partners (members) includes contract templates, virtual negotiation rooms, and negotiation objects
- Defining roles and responsibilities of VO partners
- Building trust as the base for organization collaboration
- Establishing common interoperability/integration platform
- Comparing and selecting organizations to configure the VO
- Issues related to incompatibility and heterogeneity of information sources
- VO planning [8]: Acquiring basic competency information of organizations and collaboration modalities
- Dynamically configure a new VO from autonomous organizations as VO members

Efficient creation of dynamic VOs [3] requires a proper environment that the members of new VOs are selected in it according to their capabilities and trust among them. The main goal of VBE is to improve the preparedness of its member organizations for efficiently creating VOs.

3.2 Security Management

The concept of security in virtual organizations includes confidentiality and integrity of data for secure communication, authentication, and access control to resources. Since the whole VO is as secure as its weakest member organization is, each VO member becomes responsible not only for its own security, but also for security of common resources. Definition of a curity framework is a real challenge. Due to dynamically changing environment, security management becomes a must. Security policies and mechanisms are categorized into three groups: organizational, legal, and technical. Alteration in the organizational structure of institutions and changes in information system configuration make security management a continuous process. Estimating the risk of occurrences of potential threads and their effects, determining and implementing optimal security measures, continuously monitoring the system operations, detecting proper security rules, and running them are main activities of security management [9].

3.3 Competency Management

Competency of an organization is defined as the validated capability of an organization to perform business processes, in collaboration with associated partners, having available the necessary resources (e.g. human, physical, technological), and applying known practices, with the aim to offer creation services/ products to customers. The competencies allow to perform processes and require resources as input that have product or services as output. The processes are supported by associated partners. The advance functionalities of competency management [10] include as follows:

- Automatically collecting competency data from organizations
- Competency gap analysis: This is based on matching domain competency ontology and a set of competencies existing in the VBE database
- Discovery of new competency in VBE: This is based on matching competencies needed for future business strategy and a set of competencies existing in the VBE database

Competency ontology is a part of the VBE ontology.

3.4 Trust Management

To enhance the efficiency and success of both their cooperation within the VBE as well as their collaboration in virtual organizations configured in the VBE, *trust [11]* is discussed. Some challenges in trust are presented in the following:

- Transparency: Each step taken for entire trust assessment within a VO or a VBE must be clear and transparent to all involved VBE members. Information used must be certified too
- Complexity: The complexity of multi-objective and multi-criteria nature of trust and trust level in VBEs is one of main challenges
- Causality: The future trust level of a VBE member is causally related to its role and behavior at present, and actions it has performed and events it has caused in the past

Trust accelerates collaboration among VBE members, enhances information sharing and knowledge creation, and reduces the management cost and transaction costs between the members [12]. Applying agents in implementation of virtual enterprise [13] and designing trust between them are one of challenges in this context.

3.5 Ontology Engineering

Ontology engineering [2] is discussed in VBEs in order to create virtual organizations. It includes defining classes in the ontology, arranging the classes in a taxonomic hierarchy such as subclass-super class, defining slots (properties and relations) and describing allowed values for them, and filling in the values for slots and instantiation. Ontology elements for a VBE in order to create VOs are found in structured resources such as database schemas, semi-structured resources such as XML pages and dictionaries, and unstructured resources such as related text corpora in general. The ontology is engineered by designing and developing reverse engineering methods for structured resources and developing NL parsers for semi-structured and unstructured resources. Domain experts use testing methodology to incrementally develop ontology. They also verify the ontology.

4. Conclusion and Future Work

Virtual organization is becoming a strategic characteristic applicable to any organization without physical, geographical, or structural constraints. Virtual team, virtual workplace, and virtual worker are defined in the extended enterprises. Collaborative networks or breeding environments are the source of virtual organizations. They are used for a long-term supporting network in order to enable efficient collaboration in virtual organizations and handle VO activities. At present, more than 100 existing VBEs for creating, managing, and supporting virtual organizations are studied. CARPI is one of them and includes 2068 members in textile domain [2]. This paper presents an overview of virtual organizations including base concepts and challenges. Implementing an autonomic virtual organization including self-configuration, self-healing, self-protection, and self-optimization in information and resources management is my future research.

ACKNOWLEDGEMENTS

Mohammad Reza Nami is a PhD researcher in autonomic computing domain. He got a scholarship from the MSRT (Ministry of Science, Research, and Technology) of Iran. He has more than 15 journal and conference papers. He has run many projects in formal methods, software engineering, virtual organizations, and self-managing systems. He has worked at Delft University of Technology with Prof. Stamatis and Dr. Bertels. Some of his research has been supervised by Prof. Afsarmanesh at Amsterdam University.

REFERENCES

1. Camarinha-Matos L. M. and Afsarmanesh H., *Creation of virtual organizations in a breeding environment,* In the Proceedings of INCOM 2006, 12th IFAC Symposium on Information Control Problems Manufacturing, Saint-Etienee, France, May 2006.
2. Davidow W. and Malone T., *The Virtual Corporation,* Harper Business, 1992.
3. Camarinha-Matos L. M., Afsarmanesh H., and Ollus M., *Virtual Organizations: systems and practices*, In Springer Science, 2005.
4. Nami M. R. and Tavangarian D. J., *Virtual Organizations: A New Approach in IT,* The 7th IEEE International Conference on Computer and Information Technology (CIT 2007), Aizu, Japan, October 2007, pp.93-98.
5. Dimitrakos T. et al, *Towards a Trust and Contract Management Framework for Dynamic Virtual Organizations*, Proceeding of the e-Challenges 2004, Vienna, Austria, October 2004.
6. Afsarmanesh H. and Camarinha-Matos L. M., *A framework for management of virtual organization breeding environment, PRO-VE'05*, 2005.
7. Karvonen J., Salkari I., and Ollus M., *Characterizing virtual organization and their management.* In PROVE' 05, September 2005.
8. Camacho R. et al, *An integrative approach for VO planning and launching*, PRO-VE'05, 2005.
9. Magiera J. and Pawlak A., *Security frameworks for Virtual Organizations*, In Virtual Organizations, Springer, 2005, pp.133-148.
10. Ermilova E. and Afsarmanesh H., *Competency and profiling management in VBEs,* in the Proceedings of PRO-VE '06, Springer, Helsinki, Finland, September 2006, pp. 131-143.
11. Haller J., *A stochastic approach for trust management.* In 22nd International Conference on Data Engineering Workshops (ICDEW'06), Atlanta, GA, USA, April 2006.
12. Msanjila S. S. and Afsarmanesh H., *Assessment and Operation of trust in VBEs,* in the Proceedings of PRO-VE '06, Springer, Helsinki, Finland, September 2006, pp. 161-173.
13. Guidi-Polanco F., Cubillos C., and Menga G., *The global automation platform: An agent-based framework for virtual organizations.* in PRO-VE'05, September 2005.

A RISK ASSESSMENT SYSTEM WITH AUTOMATIC EXTRACTION OF EVENT TYPES

Philippe Capet[1], Thomas Delavallade[1], Takuya Nakamura[2], Agnes Sandor[3], Cedric Tarsitano[3] and Stavroula Voyatzi[2]

[1]*THALES Land & Joint Systems*
160 boulevard de Valmy, 92704 Cedex
first_name.last_name@fr.thalesgroup.com

[2]*Universite de Marne-la-Vallee, Institut Gaspard-Monge*
5 bd Descartes, 77454 Marne-la-Vallee Cedex 2
first_name.last_name@univ-mlv.fr

[3]*Xerox Research Centre Europe*
6 chemin de Maupertuis, 38240 Meylan, France
first_name.last_name@xrce.xerox.com

Abstract In this article we describe the joint effort of experts in linguistics, information extraction and risk assessment to integrate EventSpotter, an automatic event extraction engine, into ADAC, an automated early warning system. By detecting as early as possible weak signals of emerging risks ADAC provides a dynamic synthetic picture of situations involving risk. The ADAC system calculates risk on the basis of fuzzy logic rules operated on a template graph whose leaves are event types. EventSpotter is based on a general purpose natural language dependency parser, XIP, enhanced with domain-specific lexical resources (Lexicon-Grammar). Its role is to automatically feed the leaves with input data.

1. Introduction

In various fields rational risk analysis is part of the decision making process. It is a fundamental methodological tool which helps economic and political actors to anticipate potential crises. Such an analysis is usually carried out by human experts. The first step in risk analysis is the retrieval of relevant information from available data. The amount of the data may be so large that there is a great need for tools that automate parts of the risk analysis. An early

Please use the following format when citing this chapter:

Capet, P., Delavallade, T., Nakamura, T., Sandor, A., Tarsitano, C. and Voyatzi, S., 2008, in IFIP International Federation for Information Processing, Volume 288; *Intelligent Information Processing IV*; Zhongzhi Shi, E. Mercier-Laurent, D. Leake; (Boston: Springer), pp. 220–229.

warning system should help experts to monitor massive flows of events, in the short term, and launch alerts whenever critical event sequences are detected.

For this purpose we are designing ADAC [7], an automated early warning system that provides a dynamic synthetic picture of situations involving risk. ADAC is being implemented for detecting weak signals of nuclear proliferation, in order to issue alerts about emerging nuclear risks as early as possible. Risk assessment in this domain has to process large amounts of knowledge -such as educational changes in a particular country, public statements of local leaders, covert information, diplomatic negotiations, satellite observations, etc- that can only be acquired through widely disparate channels of information. A significant amount of this knowledge is directly derivable from the events described in information newswires. At present, data concerning events are introduced into the ADAC system by human analysts.

However, the exponentially growing information flow through the internet no longer allows human analysts to keep abreast of the events referred to in the newswire sources. On the other hand, the more extensively a risk assessment system is populated the more reliable it is. Thus the use of an automatic information extraction (IE) system has become a necessary component of any risk assessment system based on the continuous monitoring of event flows.

In this article we describe the underlying principles of ongoing work: the joint effort of experts in linguistics, IE and risk assessment to integrate EventSpotter, an automatic event extraction engine, into ADAC.

This paper is organized as follows: In section 2 we describe ADAC, the risk assessment component that needs to be fed with automatically extracted events. In section 3 we present EventSpotter pointing out its innovative features compared to other event extraction systems. We argue that these features are necessary in order to meet the requirements of the subsequent risk assessment modules. In this section we underline the importance of the integration of extensive lexical resources into the event extraction system, and briefly describe their form and the principles that lead us to constitute them. We also present an evaluation of the present state of the IE system. In section 4 we present some related work in IE applied to event extraction. Finally, in section 5 we draw some conclusions and show directions for future work.

2. The Risk Assessment System: ADAC

ADAC is a dynamic risk assessment system that monitors the daily evolution of the situation in a particular domain in order to give experts a better understanding of situations involving risk. Based on a library of experts' scenarios describing typical crisis developments and on an ontology representing the domain knowledge, the system monitors a flow of incoming event in order to spot the event sequences that are likely to end up in crisis. This section is dedicated to the presentation of the various components of the ADAC system.

2.1 Scenarios

A scenario describes typical developments of a specific type of crisis, i.e. it depicts how a system moves from a normal, sound state to a critical, anarchical state. Scenarios are expressed in the template formalism. The general principle of a template is the description of a complex phenomenon as a combination (conjunction, disjunction, etc.) of less complex phenomena which again are decomposed into a combination of less complex phenomena until elementary phenomena are reached, namely the events directly observed from the input.

2.2 Ontology

The scenarios, represented by templates, are part of the knowledge base feeding the system, which is more general than a simple scenario library. It gathers all the information the system has at its disposal to perform crisis detection. It contains all the linguistic terms, organized in a subsumption hierarchy, that are necessary to link the scenarios with the input data. Locations and actors that are under watch are for instance defined in this ontology.

2.3 Event Data

The data used to feed the system are structured representations of occurring events, related to the particular type of crisis under study. The structure used to summarize a piece of information is defined by the following fields: the source reporting the information, the date and location of the reported event, the event type, the actors of the event (persons or organizations), the other persons or organizations involved in the event (other participants), the uncertainty of the event from the source's point of view (does the source report the event as a fact, is it an assumption, an opinion... ?). The choice of these fields has been inspired by the work of political scientists concerning the anticipation, monitoring and termination of wars [14].

2.4 Recognition Engine

The core of our system consists in comparing input event data and known scenarios of crisis developments, through a constrained pattern matching process. This is done by our recognition engine, which assesses the degree of match between event sequences and experts' scenarios, taking into account some, spatial, temporal and operational constraints. It may indeed be important to ensure that two events are considered as parts of the same scenario, only if they occur in a specific area, within a given time frame, while involving similar actors. The recognition degree is estimated by a similarity degree, which takes its values between 0 (null recognition) and 1 (full recognition). It evolves according to the arrival of new events which confirm or invalidate the hypothesis: each time new data match the template, the recognition degree is updated. Through this information fusion mechanism, guided by experts' knowledge, ADAC enables to detect the early signs of what usually ends up in crisis.

3. Automatic Extraction of Event Types: EventSpotter

3.1 General Properties

As we outlined above, the ADAC system calculates risk on the basis of a template graph whose leaves are event types. The role of the natural language processing (NLP) system is to feed the leaves with input data. We do this by extracting event descriptions from sentences of news articles. These extracted event descriptions are transformed by subsequent operations, which render them suitable for further automatic processing in the template.

The extraction of event descriptions is carried out with syntactic analysis using the Xerox Incremental Parser (XIP) [2]. An event is defined in terms of syntactic relationships in the sentences. Out of all the dependency relations produced by the analyzer, we consider an event description to be a predicate (verb, adjective and predicative noun) related to its arguments and modifiers.

The first operation that EventSpotter carries out with respect to the extracted event descriptions is their normalization to a unique representation structure. This operation is domain-independent since invariably every event description is extracted. The unique representation structure consists first in indicating for each event description its information source and factuality as conveyed by the information source. Furthermore we transform each event description into a set of common constituents. The constituents of events are a core, which is the name of the event, and its coordinates, whenever they are present in the sentence. We have defined the coordinates of event cores as agent(s), other participant(s), place(s) and time. The way this normalization is carried out by EventSpotter is described in a previous article [12].

The second operation that EventSpotter carries out is the association of the extracted event descriptions to the pre-defined relevant event types that constitute the leaves of the template graph in ADAC, whenever it is appropriate. This operation is domain-specific. It is carried out on the event core and its extensions, as we will describe below, and as it is illustrated by the following example taken from the corpus that we have chosen for developing our application. Sentences (2) through (4) indicate extended event cores in bold. These extended event cores are the parts of the sentences associated with (1), one of the relevant event types with respect to our domain defined in ADAC.

(1) to get involved in a cooperation in the nuclear domain.

(2) A delegation from Syria arrives in Iran **to begin negotiations on a** possible Iranian-Syrian **nuclear pact**.

(3) The Middle East Newsline reports that Iran **is preparing to receive a light water nuclear reactor** from Russia.

(4) Former chief nuclear negotiator for Iran Hassan Rowhani says Tehran **is ready to negotiate a mutual start for the Natanz nuclear facility**.

After the second operation, Table 1 is extracted.

Table 1. Representation of the extracted event (3)

Source	*Fact.*	*Actor*	*Core*	*Oth.pt*	*Place*	*Time*	*Event type*
Middle East Newsline	F	Iran	receive a light water nuclear reactor	Russia			to get involved in a cooperation in the nuclear domain

3.2 Concept-Matching

In order to match event descriptions in sentences (2) through (4) with the relevant event type (1) we use the concept-matching framework. Since we have described it previously [13], here we only recall the basic idea. Concept matching combines the bag-of-words approach with syntactic dependency parsing for extracting complex target concepts. The complex target concepts are coherent and recurrent meaning fragments of sentences, and are expressed in highly diverse ways. Within the concept-matching framework the target concepts (like (1) above) are matched whenever syntactically related chains of expressions conveying - what we call - their constituent concepts (bags of words) occur within the same sentence. We show how the concept-matching framework is applied on (2) through (4) for matching the target concept (1).

As first step, the target concept is broken down into three constituent concepts: [get involved] in [cooperation] in the [nuclear domain]. We assign general concept labels to these constituent concepts as follows: BEGIN LINK NUCLEAR.

The sentences (2) through (4) all contain words that convey each of these concepts. Moreover, these words form dependency chains in all of the sentences as shown below, thus they do in fact convey the target concept (1):

(5) A delegation from Syria arrives in Iran to <BEGIN> begin </BEGIN> <LINK> negotiations </LINK> on a possible Iranian-Syrian <NUCLEAR> nuclear pact </NUCLEAR>.

dependency chain: ... begin ... negotiations on ... nuclear pact.

(6) The Middle East Newsline reports that Iran <BEGIN> is preparing </BEGIN> <LINK>to receive</LINK> a light water <NUCLEAR> nuclear reactor </NUCLEAR> from Russia.

dependency chain: ... is preparing to receive ... nuclear reactor ...

(7) Former chief nuclear negotiator for Iran Hassan Rowhani says Tehran <BEGIN> is ready </BEGIN> <LINK> to negotiate </LINK> a mutual <BEGIN> start </BEGIN> for the Natanz <NUCLEAR> nuclear facility </NUCLEAR>.

dependency chain: ... is ready to negotiate a ... start for ... nuclear facility.

We can observe that neither the order nor the type of relationship among the constituent concepts is relevant for the match. The essential constraint of coherence is the existence of a dependency relationship among the words conveying the constituent concepts.

In order to carry out concept-matching automatically we need a general purpose natural language dependency parser as well as domain-specific resources: a set of constituent concepts, lists of words conveying the constituent concepts, a lexicon-grammar to improve the performance of the general purpose parser in the establishment of the argument and modifier dependencies and rules of the co-occurrence of the constituent concepts. The general purpose dependency parser is used for extracting all the possible dependency pairs among the words of the sentences, whereas the domain-specific resources make it possible that the relevant dependency pairs conveying the constituent concepts can be chosen out of all the dependency pairs in the sentences and associated with the target concepts.

In the following sections we will concentrate on the domain-specific resources we have used to extract descriptions of event types that are needed by ADAC to calculate risks of nuclear proliferation.

The Target Concepts and the Constituent Concepts for Nuclear Proliferation. In ADAC 103 event types are listed as relevant for inducing crisis in the nuclear domain. Table 2 is an excerpt of the list.

Table 2.

1. to work on secret nuclear programs
2. to sell military equipment
3. to get involved in a cooperation in the nuclear domain

In the entire list we propose 18 constituent concepts, whose various co-occurrence combinations cover all the target concepts. They are the following:

NEGATIVE, INTENT, BEGIN, CONTINUE, END, POSITIVE, HOSTILITY, LEGAL, SECRET, MILITARY, NUCLEAR, KNOWLEDGE, LINK, MOVEMENT, PRODUCTION, MONEY, TOOL, STATE

The granularity of the constituent concepts is subject to experimentation. If certain constituent concepts do not assure fine-grained event types, they can be broken down to several types. A word might also be assigned to several constituent concepts. Table 3 shows Table 2 marked up with constituent concepts:

Table 3.

1. to work[PRODUCTION] on secret[SECRET] nuclear[NUCLEAR] programs[PRODUCTION]
2. to sell[MONEY] military[MILITARY] equipment[TOOL]
3. to get involved[BEGIN] in a cooperation[LINK] in the nuclear domain[NUCLEAR]

For the present system we have assigned the list of words to the constituent concepts manually. We have worked on a prototype based on a corpus of news containing 4196 tokens of content words.

Table 4. Some sample constituent concepts and some words associated with them

Constituent concept	Words
NEGATIVE	contrary, lie, refute
INTENT	decide, effort, require
LINK	ally, connect, negotiate
CONTINUE	augment, emerge, regular

Lexicon Grammars. As we pointed out above we have built domain-specific lexical resources in order to ensure the precision of the extraction of the relevant dependencies in the sentences. In the general-purpose XIP parser certain dependencies, especially prepositional phrase attachment and clausal complementation cannot be handled with high precision due to word sense ambiguities on the one hand and the lack of a broad coverage lexical grammar on the other hand. Working on a domain-specific vocabulary allows us to build lexicon-grammars for this vocabulary.

A lexicon-grammar is a dictionary that provides exhaustive and detailed subcategorisation information about the predicates of a natural language such as verbs, predicative nouns and adjectives. Predicates with related syntactic and semantic behaviour are grouped together, for example, in the structure of simple sentences, in the distribution of arguments and in terms of interpretations [10]. The lexical, syntactic and semantic features provided by the lexicon-grammars are used for establishing grammatical and dependency rules. Table 5 shows an extract of the lexicon-grammar of English verbs taking a sentential complement (e.g. *Russia admitted (that Iran's program is of peaceful intent + having discussions with Iran + to providing incorrect information)*).

Table 5.

N0=: Nhum	N0=: N-hum	N0=: Nsupport	N0=: Npl obl		N0 V	N0 V N1	N0 V with N2hum N1	N1=: that S	N1=: that Ssubj	N1=: Wh-S	N1=: if S	N1=: whether S	N1=VOing W	N1=to VOing W	N1=on VOing W
+	-	+	-	acknowledge	-	+	-	+	-	-	-	-	+	-	-
+	-	+	-	add	-	+	-	+	-	+	-	-	-	-	-
+	-	-	-	admit	-	+	-	+	-	-	+	+	+	+	-
+	-	-	+	agree	-	+	+	+	-	-	-	-	-	-	+

Sentence (8) is associated to the event-type "nuclear-related agreement" due to specific syntactic features present in the lexicon-grammar, which allow XIP to extract a dependency between "agreement" and "import":

(8) An unnamed official of the Russian atomic energy ministry says that Russia has yet to receive Iran's **agreement** for Moscow **to import back radioactive fuel waste** from an Iranian nuclear power plant that Russia is building in Bushehr.

dependency chain: ... agreement ... to import back ... radioactive fuel waste

We carried out an evaluation of in what extent the lexicon-grammar resources have influenced the extraction of dependency relationships. We established a gold standard of a 100 sentences, which we compared to the output of XIP with and without the addition of the lexicon-grammar. The improvement of the performance was 36%, which is a significant difference.

4. Related Work

Event extraction is the subject of an increasing number of information extraction applications. Different systems, however, represent events in different ways. [1] describes two approaches to represent events: *"On the one hand, there is the TimeML model, in which an event is a word that points to a node in a network of temporal relations. On the other hand, there is the ACE model, in which an event is a complex structure, relating arguments that are themselves complex structures, but with only ancillary temporal information."*. Our representation is closer to the Automatic Content Extraction (ACE) model, which however, does not describe it entirely. We are not aware of any system that shares our event representation.

Apart from differences of representation, event extraction has been handled with various approaches. It is difficult to make comparisons among different systems with different purposes in this article. We will give here a brief overview of the latest systems whose main application is event extraction.

Recent applications in the field of event extraction have mainly been carried out with probabilistic or machine learning approaches, which do not need to rely on strict linguistic constraints, but which fail to extract exact semantic relationships based on sentence structure. The following articles describe various event extraction systems, and none of them shares our approach and purposes: [11] built a Retrospective news Event Detection system which merges events with existing similar events with a probabilistic approach based on bag-of-words and clustering. [15] built a prize-winning event extraction system based on machine learning with limited linguistic constraints. [4] study the tradeoffs between open and traditional relation extraction. They conclude that it seems more interesting to use traditional IE for a domain specific extraction. Finally, closer to our approach, [3] built a relation and event extraction system, but only for verb-based events.

Several works in NLP systems argue that acquiring subcategorization information is an important task for the improvement of performance (see [5; 6; 8; 9]). Some of them also put forth that manual acquisition of such resources is time and resource consuming (see [6]). However, manually-developed lexicons (enriched with subcategorization information) prove to be precise [6]. Moreover, [5] estimate that half of the parse failures is caused by inaccurate or incomplete subcategorization information [8].

5. Conclusion

In this article we have described the components of an entirely automatic integrated system of risk assessment concerning nuclear proliferation. It consists basically of two components: linguistic analysis of news articles and computation of nuclear risk. The actual integration has not taken place technically but the evaluation of the output of the linguistic component shows that conceptually it is possible, i.e. the two components are compatible. Once the integration is carried out, ours will be the first system where automatic linguistic analysis of newswire articles is used as input to a risk detection system.

This system is the result of a chain of processes where in each step the enrichment of a lower level analysis makes way to a higher level analysis. Starting from lexical analysis, continuing by syntactic parsing of free text, the output of which is then mapped into semantic role assignment, and coupled with conceptual analysis, the process goes on by carrying out operations on high-level concepts, which yields the final output.

Further work consists in the integration of the two components, which will be followed by an evaluation. We carried out a partial evaluation of the system, which we reported in previous work [12]. In a longer term perspective, the approach that we propose for nuclear risk assessment can be extended for other kinds of political risk assessment or in general to any kind of risk assessment where the risk is related to event occurrences that are reported in texts.

Acknowledgments

This research is being funded by the French national project Infom@gic.

References

[1] Ahn, D.: *The stages of event extraction.* In: Proceedings of the Workshop on Annotations and Reasoning about Time and Events, pp. 1–8. (2006)

[2] Ait-Mokhtar, S., Chanod, J-P., Roux, C.: *Robustness beyond shallowness: incremental dependency parsing.* Natural Language Engineering, 8(2/3) pp. 121–144. (2002)

[3] Aone, C., Ramos-Santacruz, M.: *REES: A Large-Scale Relation and Event Extraction System.* In: Proceedings of the sixth conference on Applied natural language processing, pp. 76–83. Seattle, Washington (2000)

[4] Banko, M., Etzioni, O.: *The Tradeoffs Between Open and Traditional Relation Extraction.* ACL (2008)

[5] Briscoe, T., Carroll, J.: Generalised Probabilistic LR Parsing for Unification-Based Grammars. Computational Linguistics, 19(1) (1993)

[6] Carroll, J., Fang. A.: *The Automatic Acquisition of Verb Subcategorisations and their Impact on the Performance of an HPSG Parser.* In: Proceedings of the First International Joint Conference on Natural Language Processing, pp. 107–114. Sanya City (2004)

[7] Delavallade, T., Mouillet, L., Bouchon-Meunier, B., Collain, E.: *Monitoring Event Flows and Modelling Scenarios for Crisis Prediction: Application to Ethinc Conflict Forecasting.* International Journal of Uncertainty, Fuzziness and Knowledge-Based Systems. (2007)

[8] Gardent, C., Guillaume, B., Falk, I., Perrier, G.: *Le lexique-grammaire de M. Gross et le traitement automatique des langues.* In ATALA (2005)

[9] Korhonen, A.: *Semantically Motivated Subcategorization Acquisition.* In: Proceedings of the ACL Workshop on Unsupervised Lexical Acquisition, 9, pp. 51–58. Philadelphia (2002)

[10] Leclere, C.: Organization of the Lexicon-Grammar of French Verbs. Lingvisticae Investigationes, 25(1), pp. 29–48 (2002)

[11] Li, Z., Wang, B., Li, M., Ma, W-Y.: *A Probabilistic Model for Retrospective News Event Detection.* In: Proceedings of the 28th annual international ACM SIGIR conference on Research and development in information retrieval, pp. 106–113. Salvador (2005)

[12] Rebotier, A., Sandor, A., Voyatzi, S., Nakamura, T., Martineau, C., Delevallade, T., Capet, P., Jacquelinet, J.: *Intelligent awareness: event extraction, information evaluation & risk assessment.* In: 3rd Language & Technology Conference, pp. 539–543. Poznan (2007)

[13] Sandor, A., Kaplan, A., Rondeau, G.: *Discourse and Citation Analysis with Concept-Matching.* In: International Symposium, Discourse and Document, pp. 147–151. Presse Universitaire de Caen, Caen (2006)

[14] Schrodt, P., Davis, S., Weddle, J.: *Political Science: KEDS-A Program for the Machine Coding of Event Data.* Social Science Computer Review. 12, 561–588 (1994)

[15] Xu, F., Uszkoreit, H., Li, H.: *Automatic Event and Relation Detection with Seeds of Varying Complexity.* AAAI Workshop Event Extraction and Synthesis, Boston (2006)

Addressing Risk Assessment for Patient Safety in Hospitals through Information Extraction in Medical Reports

Denys Proux, Frédérique Segond[1] , Solweig Gerbier and Marie Hélène Metzger[2]

[1] Xerox Research Centre Europe

6,Chemin de Maupertuis, Meylan 38240, France

Denys.proux@xrce.xerox.com, Frederique.Segond@xrce.xerox.com

[2] Service d'hygiène, épidémiologie et prévention des Hospices Civils de Lyon

Hôpital Henry Gabrielle - Villa Alice,

20 Route de Vourles BP 57, 69 230 Saint-Genis Laval cedex, France

solweig.gerbier@chu-lyon.fr, marie-helene.metzger@chu-lyon.fr

Abstract: Hospital Acquired Infections (HAI) is a real burden for doctors and risk surveillance experts. The impact on patients' health and related healthcare cost is very significant and a major concern even for rich countries. Furthermore required data to evaluate the threat is generally not available to experts and that prevents from fast reaction. However, recent advances in Computational Intelligence Techniques such as Information Extraction, Risk Patterns Detection in documents and Decision Support Systems allow now to address this problem.

Keywords: Hospital Acquired Infections, Natural language Processing, Information Extraction, Risk Pattern.

1. Introduction

Patient's security is a key issue in hospitals and monitoring adverse events is a preliminary step of a corrective or preventive action. Only a qualitative and quantitative estimate of observed adverse events in hospital can help in deciding which measures to implement. For example, in France, the incidence of adverse events was estimated [1] to 6.6 per 1000 hospital days in 2004, from which 24.1% were Hospital Acquired Infections (HAI).

Please use the following format when citing this chapter:

Proux, D., Segond, F., Gerbier, S. and Metzger, M.H., 2008, in IFIP International Federation for Information Processing, Volume 288; *Intelligent Information Processing IV*; Zhongzhi Shi, E. Mercier-Laurent, D. Leake; (Boston: Springer), pp. 230–239.

Hospital acquired infections represent an important part of adverse events in hospitals and monitoring procedures are in place in most of European countries. These procedures are mostly based on methods developed in the United States by the Centers for Disease and Control and Prevention (CDC) National Nosocomial Infection Surveillance System [2]. However, the important workload linked to these monitoring methods forced the hospitals to consider alternatives to these methods which are based on active report of HAI by the medical personnel or infection control experts. There is need for automation of part of the surveillance to backup Risk Management teams that often have not enough resources to efficiently perform this monitoring.

The use of Natural Language Processing techniques is one of the promising alternatives for monitoring adverse events in hospitals. Text Mining Techniques applied on medical reports specifically for risk assessment are still relatively new [3] because it assumes to have access to a very accurate and disambiguated terminology, to a list of factors characterizing a potential infection and finally it requires most of the time robust parsing capabilities to handle real life medical literature. Most of these systems are keywords based or based on simple pattern matching [4]. The identification and disambiguation of complex information such as HAI require not only having access to named entity recognition but also and mainly to the detection of specific semantic links appearing in text between these entities.

Therefore two key elements will be needed;

- a rich and standardized terminology to allow detecting inside text some meaningful pieces of information (such as drug names, symptoms, ...);
- a robust parser able to process long and complex sentences in order to identify key dependencies between these meaningful pieces of information.

The following paper presents such a system in the following sections, applied to monitoring of hospital acquired infections through information extraction in patient discharge summaries.

2. Hospital Acquired Infections

2.1. Definition

A Hospital Acquired Infection can be defined as: *An infection occurring in a patient in a hospital or other health care facility in whom the infection was not present or incubating at the time of admission. This includes infections acquired in the hospital but appearing after discharge, and also occupational infections among staff of the facility. If the exact status of the patient is not clearly known when he first came in a medical unit, a period of 48 hours (or superior to the incubation period if it is known) is considered to separate HAI from other kinds of infections coming from outside. As for infections related to surgery a period of 30 days is considered and extended to 12 months in case of implanted device.* [5]

2.2. Burden of disease

Studies [6] show that in Europe, the frequencies of HAI hit 5 to 10% of hospitalized patients. In the extended European Union, there are approximately 3 million identified cases and 50,000 related deaths per year. Mortality related to HAI was estimated in 2005 to 4000 deaths per year in France and 20 to 30 per cent of these deaths are estimated avoidable by adapted prevention guidelines.

HAI related costs are greatly dependent on the type of infection and on the patient's risk factors. The costs associated to HAI ranged from 500 € for a urinary infection up to 40 000 € for a serious bacteraemia in Intensive Care Units (ICU) [7]. In France, estimating that the number of HAI by year is 750 000 and that the preventable part of these cases is 30%, the overcharge for the health system may represent a total cost between 0.11 and 9 billion €.

2.3. Monitoring Systems

Automated surveillance is defined by Wright et al. [8] as a process of obtaining useful information from infection control data through the systematic application of medical informatics and computer science technologies. This definition recovers very different ways of processes.

The first way of process is based on the combination of different hospital databases (bacteriological data, antibiotic exposure, claim data…). Different studies have demonstrated the efficiency of systems based on the combination of bacteriological data, antibiotic exposure or discharge diagnoses [9]. In France, Bouam and al [10] evaluated the sensitivity of automated nosocomial infections detection based on bacteriological databases to 59% and the specificity was 91% compared to manual detection. A Danish study [11] showed that the sensitivity of nosocomial infections detection was higher by combining different infection parameters (microbiology, antibiotic treatment, leucocytes counts, C-reactive protein concentrations) (94%) than by using each infection parameter separately (61% to 82%). However the specificity was lower (47% for combined parameters vs. 53% to 70% for each parameter used separately.

A second way of automated process is based on using natural language processing of discharge summaries. There is no national guideline or obligation whatsoever to standardize recording systems neither in private clinics nor in public hospitals. However information exists and is organized in a way or another. Main clinical events occurring during a patient's hospitalization are recorded in the patient's record by the medical staff. A summary is written at the hospital discharge which is the main source of communication between the various medical units.

But today there is no real standardized summary of this information and medical staff can write this discharge report on the way they want. It stresses therefore the need for an automated tool able to scan daily reports, to mine information written in these texts in order to detect potential risk patterns and to send alerts to appropriate people.

Very few experiences were already performed [3]. Melton and al. used for instance the MedLEE natural language processor for the detection of adverse events, comprising nosocomial infections. The sensitivity to detect adverse events was evaluated to 28% (IC95% = 17-42) and the specificity to 98,5% (IC95% = 98,4 – 98,6) .We can hypothesize that the low sensitivity of this tool is linked to the broad type of adverse events searched (venous thrombosis, post-operative wound, perioperative myocardial infarction, falls…). The medical language being very complex, the use of natural language tools for the detection of adverse events should be developed by specific adverse events topics (nosocomial infections, therapeutic adverse events, …).

3. A strategy for risk assessment using natural language technology on patient discharge summary

3.1. First step: develop interoperable information extraction systems

It appears that information recording system in hospitals, is not always the top priority with respect to investments. Even if the current tendency is to computerize all data to make them available to electronic databases and for automated processes some hospitals are still relying most of paper based documents as some other have make the move to the digital world. There is not national obligation to normalize these systems. Each hospital, and some time each department, can decide which equipment to adopt and deploy. The result of this is a complete mess of heterogeneous systems not really interoperable where information is duplicated and not easily available for global analysis. Interoperability is still an important issue as stressed by EU reports [12].

The HAI surveillance system must not be specific to a given hospital or department but should be operational at a National level. This step implies developing processes and ad-hoc methods to gather required documents from local databases.

3.2. Second step: anonymization of patient's records

Medical data are highly sensitive. At that point one important task is to anonymize these data. This means removing all personal information related to people or places (in order to protect patients' privacy). This means that not only people names should be removed but also any information that could lead to an identification such as personal address, phone number, social security number, and so on. This is often required by specific national regulation. While at the moment anonymisation of patient records is done manually, natural language techniques specifically designed to detect this kind of Named Entities [13] can be applied here to perform this task.

In order to do so and also for the remaining text processing steps we are using the Xerox Incremental Parser [14] that combines five linguistic processing layers which are: pre-processing (tokenization, morphological analyzer and part of speech tagging); named entities; chunking; dependency extractions between words on the basis of sub-tree patterns over chunk sequences and finally a combination of those dependencies with boolean operators to generate new dependencies or to modify or delete existing dependencies. XIP comprises an engine and a meta-language that allows users to write grammar rules or add words in the lexicon. XIP integrates also a Named Entity Recognition module.

4. The different linguistic steps to be achieved for hai surveillance

4.1. Entity detection

Once documents have been normalized and anonymised they can be processed by a Terminology Server in order to identify and locate all Named Entities that will be useful for the remaining decision process (e.g. drug names, symptoms, processes, dates). The goal of this step is twofold: to perform a Part of Speech analysis to allow a further computation of syntactic dependencies, and then to detect and disambiguate at a semantic level all key entities that will be involved in the risk pattern detection step.

Furthermore in the context of information extraction and risk analysis a proper recognition of specific vocabulary allows also to add a semantic tag to some words or multi-word expressions that can be involved in the description of an adverse event. This step will be performed by the Named Entity Recognition module enriched with some specialized terminology contained in medical structured terminologies. Indeed, terminological resources, and to be even more specific Taxonomies such as SNOMED[1] for instance, are very important at this step. They allow a system to identify these entities with respect to their definition in these dictionaries. These entities can be composed of several words (or tokens). In this case specific detection rules apply to regroup all these words under a same semantic tag. In the context of HAI, these entities, taken to the largest extend, can be drug names (e.g. "Tienam"), disease name (e.g. "Surgical site infection"), exam (e.g. "abdominal ultrasound"), symptoms (e.g. "abdominal pain"), etc.

Applying now the XIP parser to texts enables the system to detect chunks of related words. Coupling this general tagger, the XIP chunker with a medical terminology infrastructure like for instance SNOMED enables the system to semantically tag the different concepts.

"*The postoperative consequences were marked by abdominal pain and fever due to multiple intra-peritoneal abscesses and peritonitis without anastomotic dehiscence that required a peritoneal toilet on September 29th of this year. It was an infection with Klebsiella only sensitive to Tienam which was probably facilitated by the preoperative biliary drainage and the splenectomy. The evolution was finally favorable.*"
Detected Entities:
SYMPTOM(postoperative consequences)
SYMPTOM(abdominal pain)
SYMPTOM(fever)
DIAGNOSIS (multiple intra-peritoneal abscesses)
DIAGNOSIS(peritonitis)
DIAGNOSIS(infection)
PROCEDURE(peritoneal toilet)
TREATMENT(Tienam)
BACTERIA(Klebsiella)

Figure 1: Named Entity Detection

4.2. Risk pattern detection

Once a patient Discharge Summary has been processed to assign POS tags and identify Named Entities, the next step is to detect some typical combinations of named entities that may be involved in the description of an adverse event.

Characterizing these events is not simply identifying some keywords inside texts; it is about finding special relations between these keywords. Therefore a syntactic analysis is required to detect the potential links, and more specifically the order of these relations. This can be simply summarized by trying to found: What produces what to whom when and how.

The first step consists in processing each sentence of a report to compute all syntactic dependencies. This is done thanks to a set of grammar rules designed for

[1] http://www.snomed.org/

common language. XIP provides already grammar rules for almost 10 different languages including for example French and English. This rules applies on the POS tags assigned to each words (or tokens) at preceding step. Syntactic dependencies extraction does not need to be customized for a specific domain provided that it has been done for the lexical level.

What need to be customized for the domain is the rules to characterize key information searched inside texts. For the detection of HAI it includes the detection of various types of information such as:

where does the situation takes place

who is the patient (male, female, young, old)

what are the treatment or drug involved

what symptoms are detected

are characteristic adverse events terms appearing inside the text (e.g name of a virulent bacteria)

The connection between these elements is important because according to their order it may characterize an HAI or just a normal case. In order to detect these elements specific rules have to be designed that takes into account both the semantic tags assigned to words or multi-words expression thanks to domain specific terminologies that help identify symptoms and drug names for example, and the detected syntactic relation between these entities.

These rules have to be defined by experts from the domain. In this case this is experts from surveillance groups that already spent time reading report to find potential indication about HAI case. They must formalize what are the criteria they use to say whether or not if there is a potential HAI case emerging from a report. Once these rules are formalized, then linguist can convert them into parsing rules than can be processed by the text parser.

The result of such analysis can be illustrated by the following example that characterize key information element that will be used when trying to find a match between what is extracted from the text and potential HAI scenario.

"The postoperative consequences were marked by abdominal pain and fever due to multiple intraperitoneal abscesses and peritonitis without anastomotic dehiscence that required a peritoneal toilet on September 29th of this year. It was an infection with Klebsiella only sensitive to Tienam which was probably facilitated by the preoperative biliary drainage and the splenectomy. The evolution was finally favorable."

Dependencies between pertinent entities and events

Symptom (pain, without, dehiscence)

Preliminary_Condiction (yes, pain)

Preliminary_Condiction (No, dehiscence)

Detailed_Symptom (abdominal, pain)

Location (abdominal)

Prescribed_AntiBio (Tienam)

Figure 2 : Detected Syntactic dependencies

4.3. *Risk assessment*

Once some key entities and specific links among them have been detected inside a text, the next step is to evaluate a potential match with predefined scenarios characterizing HAIs.

In order to do so, these scenarios which detail all the criteria that are taken into account to define one specific HAI, have to be formalized by experts. They must details both all the elements (symptoms, drugs, ...) that can be involved in a case definition and also the various types of links that should exist among them.

At this level several strategies are possible. One might consist in simply remaining at the sentence level to find direct ordered syntactic links between key elements. This can be illustrated for example by the detection in a single sentence of a symptom that is the consequence of a new treatment (or drug prescription that must belong to a specific category of drugs such as Anti-Biotic) which produces the following effect (or symptoms).

However, HAI are complex to characterize and generally involve various different elements that must occur in a specific order. This is why all the needed information to decide whether or not we face an HAI is generally not contained in one single sentence. Other information than just dependencies between Events are therefore part of the reasoning process. According to input documents metadata and localization (sections where the information is detected) can also be taken into account to make the decision. Paragraphs ordering as well as dates inside these paragraphs provide useful data to build a timeline that helps classifying information between actions and consequences. Therefore it is important to build a complete discourse analysis to take into account all these elements. This requires some kind of discourse representation mechanisms, and to do some decision support systems designed to formalized medical knowledge can be well adapted to do so.

Ontologies are important at this level because it allows to formalize a scenario at an abstracted level which reduce the number of cases the knowledge expert has to take into account to cover all possible combinations of keywords that may be involved into the definition of one single case. Ontologies provide hierarchies of terms (Drug names, symptoms, ...) this allows for example to state simply in one scenario that if a specific type of anti-biotic is detected inside a text in combination of a specific type of bacteria then this related to an HAI. There will be therefore a link made between the semantic tag assigned to the elements detected inside text and the abstracted concepts used inside the scenarios thought the use of such Ontologies that will provide the link between these two elements.

One last element that should be taken into account for HAI detection is flexibility and this because most of the time HAI are not clearly indicated inside text. There could be pieces of evidences but not a clear statement because for example the case has not been detected by the medical staff as so, and therefore not detailed explicitly. This means that several levels of HAI detection confidence should be taken into validating a detection. Some elements can be very characteristic such as the name of a given bacteria (e.g. “infection with Klebsiella”), some strong candidate such as the use of a specific type of antibiotic drug in specific department (e.g. “tienam” and “Intensive Care Unit”) and some require a combination with various other elements to truly characterize an HAI. The alert mechanism must therefore be able to compute the level of HAI likelihood according to the elements extracted from text that match a given scenario.

5. Plan and next steps

A Patient Discharge Summary Analysis Strategy is currently investigated in the context of a project that is starting up between the Lyon University Hospital and the Xerox Research Centre Europe to apply state of the art Computational Intelligence Techniques to address a problem jeopardizing public health. This project will be developed in close collaboration between HAI surveillance experts and Linguistic and Knowledge Management experts in order to design the necessary set of rules to identify HAI from medical reports.

On a first hand only some departments and infections will be targeted. These are those related to the highest risks and that have the highest impact on human health. These departments are: Intensive Care Unit and Surgery.

A consistent set of reports containing HAI cases will be selected and highlighted by experts for system design and validation. We are currently building the first version of the system architecture focusing on the detection of the following events:

- Context (e.g. “re-entry”, “Surgery”, “HAI”, …)
- Clinical Parameters (e.g. “fever”, “inflammatory trace”, “pulmonary secretion”, “cough”, …)
- Biological Parameters (e.g. “bacteriological exam”, …)
- Biochemical Parameters (e.g. “white-cell > 10 000/mm3”, …)
- Treatments (e.g. “specific anti-biotic drugs”, …)

The real impact of such a project remains to be determined by experiments. In particular, we need to evaluate how much relevant information is present in the patient record.

6. Conclusion

Hospital Acquired Infection is a major issue that has a very important impact both for the patient and for added medical cost. Providing tools to shorten the time and effort necessary to discover and react against HAI is crucial to reduce this impact.

In this paper we presented a strategy that aims at applying Natural Language Processing techniques to mine patient Discharge Summaries in order to identify HAI. This strategy implies a strong collaboration with HAI surveillance experts in order to formalize the detection rules land linguist to convert these rules into appropriate grammars for advances parser and decision mechanisms to trigger alerts. This will be made in the context of a collaboration started between XRCE and HAI surveillance experts from the Lyon University Hospital to design a control and prevention system able to analyze medical reports for HAI detection.

Reference

1. P. Michel, J. Quenon , A. Djihoud, S. Tricaud-Vialle et al. Les événements indésirables graves liés aux soins observés dans les établissements de santé : premiers résultats d'une étude nationale. Etudes et résultats DRESS 2005(n°398).
2. Emori T, Culver D, Horan T, Jarvis W, White J, Olson D. National Nosocomial Infections Surveillance System (NNIS) : description of surveillance methods. American Journal of Infection Control 1991;19(1):19-35.
3. Murff HJ, Forster AJ, Peterson JF, Fiskio JM, Heiman HL, Bates DW. Electronically screening discharge summaries for adverse medical events. J Am Med Inform Assoc 2003;10(4):339-50.
5. Prevention of hospital-acquired infections: A practical guide. 2nd edition. World Health Organization. http://www.who.int/csr/resources/publications/drugresist/WHO_CDS_CSR_EPH_2002_12/en/
6. H, S. E. Humphreys. "Prevalence surveys of healthcare-associated infections : what do they tell us, if anything?" Clin Microbiol Infect 2006; 12: 2-4.
7. S. D. Bärwolff, C. Geffers, C . Brandt, R.P. Vonberg, et al. "Reduction of surgical site infections after caesarean delivery using surveillance." Journal of Hospital Infection 64: (2006) pp. 156-161
8. Wright M. Automated surveillance and infection control:toward a better tomorrow. Am J Infect Control 2008;36:S1-6.
9. Bellini C, Petignat C, Francioli P, Wenger A, Bille J, Klopotov A, Vallet Y, Patthey R, Zanetti G. Comparison of automated strategies for surveillance of nosocomial bacteremia. Infect Control Hosp Epidemiol 2007;28(9):1030-5.
10. S. Bouam, E. Girou, et al. "An intranet-based automated system for the surveillance of nosocomial infections: prospective validation compared with physicians' self-reports." Infection Control and Hospital Epidemiology (2003) 24(1): pp. 51-55.
11. Leth, R.A. and J.K. Moller, Surveillance of hospital-acquired infections based on electronic hospital registries. J Hosp Infect, 2006. 62(1): p. 71-9.
12. eHealth for Safety. Impact of ICT on Patient Safety and Risk Management. European Commission. Information Society and Media. ISBN 13 978 92 79 06841 6.
13. C. Brun, C. Hagège. Intertwining deep syntactic processing and named entity detection. ESTAL 2004, Alicante, Spain, October 20-22, 2004.
14. S. Aït-Mokhtar, J.P. Chanod, (1997) Incremental Finite-State Parsing. In Proceedings of the Fifth Conference on Applied Natural Language Processing (ANLP'97), Washington March 31st to April 3rd, 1997, pp.72-79.

An SMS-based System Architecture (Logical Model) to Support Management of Information Exchange in Emergency Stuations. poLINT-112-SMS PROJECT

Zygmunt Vetulani, Jacek Marciniak, Paweł Konieczka and Justyna Walkowska

Adam Mickiewicz University, Department of Computer Linguistic and Artificial Intelligence, ul. Umultowska 87, 61-714 Poznań, Poland, {vetulani, jacekmar, pawelk, ynka}@amu.edu.pl

Abstract: In the paper we present the architecture of the POLINT-112-SMS system to support information management in emergency situations. The system interprets the text input in form of SMS messages, understands and interprets information provided by the human user. It is supposed to assist a human in taking decisions. The main modules of the system presented here are the following: the SMS gate, the NLP Module (processing Polish), the Situation Analysis Module (SAM) and the Dialogue Maintenance Module (DMM).

Keywords: artificial intelligence, computer understanding systems, human-computer interaction, crisis management tools, incoming information processing, text understanding, information integration, contradiction solving, decision making

1. Introduction

In this paper we present the architecture of the POLINT-112-SMS system: a computer system supporting the gathering, processing and interpretation of information on events and situations reported by different informers in the text message form (in future version also in the spoken form). The following assumptions are made:

- the information may be sent by different informers, who do not cooperate with each other,
- the information concerns a specific situation or event,
- the information is sent by means of an SMS message in natural language (Polish) or in controlled natural language (a subset of Polish); the system

---

Please use the following format when citing this chapter:

Vetulani, Z., Marciniak, J., Konieczka, P. and Walkowska, J., 2008, in IFIP International Federation for Information Processing, Volume 288; *Intelligent Information Processing IV*; Zhongzhi Shi, E. Mercier-Laurent, D. Leake; (Boston: Springer), pp. 240–253.

has passive language competence, i.e. it can understand and process information,
- the information inputted into the system may be untrustworthy, incomplete or imprecise; also, contradictory statements may occur,
- the system is supposed to process the information to the extent allowing it to display (visualize) the state of the situation to the user and to answer user questions,
- the information is sent to the system and (possibly) also to a human operator.
- The communication mode has been limited to text due to the following reasons:
- there is no speech-to-text technology (even for English language) advanced enough to make it possible for the system to understand speech in extremely noisy conditions or when speaker's pronunciation is sloppy, distorted or highly regional,
- the system is to be used in the specific environment where noise or security reasons make the usage of text mode the most appropriate; e.g. in football stadiums during important events where the use of speech is not advisable because of both technical (noise) and logistic (safety of the informer) reasons.

A typical example of the system's application under the above assumptions is supporting the process of crisis situation management (a situation that poses danger to public safety), where decisions have to be made based on a large amount of information coming from different sources. In particular, this applies to mass events (sports games, big artistic events) and natural disasters. The common feature for this kind of situations is their variability and dynamics. This is why they need to be monitored by several observers who will report from various locations in different moments. As a typical case we selected high-stake football games (such as UEFA European Football Championship).

Compared to traditional methods of event reporting (telephone communication between the informer and the emergency center), a significant quality improvement is expected thanks to the computer-assisted integration of information coming from distributed informers, the on-line verification of the coherence of data, and the high credibility of the information sources. This goal can be achieved by using POLINT-112-SMS software to understand text and to process messages.

The practical goal of the work described in this article is to create a tool assisting a human in crisis management. By crisis management we mean undertaking preventive or repair actions by a human or a team, from now on referred to as Crisis Management Centre (CMC). We assume that CMC uses data acquired from informers, who can be ether professionally-trained experts or outside persons, who input information in a mode similar to 112 emergency telephone service, but using SMS messages instead of voice as the communication medium.

In traditional crisis management models, information is received and interpreted by professionally trained human operators. The fundamental problem here is the problem of communication bottlenecks when large amount of information tries to reach the CMC at the same time. When this problem is addressed by involving more operators, information may be lost, may remain unconnected (when two operators describe different aspects of the same situation) or even contradictory. The automation (or partial automation) of information gathering and processing may help solve this problem. Within this project we assume that the information is sent directly to the computer system that processes it for CMC use.

System's main functions are:

a) to collect information sent by the informer (SMS message),

b) to process (understand) the information to construct a coherent model of the situation/event in real-time,

c) to integrate data from different sources,

d) to perform some of the operator's duties when all the operators are busy.

Figure 1 presents a possible application context of the POLINT-112-SMS. The prototype being developed now will be tested in context of public order protection during a football match attended by a large number of fans.

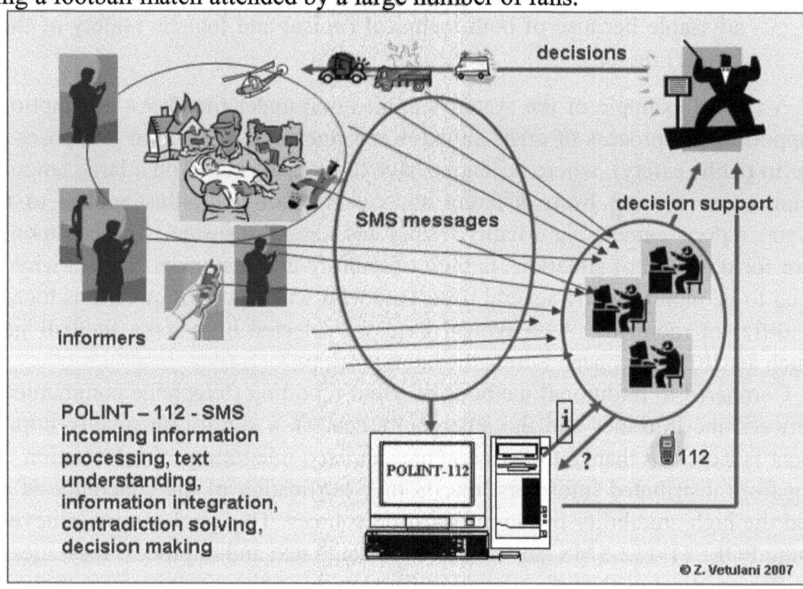

Figure 1. Application context of the POLINT-112-SMS system

2. LOGICAL MODEL

The logical model of the POLINT-112-SMS system, constituting the basis for the implementation in progress, has been developed with participation of experts with practical experience in the field of sport events security. As empirical background we considered a corpus of SMS messages collected in experimental setting. The messages were gathered in controlled conditions (experiments with participation of PPBW (Polish Platform for Homeland Security) to construct a linguistic model of SMS communication in Polish language in some precisely defined types of situations (cf. also (Fairon & Paumier 2006) and (Walkowska 2008)).

2.1. Assumptions about the logical model

The complexity of the processes that the system is expected to support has led to distinguishing 3 Entity Sets, that will be used to store data and reason about the events. These are Reports, Events and Situations.

Report – an entity designed to store data gathered during interaction with one specific informer. It is kept in the system for a determined period of time and moved to an archive when it expires. A Report is always assigned to at least one Event. If a Report cannot be assigned to any Event already existing in the system, then a new Event is created. After the Report is created, the system must decide about what Event(s) (a fight, a fire) it should be tied to. The type of the Event determines the mode of possible system-user dialogue to feed the system with required information. The system formulates questions to obtain as much information on Events tied to the Report as possible. E.g. or a Fight Event this may include questions about location, number of participants, danger for external people, etc.

Event – an entity representing a real-life situation (accident, crime, fight) reported by at least one informer. One Event has at least one Report assigned to it, which stores pieces of information. One Event organizes data from possibly various Reports. Each Event may contain:

- the most up-to-date (according to the system) information about the event,
- reliability assessment for each partial piece of information,
- information about contradictory elements of Reports,
- information about false data discovered in Reports.

The system tries to gain the maximal amount of information on the Event. It will query the informer when the introduced information is untrustworthy, contradictory or false. If the course of the dialogue (especially in the initial phase) does not make it possible to assess whether the inputted data concerns an Event already present in the system, an auxiliary unification question (e.g. about the location of the Event) may be asked.

Situation – an entity representing an important situation concerning many people (e.g. public order disturbance, riots, accidents with a significant number of victims). Such a situation is identified and the corresponding Situation entity is generated by the system automatically (using Situation Templates). This may also be done by the Analyst who has access to the events controlled by the system. At least one Event is assigned to each Situation. The Situation contains:

- information about Events tied to the Situation,
- information about the completeness of data in the Situation,
- information about how important the Events in the Situation are.

While accepting a Report concerning an Event that is tied to the given Situation, the system may generate further questions to the informer about different Events in connection to this Situation in order to complete its understanding.

2.2. Components

The system's architecture is presented in Figure 2. The components' tasks are as follows:

SMS Gate is a module allowing SMS communication with the informer by means of SMS messages. It is formed of two submodules, one of which is responsible for sending messages, the other one for receiving them. The SMS Gate communicates directly with the NLP Module.

The NLP Module is the main module responsible for processing text input to the System. In the final version of the system, the module will be responsible for question generation, but at this point the question generation functions are performed by DMM. The NLP Module communicates directly with the SMS Gate and with DMM.

Dialogue Maintenance Module (DMM) is responsible for dialogue with the informer. It takes into account the data controlled by the Situation Analysis Module. Thanks to the DMM, the NLP Module focuses on transforming single sentences into data structures without storing and processing these structures. DMM communicates directly with the NLP and SAM modules.

Situation Analysis Module (SAM) is responsible for reasoning. It acts as the „brain" of the system. It controls a number of subordinate modules, presented in points 5-12 (at this point some of them are integrated with SAM). SAM reasons about the structures without directly communicating with the informers. SAM communicates directly with DMM.

Knowledge About the World Module stores general knowledge and is used as the system's knowledge base. It may contain knowledge such as firemen reaction procedures, city maps in the GIS format and other information.

PolNet Module. PolNet is a WordNet-type ontology. Apart from the basic relations of hyponymy / hiperonymy it also contains relations that facilitate reasoning.

Reports Module stores information obtained from users in the form of Reports.

Events Module stores information about Events. Each Event is tied to at least one Report. The information stored in this module can be directly accessed by the Analyst

Event Recognition Module is responsible for creating new Events in the Events Module.

Situations Module stores information about Situations. Each Situation is tied to at least one Event. The information stored in this module can be directly accessed by the Analyst.

Situation Recognition Module is responsible for creating new Situations in the Situations Module..

Reaction Module's task is to inform the Dispatcher at the Crisis Management Centre that an action should be taken (e.g. sending an ambulance).

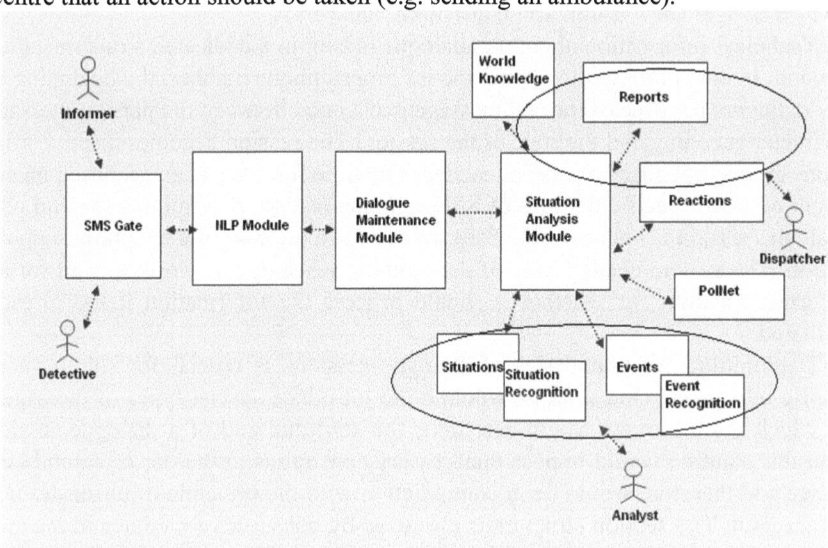

Figure 2. The logical model for the Polint-112-SMS system

3. Components implementation

3.1. System input – the SMS Gate

The SMS Gate is used for sending and receiving SMS messages. Currently it consists of a physical device (SMS terminal) and an application enabling communication with the device. The component's main tasks are: informer identification (by their phone No.), merging multipartite messages (i.e. messages too long to fit in 160 characters) into one message, detection and standardization of the encoding, and detection of the beginning and the end of a single dialogue session with the user. The informer's interaction with the system comes down to exchanging SMS messages (new information, questions, answers) .

Technical information about the dialogue is kept in a dedicated structure called session. It stores information about the informer's phone number, the beginning of the dialogue, the time of the last message exchanged between the parties, message character encoding and the state of the session. The session becomes inactive after a preset time boundary has been reached. The time limit has been proposed on account of some specific features of SMS communication: determining the end of a dialogue session is not as straightforward as it is in the case of a telephone conversation. The system needs a way of determining whether it is worth to wait for an informer's answer, or whether it should process the information it has already gathered.

Determining the boundaries of dialogue sessions is crucial for solving anaphoric references. One solution would be to introduce special types of messages, in which the informers would determine the start and end of a dialogue session (but this solution would impose unnecessary constraints to the use of natural language and therefore would be in contradiction with the principle of unconstrained NL access). The session structure is also used by consecutive modules in the system, especially by the Dialogue Maintenance Module.

The prototype implementation of the SMS Gate is a Java application that communicates with PROLOG modules by SWI-PROLOG's API. This application is capable of accepting messages sent to the SMS terminal and carrying their content to further modules and of sending the module's output to the user. An additional window can be opened to monitor the informer's communication with the system.

Within the prototype implementation of the system it is also possible to input messages from the keyboard. This type of the communication may be considered as a regular communications mode and it can be used in the target version for facilitating interaction with the system by the operator (e.g. with the role of system analyst).

In Figure 3 below we show a screenshot of a sample session.

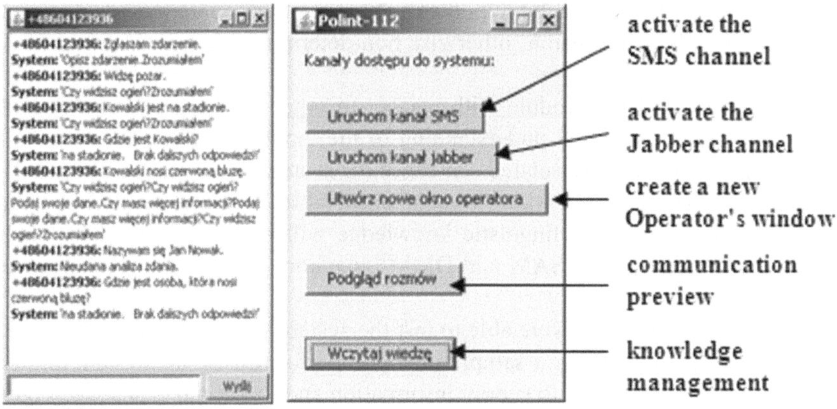

Figure 3. A sample dialogue session in the SMS Gate's window

3.2. The NLP Module

The NLP Module is based on the POLINT system, initially developed as a text understanding system which answers the user questions (both questions and answers in Polish). Several prototypes of the POLINT system were implemented during 1990ies and in the past couple of years initially in Arity-PROLOG. Using these prototypes the user may ask questions about facts collected in a PROLOG data base. The methodological and linguistic foundations of POLINT have been published in (Vetulani 1989) (see also (Vetulani & Marciniak 2000) and (Vetulani 2004)).

For the needs of this project, POLINT was re-implemented in the SWI-PROLOG and adapted to new tasks, in particular gathering information from the user.

POLINT (Vetulani 1997) was a language understanding system including several modules:

- dictionary (lexicon-grammar),
- preanalysis module for parsing heuristics,
- interpretable grammar rule set (PROLOG clauses),
- semantic module,
- knowledge base (in form of PROLOG facts and clauses).

POLINT is a real time system due to appropriate use of heuristics which substantially reduce non-determinism of the top-down parsing mechanism (inherited from PROLOG). Heuristics take into account words in the input string, extract from the system dictionary the syntactic information contained in the lexical entries and calculate heuristics. These operations are executed in linear time. Heuristics permit to generate syntactic hypothesis about the input sentences and therefore substantially reduce the search (otherwise non-deterministic) (eg. (Vetulani 1997, 2004)).

The role of the NLP Module with respect to other elements of the POLINT-112-SMS consists in partial understanding of the input text. The NLP Module is responsible for processing isolated sentences (or sentence equivalents). In particular, resolution of problems which remain unsolvable without considering larger context and/or some extra linguistic knowledge will require involvement of the other system modules, i.e. SAM and DMM (anaphora, identification of event actors etc.).

At the present stage we were able to test the system's basic understanding functionalities. The following is a sample dialogue performed by the system and the user. The user was allowed to supply information and to ask questions (see Figure 4). In the dialogue presented in Figure 4, the involvement of the SAM/DMM functionalities was very restricted.

USER: Kowal nosi bluzę i czarne spodnie. Kowal i Wolski są na murawie. Kowal i Wolski należą do bojówki. *(Kowal is wearing a blouse and black trousers. Kowal and Wolski are on the football field. Kowal and Wolski are members of a hooligan squad)*

SYSTEM: Zrozumiałem'*(Understood)*

USER: Osoba, która nosi czarne spodnie, jest niebezpieczna. Kowal i Wolski atakują policjantów kamieniami. *(The person who wears black trousers is dangerous. Kowal and Wolski are attacking policemen with stones)*

SYSTEM: Zrozumiałem *(Understood)*

USER: Kto atakuje policjantów? *(Who is attacking the policemen?)*

SYSTEM: Kowal. Wolski. Brak dalszych odpowiedzi! *(Kowal. Wolski. No more answers!)*

USER: Kto jest niebezpieczny? *(Who is dangerous?)*

SYSTEM: Kowal. Wolski. Brak dalszych odpowiedzi! *(Kowal. Wolski. No more answers!)*

USER: Czy istnieje niebezpieczna osoba, która nie została złapana? *(Is there a dangerous person who has not been captured?)*

System: 'Tak, kilka, w szczególności istnieje: Kowal !' *(Yes, a few persons, in particular Kowal!)*

Figure 4. A sample dialogue session

3.2. Dialogue Maintenance Module (DMM)

The DMM's main tasks are as follows:

- DMM receives and processes data structures.
- If the data structure created from a sentence by the NLP Module lacks an important argument, then DMM consults the informer about its value be-

fore passing the structure to SAM. The importance of arguments is expressed by means of their priorities.

- If SAM needs to confirm or to fill a slot value in a structure (e.g. the color of clothes of a tracked person – slots correspond loosely to predicate arguments), then the module marks the slot and sends the structure to DMM. DMM chooses an informer that may have information on the subject based on the user dialogue history and asks the question.
- For any incoming data structure, DMM needs to decide whether the structure contains completely new information, or is a continuation of previous information (then structures should be merged), or is an answer to one of the previously asked questions.
- DMM tries to maintain and expand the user model. There are different types of users – information from registered police informers is to be treated with more trust than information from an anonymous user. User type influences DMM's communication mode. Some types of informers cannot communicate with the system too often, because their function cannot be revealed to people surrounding them, so questions to them should be grouped and sent rarely. If a user takes too much time answering questions, DMM will most likely choose somebody (at similar position) else to ask for urgently needed information.
- One of DMM's most important functions is to solve anaphoric references. If the NLP Module discovers a reference of this kind (as in "He hit her."), it marks the corresponding slots. When DMM receives such structure, it tries to find the referenced value in the recent user dialogue history.
- There is a number of structures that DMM passes to SAM with almost no processing. These include structures used to indicate that the informer has asked a question or asked for notification when a described situation occurs (e.g. "Please inform me when Piotr Kowalski enters sector 5."). For such structures, DMM's task is only to remember which user asked for information, in order to sent them the answer/notification later.
- As the NLP Module is limited to understanding (questions, affirmative sentences and orders), DMM is charged with question generation. It keeps partially predefined questions for values of each slot in each structure, also in nested structures. It chooses the question form based on the slots that are already filled (e.g. a question for a person's first name can be formulated using their surname or nickname) and on the questions that have already been asked. DMM tries not to repeat question forms or questions. If a informer does not answer a question or says that he does not know the answer, DMM remembers the fact and does not try to ask again.

DMM is being implemented in PROLOG. It operates on data structures that also play the role of transport structures between the NLP Module and DMM, and between DMM and SAM. The NLP Module fills the structures with as much information as it can extract from single sentences. As stated in the previous section, some of DMM's most important tasks are merging structures received from the NLP Module, solving anaphoric references and asking (i.e. choosing and generating) questions about missing pieces of information that are considered crucial.

Structure merging is based on PROLOG list unification. After receiving a structure generated from a sentence sent by an informer that had communicated with the system a short time before, DMM tries to merge the structures. If the same kind of structure has been received (e.g. one describing a person), but the information inside is different (or partially different), DMM checks for conflicts. If there is a conflict, meaning that a value in a particular slot differs among the structures, then DMM either considers the structures separate (e.g. when different surnames are given) or asks for clarification (e.g. when different nicknames are given, it can ask if they both refer to the same person). When there are no conflicts, it is assumed that the information carried by the structures is complementary, and the structures will be merged. After having merged the structures, or adding a new structure if unification was not possible, DMM checks for missing information. Every slot in the structures (representing every possible piece of information that the system is capable of processing) is given a priority value at the start of the system. If a slot with priority above some predefined threshold remains not filled, then DMM asks for its value before sending the structure to SAM (it will send the structure anyway if the informer does not know the answer or if it does not respond within a given period of time). Thresholds may be different depending on types of informers.

DMM keeps a list of all structures sent by the NLP Module and of all questions it has asked. Because of this, it is able to assess that an incoming structure is the answer to one of its questions in a manner similar to structure merging described in the previous paragraph. Keeping a history of user input allows DMM to choose the best informer to ask when SAM forces a question by looking through structures sent by informers and finding one containing similar information (e.g. a structure in which an informer described an event close to a place about which SAM want to receive more information).

The situation is very similar when it comes to anaphoric references. If the first structure sent by the NLP Module, generated based on the informer's input, describes an event in which two people participate („Kowalski is throwing stones at Nowak.") and the second structure describes a person, but the person is not named („He is very aggressive."), the NLP Module will mark the corresponding slot (representing the person's data) as anaphoric. DMM will then test the latest structures sent by the same informer, looking for structures representing persons that might match the event. If in the last event more than two people are present (as is the case in the example), it will choose the person that was more active. Coming back to the example: DMM will decide that „he" in „He is very aggressive" is Kowalski. (Of course, if Kowalski is throwing stones at Nowak, the Situation Analysis Module will mark him as aggressive anyway.)

The DMM only reasons within one dialogue session. It does not try to merge structures sent by different informers on its own. It is the Situation Analysis Module that is responsible for combining information sent by different informers. When SAM forces a question upon the DMM, the DMM starts a new dialogue session with the informer.

3.3. *Situation Analysis Module (SAM)*

The Situation Analysis Module is responsible for collecting knowledge based on the information from the informers and for reasoning with the knowledge in order to deduce new facts. Its main tasks are: management of information about individuals, linking new information about entities with information stored in the knowledge base, recognizing Event types (using built-in context-related Event templates) and managing knowledge about Events and Situations (linking participants of Events and Event type structures, detecting dangerous objects, etc.).

There are three categories of SAM data structures:

a) Structures describing entities and relations between them.

Two types of entities have been distinguished: animate (individuals and groups) and inanimate (objects, artefacts). Special structures have been added to represent the relation of possessing objects by individuals and groups. Examples of entity structures are shown below:

- PERSON(id, name[], surname[], alias[], function, sex, appearance(heightCm, hair_colour, hair_length, eye_colour, skin_colour, has_moustache, hair_beard, is_dressed, identifying_articles[], clothes(article, pattern)[]), mood[], physical_state[]),
- GROUP_MEMBER(group_type, person_id, group_id, position_in_group)
- ARTICLE(id, idPolNet, size, colour, is_dangerous),

b) Structures describing Reports, Events and Situations

The most important structures from the point of view of SAM are those representing Events. Such structures contain current information about real-life, potentially dangerous situations reported by the informers. Examples of Event structures are shown below:

- EVT_BATTERY(id, aggressors[], victims[], articles[]),
- EVT_UNREST(id, participants[]),
- EVT_DESTROYING(id, participants[], destroyed_place, articles[]),
- EVT_FIGHT(id, participants[], articles[]).

c) Structures describing referential points in space and space-time relations between entities, Events and places.

The location of entities and Events is represented in the knowledge base by means of special structures called landmarks. They describe the entities' and Events' location in the space of referential points. Referring to them by their names, the informer inputs data about their location, specifying temporal and spatial relations between entities ("individual A is standing next to individual B"), between entities and Events ("individual A is involved in a fight in sector X"), between Events ("fans of opposite teams met, and then they started fighting"), between landmarks and entities ("the suspect is in the guests sector), between landmarks and Events ("riots in the guest sector"), or between different landmarks (sector A is to the right of sector B). Relations of this type can be static ("to the north of X") or dynamic ("right behind X's back"). Spatial relations in the Situation Analysis Module are translated into directional matrices, on which calculations are carried that determine new space-time relations.

Examples of space-time structures are shown below:

- LANDMARK_SECTOR(place(id, idPolNet, name, place_state(is_peace, is_smoke, is_fire, people_inside)), team, capacity),
- TIMESPACE_RELATION(object1_id, object2_id, matrixes[], space_distance, time_distance, orientation).

After consultation with experts a document describing business processes was prepared. The processes were used to create an experiment during which participants sent SMS messages reporting observed course of events. Analysis of the collected corpora allowed for creation of predefined Event templates for situations in the chosen context. Situation details important from the point of view of knowledge processing have been identified. The type of the Event influences the way in which the dialogue is managed and determines the set of questions asked by the system. If during a dialogue session it turns out that the informer is describing a type of Event different from what was assumed at the beginning, the dialogue mode changes.

When new information is inputted into the system, SAM checks if it is possible to tie the incoming information (forming a Report) to an Event or Situation already present in the knowledge base. If SAM suspects that such relation occurs, it asks questions (i.e. forces the Dialogue Maintenance Module to ask questions) that may confirm it. After confirming the relation SAM will try to gather missing information about the Event/Situation.

4. Conclusions

A system based on the presented architecture can satisfy the needs of a number of user categories. When used in a crisis situation or a potential crisis situation (e.g. large scale football event or another type of mass event) the system might have the following users:

The Informer, is a person (not necessarily professional) which reports on an accident, a crime, an incident, etc. The Informer might be in a state of vexation, stress or fear. Hence, the data obtained from them may be incomplete or imprecise, and the mode of conveying the information may be chaotic or clumsy.

The Detective is a employee of emergency services (police, fire service) working in the field, supposed to report an accident, a crime, an incident or a significant change in the monitored situation, etc. It is assumed that he/she has been trained to work under crisis conditions.

The Analyst works for emergency services trained to recognize critical situations.

The Dispatcher is an emergency services employee responsible for making decisions about the actions that should be taken.

Identification of the above user categories introduces new quality into the technologies of crisis situation management. Systems with text based communication competence (as it is the case of POLINT-112-SMS) apt to collect and process knowledge, open new possibilities to obtain information about events from a large number of informers in situations that call for quick decisions.

ACKNOWLEDGEMENTS

The research presented in this paper was partially covered by the on-going Polish Government research grant R00 028 02 "Text processing technologies for Polish in application for public security purposes" (2006-2009) within the Polish Platform for Homeland Security.

References

Fairon C., Paumier S. (2006): A translated corpus of 30,000 French SMS; in: Proceedings of LREC 2006. Genova.

Vetulani Z. (1989): Linguistic problems in the theory of man-machine communication in natural language. A study of consultative question answering dialogues. Empirical approach. Brockmeyer, Bochum.

Vetulani Z. (1997): A system for Computer Understanding of Texts, in: R.Murawski, J. Pogonowski (eds.), Euphony and Logos (Poznań Studies in the Philosophy of the Sciences and the Humanities, vol. 57) Rodopi, Amsterdam-Atlanta, 387-416.

Vetulani Z., Marciniak J. (2000): Corpus Based Methodology in the Study and Design of Systems with Emulated Linguistic Competence; in: Dimitris N. Christodoulakis (ed.), Natural Language Processing - NLP 2000, Lecture Notes in AI, no 1835, Springer, 346-357.

Vetulani Z. (2004): Komunikacja człowieka z maszyną. Komputerowe modelowanie kompetencji językowej, Akademicka Oficyna Wydawnicza EXIT, Warszawa.

Walkowska J. (2008): A corpus of real-life and experimentally collected Polish SMS messages (manuscript).

Semi Automatic Ontology Instantiation in the domain of Risk Management

Jawad Makki[1], Anne-Marie Alquier[1] and Violaine Prince[2]

[1] Université Toulouse 1, 2 rue du Doyen Gabriel Marty, 31042 Toulouse
Jawad.Makki@univ-tlse1.fr, Anne-Marie.Alquier@univ-tlse1.fr

[2] Université Montpellier 2, LIRMM-CNRS, 161 rue Ada, 34392 Montpellier
prince@lirmm.fr

Abstract: One of the challenging tasks in the context of Ontological Engineering is to automatically or semi-automatically support the process of Ontology Learning and Ontology Population from semi-structured documents (texts). In this paper we describe a Semi-Automatic Ontology Instantiation method from natural language text, in the domain of Risk Management. This method is composed from three steps 1) Annotation with part-of-speech tags, 2) Semantic Relation Instances Extraction, 3) Ontology instantiation process. It's based on combined NLP techniques using human intervention between steps 2 and 3 for control and validation. Since it heavily relies on linguistic knowledge it is not domain dependent which is a good feature for portability between the different fields of risk management application. The proposed methodology uses the ontology of the PRIMA[1] project (supported by the European community) as a Generic Domain Ontology and populates it via an available corpus. A first validation of the approach is done through an experiment with Chemical Fact Sheets from Environmental Protection Agency[2].

Keywords: *Information Extraction, Instance Recognition Rules, Instantiation, Ontology Population, POS tagging, Risk Management, Semantic analysis.*

1. Introduction

Risk Management is as a rule assisted by decision support, which relies on a risk knowledge base (supposed to be or become a corporate memory) and a cognitive framework adapted to risk [1]. Our work focuses is mostly on the knowledge

---

[1] PRIMA project : Project Risk Management, IST-1999-10193, 00-02.

[2] EPA : U.S. Environmental Protection Agency www.epa.gov/chemfact

---

Please use the following format when citing this chapter:

Makki, J., Alquier, A.M. and Prince, V., 2008, in IFIP International Federation for Information Processing, Volume 288; *Intelligent Information Processing IV*; Zhongzhi Shi, E. Mercier-Laurent, D. Leake; (Boston: Springer), pp. 254–265.

acquisition process related to the risk knowledge base. This acquisition process raises specific problems and difficulties: knowledge and expertise are sensitive, scattered, hidden or unclear; moreover, knowledge is highly specialized, although its implementation is very multi/inter-disciplinary. PRIMA represents the initial work of defining a Generic Domain Ontology, validated in industrial context, and kernel for further developments in the fields of ontology extension or content extension.

There is a variety of technologies involved into risk management systems that have been applied to support acquisition, creation, application and generation of organizational knowledge processes, such as: Databases and data warehouses, decision support system, expert systems, intelligent agents, data mining, ontologies, etc.

Our research focuses on ontology technology as the backbone to support the construction and the population of the Risk Knowledge Base, because of its power of expressivity and knowledge reuse capability.

Ontology is an explicit formal specification of a shared conceptualization of a domain of interest [3]. Ontology plays an important role in many kinds of applications especially in semantic web applications and knowledge management applications; it is widely used as a knowledge representation tool for domain knowledge. It defines concepts and relations between these concepts in order to represent knowledge in a specific domain. Ontology is well prepared by knowledge managers and domain experts. But it is a laborious, time consuming, tedious, cost-intensive and complex task to find concepts, to build relations and to add new instances in the ontology. Therefore there has been a growing interest in the (semi) automatic learning and populating ontologies.

In this paper we focus on ontology population. We propose a Semi-Automatic Ontology Instantiation approach that aims at enriching a Generic Domain Ontology by acquiring new instances of concepts from texts. Domain-specific ontologies are preferable since they limit the domain and make the applications feasible [4].

We have experimented our methodology in the domain of risk management by populating PRIMA ontology with instances through Chemical Fact Sheets from Environmental Protection Agency.

The rest of this paper is organized as follows. in Section 2 we present the State of the Art. In Section 3 we describe in details our approach of Ontology Instantiation. In Section 4 an example experiment is detailed. Finally, in Section 5 we draw conclusions for further work and a future evaluation.

2. State of the Art

2.1 Risk knowledge base within Risk Management and Business Intelligence

In every ontology approach, the definition of the sphere of work, the scope characterization, is compulsory to context understanding, requirement identification, usable sources recognition and functional analysis of users requirements. This is even more true in the area of risk management, which is a very generic problem, applying to all types of situations extending to:

- Varied levels of support, from individual commitment, business management to social problems. Here we aim to support the performance management of a company using risk, called management by risk. The general idea is that most business decisions are based on risk-taking - in the sense of opportunities as well as dangers.
- Every type of risk. For example, to consider whether the materials used in a new product have hazardous impacts of are environmentally friendly, many sources should be consulted, many of them being outside the company. Here we focus on a specific type of risk.

A risk knowledge base would capture as much knowledge as possible, capitalizing on all sources potentially useful, external or internal.

Internally, a risk knowledge base capitalizes the design, development, certification, operation and lessons learnt from the past.

But external knowledge is more useful is the field of strategic decision making [2] and Business Intelligence. Helping strategic decision makers is enabling them to operate more efficiently various data sources to get a better understanding of their organization and competitive environment.

It is then necessary to search for risk knowledge. Risk Management involves different organizations, at various levels. Knowledge is scattered in distinct systems and services. Extracting relevant knowledge is not just a raw data exchange with only the corresponding syntactic and semantic conversion issues well known in databases.

But this search should not be extensive: It is impossible and it would even be harmful to incorporate any type of risk for any type of organization in a risk knowledge base. It is necessary to focus on the needs related to specific situations.

Thus, knowledge acquisition cannot be fully automated; it should be rather guided by an expert, in a semi-automatic way. This expert is in charge of bringing together, from different sources, the domain-specific knowledge, in order to reuse it as a basis for risk and business intelligence, and to allow afterwards the simulation support in risk management. The knowledge-acquisition expert would in fact reengineer risk-oriented knowledge resources (databases as well as textual resources), subsequently mapping them to a central bone structure, an Enterprise Risk Management Mechanism.

Knowledge capture in heterogeneous, informal sources can be helped by the complex central ontology for classifying and managing risks provided by PRIMA. It includes domain, task, and problem-solving ontologies validated in several industrial contexts.

The semi-automatic acquisition process offers the following outputs:

- Meta-knowledge (all the classification methods are included in the knowledge base described by PRIMA).
- Risk identification (the ontology is a generic host structure, but evolution is possible with appends or changes)
- Detailed risk description (the cognitive framework ontology is a generic host structure, but evolution is possible with additions or changes).

2.2 Natural Language Processing (NLP) for Information and Knowledge Extraction

Natural Language Processing (NLP) has been largely addressed these last years as a proficient technology for text mining in order to extract knowledge: Relevant literature is so abundant that extensively referencing its items is a contribution by itself. Therefore, we will stick here to papers exploring text mining and NLP in applications related to Risk Management or to papers that inspired our model and methodology.

Two types of relationships between NLP and risk management can be found: Those dealing with risk definition in documents, assessing the difficulty of probability assignment to terms (natural language items) related to risk definition and management [5]. Probability is re-interpreted as a confidence value in a fuzzy logic approach to risk inference from a natural language description [6]. These two representative works in literature tackle a crucial issue in risk ontologies extraction from texts, documents or discourse (oral/written): Terminology is not as precisely defined as in domains like medicine or biology, risk assessment by experts in the shape of sentences does not naturally lead to an obvious formalization. Words and phrases are various, ambiguous, stylistic figures are numerous (metaphors, emphases, understatements). This drives researchers to reconsider knowledge extraction from texts as a more complex process than those described in the abundant biomedical terminology extraction literature (e.g. [7] which deals with one of the most typical aspects of knowledge extraction, Named Entities, and their insertion in a domain taxonomy). Researchers such as [8] have acknowledged the gap between textual input and knowledge as a structural pattern for a given domain: Authors suggest annotating corpora in order to provide clues for an efficient knowledge extraction. Annotation means a human intervention: It seems that more and more works recognize human judgment as an important element in the extraction process loop, a fact upon which our own approach is based (in section 4).

This is set up to reduce the liabilities of an automatic natural language processing extracting knowledge in such a difficult environment.

Our own approach benefits from existing NLP techniques in order to extract knowledge from natural language text. These techniques involve part-of-speech (POS) tagging in order to filter the most interesting categories, semantic networks to retrieve semantic relationships between phrases as concept instances, syntactic and semantic knowledge to build concept recognition heuristics applied to texts. More precisely we used TreeTagger [9] as a POS tagger providing a basic syntactic structure for text. For semantic relation extraction, we relied on WordNet [10], in order to expand some specific words with related terms. This expansion increases the chance of matching with other semantically similar terms and decreases the problem of linguistic variations. We also used it for the acquisition of synonyms. Last we relied on the predicative power of verbs to derive our concept recognition rules described in section 3.

2.3 Ontology population with NLP techniques

Ontology population is the process of building the Knowledge Base. It consists of adding new instances of concepts and relations into an existing ontology. This process usually starts after the conceptual model of ontology is built.

As said in the introduction, building ontology and instantiating a knowledge base manually are a time-consuming and cost-intensive process. Therefore in recent years there have been some efforts to automate it. New approaches for (semi) automatic ontology population have emerged and considerably increased. These approaches are based on various techniques. ArtEquAKT [11]-[14] is a system that automatically extracts knowledge about artists from the Web, populates a knowledge base and uses it to generate personalized biographies. ArtEquAKT uses syntactic analysis to get the Part-Of-Speech and employs Semantic analysis to perform named entity recognition and extract binary relations between two instances. ArtEquAKT applies a set of heuristics and reasoning methods in order to remove redundant instances from the ontology.

LEILA [15] is an automatic approach that can extract instances of arbitrary given binary relations from natural language. LEILA uses a deep syntactic analysis and statistical techniques to learn the extraction patterns for the relation.

Reference [4] describes a pattern-based method to automatically enrich a core ontology with the definitions of a domain glossary. Reference [4] applies a method in the domain of cultural heritage. It is an automatic approach that extracts instances from semi-structured corpora (Art and Architecture Thesaurus) with the help of manually developed extraction patterns.

SOBA [16] is an information extraction system that automatically extracts information from heterogeneous sources (semi-structured data such as tables, unstructured text, images and image captions) and populates a knowledge base by using a standard rule-based information extraction system in order to extract named entities. These entities are converted into semantic structures with the help of special mapping declarative rules. SOBA addresses the problem of entity disambiguation by performing simple checks during instances creation.

These current approaches are based on various techniques; e.g. automated pattern recognition and extraction, statistic analysis, syntactic analysis, semantic analysis, mapping rules, etc. They differ from each other in some factors and have many features in common. Reference [17] defined the major distinguishing factors between ontology construction approaches. These factors are classified in the below categories "dimensions":

1. Elements learned: Concepts instances, relations instances.
2. Starting point: Domain ontology, Domain specific texts, POS Tagger, Syntactic/Semantic analyzer, additional resources (like WorldNet).
3. Learning approach: Statistical, logical, Linguistic based, Pattern extraction, Wrapper induction, combined.
4. Degree of automation: Manual, Semi-automatic (User Intervention), Cooperative, Full automatic.
5. The result: List of concept instances, List of relation instances, Populated Ontology.
6. Domain Portability: Limited, Domain specific, Fairly portable.

Risk management is multi domain, multi corpora with unstructured knowledge and sometimes with scarce knowledge. Machine learning approaches can not apply, so we needed to have a portable approach. Moreover as explained by [8] sole automatic approaches may misinterpret texts fragments which would be frequent as well as risky especially in the risk management domain. Last sticking with only one calculation method (symbolic, statistical) would deprive the system of the benefits of the other. Therefore, we have developed an appropriate method meant to be portable, semi-automatic and mixing several techniques. It is detailed in next section.

3. Our Approach

Our approach of ontology population is based on combined statistical, syntactic and semantic techniques. It starts with an initial generic ontology and a corpus of unstructured documents in a given domain, and produces a populated ontology as a result of the population process.

The main steps of our approach are the following:

1. Annotation with part-of-speech tags
2. Semantic Relation Instances Extraction
3. Ontology Instantiation process

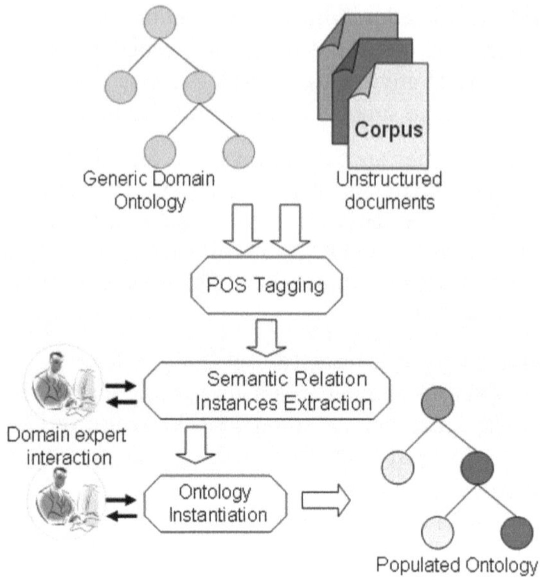

Fig. 1 Outline of the method.

There is a loop between step 2 and 3 in which human interaction adjusts automatically extracted information and knowledge. The outline of the method is summarized in Fig. 1 and the three steps are detailed hereafter.

3.1 Annotation with part-of-speech tags

The corpus (i.e. any set of texts about risk considered as the source for knowledge extraction) is processed with TreeTagger. TreeTagger annotates texts with POS and lemma information. As a result, this step produced for each word wi in the corpus, a string of POS tag or a syntactic category posi (e.g. NN for nouns, VB for verbs, JJ for adjective, etc…). These tags will be used as a filter to extract the frequent verbs in next steps; it plays an important role also in the syntactic analysis.

3.2 Semantic Relation Instances Extraction

A semantic relation between two concepts may be expressed by a verb in natural language texts. Verbs represent an action or a relation between entities (concepts) in sentences. As a result, this step aims at generating semantic relation instances between concepts by extracting all frequent verbs from the POS annotated corpus in the previous step. These verbs are assumed to be associated with existing relations between two concepts from the ontology, which can be valuable for populating the generic domain ontology provided.

Let R_{ab} be a semantic relation between two concepts C_a and C_b of the ontology ($C_aR_{ab}C_b$). The idea is to construct from the annotated corpus, a list of verbs LV_{ab} associated to R_{ab} where each verb can link the two concepts C_a and C_b. this list will be validated by a domain expert.

The list of verbs LV_{ab} associated to R_{ab} is built by : 1) synonyms of R_{ab} generated by the lexical resource WordNet, 2) frequent verbs extracted from the annotated corpus (simple frequency counting) 3) Human interference by a knowledge manager or a domain expert where his role consists in validating the candidate set of verbs associated to R_{ab}.

In brief, this step of the method takes as an input the POS annotated corpus and the generic ontology and produces for each semantic relation R_{ab} between two concepts C_a et C_b of the ontology, a list of verbs LV_{ab} associated to R_{ab} where each v_i of LV_{ab}, v_i can semantically connect C_a and C_b.

$LV_{ab} = \{v_1, v_2, \ldots v_n\}$ where $\forall\ v_i \in LV_{ab}\,.\ \exists\ C_a v_i C_b$

3.3 Ontology Instantiation process

From the list of verbs LV_{ab} semi automatically extracted from the corpus and for each verb V_{ab} of LV_{ab}, this step aims at identifying and extracting all triplets ($segment_i$,V_{ab},$segment_J$) from the set of sentences of the annotated corpus.

A triplet ($segment_i$,V_{ab},$segment_J$) is extracted from a sentence S that contains a verb V_{ab} of LV_{ab}. S is composed from a set of words wi like S= $w_1 \ldots w_i\ V_{ab}\ w_J \ldots w_n$. $segment_i$ in triplet represents $w_1 \ldots w_i$ (i.e. the words left of the verb) and $segment_j$ represents $w_j \ldots w_n$. (i.e. the words right of the verb).

At a second phase, each extracted triplet is proposed to a syntactic structure recognition procedure; this procedure is based on a set of predefined Instances Recognition Rules. To initiate the ontology population process, these rules have been created manually by testing (we contemplate to automate this process in a further step with learning algorithms such as association rules if they prove to be numerous or if those we built up don't cover the problem). Rules can recognize a certain amount of linear words configurations. They are able to identify and generate an instance triplet (Instance_of_C_a, Instance_of_R_{ab}, Instance_of_C_b) from the extracted triplet (segmenti,V_{ab},segmentj).

However, these Instances Recognition Rules can be expanded with time through the addition of new rules in order to enhance the performance and the accuracy of the knowledge extraction method.

As a result, this procedure generates Instance triplets that have the form of ($Instance_a$,V_{ab}, $Instance_b$) where $Instance_a$ is an instance of concept C_a, $Instance_b$ is an instance of concept C_b and V_{ab} in an instance of relation R_{ab} that connect $Instance_a$ and $Instance_b$.

We distinguish in Table 1 some of the Instances Recognition Rules:

Table 1 Some Instances Recognition Rules

Rule	linear words configurations	associated instances triplets ($Instance_a$, V_{ab}, $Instance_b$)
R1	$w_1 \ldots w_i\ \mathbf{V_{ab}}\ w_j \ldots w_k$	$(w_1 \ldots w_i, \mathbf{V_{ab}}, w_j \ldots w_k)$
R2	$w_1 \ldots w_i$ DT $w_j \ldots w_k\ \mathbf{V_{ab}}\ w_l \ldots w_m$ where DT = that	$(w_j \ldots w_k, \mathbf{V_{ab}}, w_l \ldots w_m)$
R3	$w_1 \ldots w_i, w_j \ldots w_k$,MD $\mathbf{V_{ab}}\ w_l \ldots w_m$ where MD = can	$(w_1 \ldots w_i, \mathbf{V_{ab}}, w_l \ldots w_m)$
R4	$w_1 \ldots w_i\ \mathbf{V_{ab}}\ w_j \ldots w_k$ CC $w_l \ldots w_m$ where CC = and	$(w_1 \ldots w_i, \mathbf{V_{ab}}, w_j \ldots w_k)$ $(w_1 \ldots w_i, \mathbf{V_{ab}}, w_l \ldots w_m)$
R5	$w_1 \ldots w_i$ CC $w_j \ldots w_k\ \mathbf{V_{ab}}\ w_l \ldots w_m$ where CC = or	$(w_1 \ldots w_i, \mathbf{V_{ab}}, w_l \ldots w_m)$ $(w_j \ldots w_k, \mathbf{V_{ab}}, w_l \ldots w_m)$
R6	$w_1 \ldots w_i$ VBZ/VBP $\mathbf{V_{ab}}$ IN $w_j \ldots w_k$ where pos($\mathbf{V_{ab}}$) = VVN and IN = by and VBZ = is / VBP= are	$(w_j \ldots w_k, \mathbf{V_{ab}}, w_1 \ldots w_i)$

The produced Instances triplets will be validated by a domain expert. Having the triplet in this form « word1…wordi + Verb + wordj…wordk» facilitate the identification of instances of concepts/relations for the generic domain ontologies by the decision maker. Finally this validation instantiates the ontology and finishes the population process.

4. Experiment

In this section, we describe the application of our method for an example experiment in the domain of risk management.

In this experiment we use the ontology of PRIMA (the risk analysis reasoning model defined in PRIMA) as a generic ontology, and a corpus consists of 20 Chemical Fact Sheets (in English) provided by the Environmental Protection Agency.

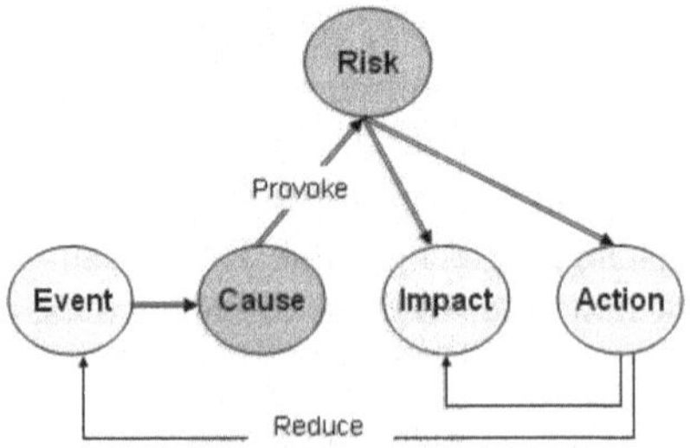

Fig. 2 Part of the Generic Ontology of PRIMA.

The ontology of PRIMA contains a set of concepts describing risk and its insertion in a technical chain of work. Risk itself is described through 7 high level entities (or objects), the relations between those entities, plus relations with items external to risk (cost for example). Only two concepts and one relation were used for the experimentation in order to populate the causal chain of PRIMA and more specifically to instantiate the two concepts «Risk» and «Cause» and the relation «Provoke» that connects them.

After applying a POS tagging on the EPA corpus, we built the list of verbs LV_{ab} associated to Relation R_{ab} "Provoke" by getting the synonyms of relation "Provoke" and extracting all the frequent verbs associated to this relation from the EPA annotated corpus. Human intervention has validated the final list LV_{ab}.

In a second phase, we extracted all the triplets (segmenti,V_{ab},segmentj) and proposed them to the syntactic structure recognition procedure. This procedure generated 150 Instances triplets. 85% of these Instances triplets are evaluated as accepted instance triplets. Table 2 shows some results of our method.

Example:

For V_{ab} = «cause» and for this entry "dermal Prolonged exposure to acetaldehyde can cause burns and erythema in humans", the Instances recognition rule R4 is applied and we get two instances triplets as following:

- *(Prolonged dermal exposure to acetaldehyde, Cause, erythema)*
- *(Prolonged dermal exposure to acetaldehyde, Cause, burns in humans)*

Table 2 Part of the Generic Ontology of PRIMA

«Cause»	«Provoke»	«Risk»
Exposure to large amounts of chlorobenzene	cause	Adverse nervous system effects
Repeat exposure to nitrobenzene in air over a lifetime	Cause	cancer in animals
Prolonged dermal exposure to acetaldehyde	Cause	erythema
Prolonged dermal exposure to acetaldehyde	Cause	burns in humans
Methanol exposed to an open flame	explode	Explosion
Humans Toluene ingestion	result	severe central nervous system depression
Exposure to moderate amounts of chlorobenzene in air	Cause	Testicular damage in animals
Nitrobenzene	Cause	Adverse reproductive system effects
Chlorobenzene has potential	Produce	adverse reproductive effects in human males
Repeatedly breathing large amounts of toluene	Cause	permanent brain damage

5. Conclusion and Future Work

In this paper, we presented an appropriate method for Semi-Automatic Ontology Instantiation from natural language text, in the domain of Risk Management. It's based on combined NLP techniques using human intervention for control and validation. First experimental results show that the approach reached 85 % of accepted Instances triplets. This percentage is satisfactory results encouraging us to go further:

- In populating other PRIMA concepts and relations within a given domain (here the chemical risk)
- In populating PRIMA generic ontology in other risk domain without extensive reworking.

Semantic relation extraction is not a domain dependent process and recognition rules are by definition domain independent (they are linguistic knowledge).
Since we rely so heavily on NLP, NLP limitations have a crucial impact on our method. For instance, POS disambiguation if not provided by the tagger could hamper recognition rules results («result» and «cause» are both noun and verb). Therefore, a deeper syntactic analysis than the one provided by TreeTagger, is investigated (we agree with LEILA authors and their choice of a real grammatical analysis).
However, our method ensures a real portability from a given domain to another if a generic ontology exists somewhere which is the case in risk management. It is flexible (easily supports enhancement), useful for expert knowledge expression (it suggests word associations to risk experts which might give them a decision support).

REFERENCES

1. Alquier A.M. & Tignol M.H., 2007. "Management de risques et intelligence économique", Economica. ISBN : 2717852522.
2. Ansoff H.I., 1990. Implanting Strategic Management, Practice Hall.
3. T. Gruber. Towards principles for the design of ontologies used for knowledge sharing. Int.J. of Human and Computer Studies, 43:907–928, 1994.
4. R. Navigli and P. Velardi. Enriching a Formal Ontology with a Thesaurus: an Application in the Cultural Heritage Domain. In Proceedings of the 2nd Workshop on Ontology Learning and Population: Bridging the Gap between Text and Knowledge – OLP 2006, pp. 1 – 9, Sydney, Australia, July 2006
5. Hillson, D. 2005 "Describing probability: The limitations of natural language."Proceedings of EMEA, Edinburgh, UK.
6. Huang, C.F.Risk 2007 "Analysis with Information Described in Natural Language ". In Computational Science, Proceedings of ICCS2007, Lecture Notes In Computer Science, Springer Verlag.

7. Liang T, Shih PK 2005 Empirical Textual Mining to Protein Entities Recognition from PubMed Corpus, Proceedings of the10th International Conference on Applications of Natural Language to Information Systems, NLDB 2005, Alicante, Spain. Lecture Notes in Computer Science. Springer Verlag. Pp 56-66.
8. Navarro B., Martínez-Barco P. and M.Palomar, 2005. "Semantic Annotation of a Natural Language Corpus for Knowledge Extraction" 10th International Conference on Applications of Natural Language to Information Systems, NLDB 2005, Alicante, Spain. Lecture Notes in Computer Science. Springer Verlag.
9. TreeTagger: a language independent part-of-speech tagger http://www.ims.uni-stuttgart.de/projekte/corplex/TreeTagger
10. Miller, G. and McDonnell, J. S. 2003. "WordNet 2.0." A Lexical Database for English, Princeton University's Cognitive Science Laboratory. http://WordNet.princeton.edu
11. S. Kim, H. Alani, W. Hall, P. Lewis, D. Millard, N. Shadbolt and M. Weal. Artequakt: Generating Tailored Biographies from Automatically Annotated Fragments from the Web. In Proceedings of Workshop on Semantic Authoring, Annotation & Knowledge Markup (SAAKM'02), the 15th European Conference on Artificial Intelligence, (ECAI'02), pp. 1-6, Lyon, France 2002.
12. Alani H., Sanghee K., Millard E.D., Weal J.M., Lewis P.H., Hall W., and Shadbolt N., Automatic Extraction of Knowledge from Web Documents, In: Proceeding of (HLT03), 2003.
13. Alani H., Sanghee K., Millard E.D., Weal J.M., Lewis P.H., Hall W., and Shadbolt N., Web based Knowledge Extraction and Consolidation for Automatic Ontology Instantiation, In: Proceedings of the Workshop on Knowledge Markup and Semantic Annotation at the Second International Conference on Knowledge Capture (K-CAP 2003), Florida, USA, 2003.
14. H. Alani, S. Kim, D.E. Millard, M.J. Weal, W. Hall, P.H. Lewis and N.R. Shadbolt (2003), "Automatic Ontology-Based Knowledge Extraction from Web Documents", IEEE Intelligent Systems, 18(1), pp. 14-21.
15. F.M. Suchanek, G. Ifrim and G, Weikum. LEILA: Learning to Extract Information by Linguistic Analysis. In Proceedings of the 2nd Workshop on Ontology Learning and Population: Bridging the Gap between Text and Knowledge – OLP 2006, pp. 18 – 25, Sydney, Australia, July 2006.
16. P. Buitelaar, P. Cimiano, S. Racioppa and M. Siegel (2006), "Ontology-based Information Extraction with SOBA", In Proceedings of the International Conference on Language Resources and Evaluation, pp. 2321-2324. ELRA, May 2006.
17. M. Shamsfard, and A. Abdollahzadeh Barforoush. The state of the art in ontology learning: a framework for comparison. The Knowledge Engineering Review (2003), 18: 293-316 doi:10.1017/S0269888903000687

Author Index

MIX
Papier aus verantwortungsvollen Quellen
Paper from responsible sources
FSC® C105338

If you have any concerns about our products,
you can contact us on
ProductSafety@springernature.com

In case Publisher is established outside the EU,
the EU authorized representative is:
Springer Nature Customer Service Center GmbH
Europaplatz 3, 69115 Heidelberg, Germany

Printed by Libri Plureos GmbH
in Hamburg, Germany